UNITED KINGDOM
KINGDOM
BUSINESS
GATEWAY TO
EUROPE

UNITED KINGDOM,
BUSINESS
GATEWAY TO
EUROPE

Consultant Editor:
Timothy R V Foster

Published in association with
The Department of Trade and Industry

with endorsement from
The British-American Chamber of Commerce
and
Canada-United Kingdom Chamber of Commerce

KOGAN
PAGE

Published in 1998

Kogan Page Ltd
120 Pentonville Road
London N1 9JN
kpinfo@kogan-page.co.uk
© Kogan Page 1998

British Library Cataloguing in Publication Data

A CIP record for this book is available from the British Library.

ISBN 0 7494 2748 5

Typeset by JS Typesetting, Wellingborough, Northants.
Printed in Great Britain by Bell and Bain Ltd, Glasgow

The American School in London

2-8 Loudoun Road
London NW8 0NP
Tel 0171-449 1200
Fax 0171-449 1350

The coeducational, independent day school
offering a challenging American curriculum
for children aged 4 to 18

TECHNICAL AND INFORMATION SUPPORT FOR THE FOOD AND DRINK INDUSTRY IN A GLOBAL MARKET PLACE

Professor Colin Dennis, Director-General
Campden & Chorleywood Food Research Association
Chipping Campden, Gloucestershire. GL55 6LD, UK.

The production of safe, wholesome and profitable products must be the minimum aim of any food and drink company. As the trade in processed food products, ingredients and raw materials becomes increasingly global this aim requires consideration of an enormous range of demanding legislation, processing, packaging, quality, safety and consumer issues. These in turn rely on up-to-date scientific and technical information as well as knowledge of legislation, the market place and consumer trends.

In such a business environment an increasing number of companies are utilising the services of an independent dedicated scientific, technical and information centre such as the Campden & Chorleywood Food Research Association (CCFRA) based in Chipping Campden, Gloucestershire in the United Kingdom. This is reflected in the rapid increase in its membership. Since its creation in January 1995, by the merger of the Campden Food & Drink Research Association and the Flour Milling & Baking Research Association, CCFRA has attracted almost 500 new member companies which utilise the extensive range of services.

The Campden & Chorleywood Food Research Association is now the largest membership based independent food drink research centre in the world and proud to serve over 1500 companies in 55 countries. CCFRA brings together the skills and facilities that food and drink companies need to ensure safety, quality, efficiency and innovation within their business. It undertakes research and development and provides consultancy, training and information services for the many industries associated with agriculture, food and drink manufacture, distribution, retailing and food service: in essence those companies which make up the food supply chain.

As an independent organisation, CCFRA is able to invest in technologies, skills and quality management systems to the benefit of its members in the agri-food industry. This continuous programme of investment ensures essential processing and laboratory facilities for research, process and product development and the wide range of information, scientific and technical support services.

CCFRA has also established and is a key player in an extensive range of networks of contacts in Europe, thus expanding its knowledge of the European market place including consumer and legislative requirements. For example through the European Sensory Network, the European Food Law Group and the European Hygienic Equipment Design Group, CCFRA has been able to assist North American companies who wish to enter the European market place. Such work has included extensive consumer research in different European countries and advice on the legislative and hygienic requirements within the UK and the European Union.

In addition in January 1998, CCFRA established its first wholly owned subsidiary in Budapest, Hungary to serve the food and drink industry in Hungary and neighbouring Central and Eastern European countries. Campden & Chorleywood Élélmiszeripari Fejlesztési Intézet Magyarország Kht has a team of experienced food scientists and technologists providing training and consultancy on HACCP, quality management, new product development, market research, hygiene, food and environmental law and factory auditing.

The technical support provided by CCFRA ranges from totally confidential work for an individual company to public domain information. The latter tends to be work funded by the public sector. In addition, results of work funded by part or all of the membership can be made public if members agree. However, any work done on behalf of an individual company or group of companies remains totally confidential unless the client(s) wishes to make the information more publicly available. Many companies use the Research Association to undertake an independent assessment of their products, for example analytical kits or systems, equipment, functionality of ingredients or packaging materials and systems. In such cases the independent assessment can then be used by the companies in support of their products. Thus the type of support provided by CCFRA varies according to the situation and circumstances of the client concerned.

One of the main advantages of using a centre dedicated to the scientific and technical needs of the food and drink industry is the wide range of on-site facilities and staff expertise available. Many of the scientists and technologies within the Centre are internationally renowned for their innovative research in their specialist areas which combined with industrial and practical experience provides a resource which is closely tuned to the needs of industry. In addition the specialist facilities, whether laboratory or pilot plant, provides access to up-to-date equipment. This, combined with a multidiciplinary approach to solving problems, provides one of the most effective scientific and technical resources available to the food, drink and associated industries. Indeed, one of the major benefits of a membership based Research Association is that companies share the cost of research and technical development in generic non-commercially sensitive areas. For example the current annual value of the collaborative member funded programme is approaching $3m US. Access to the results of such a programme can be achieved by an annual subscription (dues) of between $5,000 to $30,000 depending on the size of the company. In addition each member company is able to use 20% of the annual dues each year for free confidential consultancy, training or research and development. Any additional confidential work is charged at a preferential rate and each member only pays for the time they require the resource.

The following are just a few examples of work funded collaboratively by members which have provided the essential knowledge and skill based to assist companies in solving problems and developing opportunities.

The organoleptic (sensory) properties of food and drink are obviously paramount in determining a successful food product and thus the systematic and appropriate consumer research and sensory techniques are essential components of any new product development programme. Extensive skills and methods have been developed for the approaches to product matching, product mapping, product reformulation, product specification and control, shelf-life studies and determining product acceptability. These combined skills of consumer research and sensory analysis have been used widely by member companies in meeting the needs of consumers and especially where companies are contemplating new markets in different cultural and geographical areas.

CCFRA has also provided invaluable knowledge and information to North American companies about the UK and European market place in terms of new product trends and consumer views and attitudes.

Having the ability to predict the behaviour of formulations on, for example, product shelf life is also of great benefit to the development technologist. CCFRA is continuing to develop a series of computerised knowledge based systems in support of the baking industry. Aw Calc and Fault DoC are two such tools already available. Aw Calc is a versatile tool for calculating water activity and predicting mould free shelf-life for perishable products and has applications both in product development and production. The system will help by advising on the adjustment of formulations to achieve Aw targets and on the effects of mould inhibitors. A wide range of products can be processed through Aw Calc which has specific databases for baked products, unbaked toppings and fillings, baked fillings, high fruit products and composite products.

FAULT DoC (Fault Diagnosis of Cakes) assists manufacturers of cakes and sponges in the diagnosis of faults and optimisation of product quality. It suggests corrective actions to remedy problems or lack of specific characteristics in cakes whether they be physical e.g. uneven crumb structure or textural e.g. dry eating. These corrective actions are prioritised for production, ingredient quantities or ingredient qualities. Explanation and additional information on causes

of faults and associated remedial action are also provided thus saving valuable time and potential product losses. Apart from its use in optimisation, FAULT DoC can be used for cost-effective product development and training.

Another priority skill area for CCFRA is process modelling, especially aspects which enhance product safety and minimise commercial losses due to process deviations or reduce time to market for new products and processes.

CTemp is an example of a CCFRA product which can be used to predict the temperature history of packaged foods during a given thermal process.

It permits the rapid modelling assessments of the lethal, nutritive and cooking effects of thermal processes. Process deviations which inevitably occur in commercial production require to be made on what to do with a batch of product which could be worth several thousand dollars. CTemp has been used many times to provide a retrospective view on the Fo reduction attributed to a process deviation and has proved to be a very cost effective way of making informed and appropriate commercial decisions. CTemp only takes a few seconds to model a typical sterilisation process and essentially can be run in real time assuming the deviation is reported immediately.

CCFRA is also actively involved in using computational fluid dynamics (CFD) for applications in the food industry. It has the potential to benefit many food processing operations involving the flow of fluid such as water, air or non-Newtonian fluids as typified by most foods. Areas of current interest are in drying, mixing, refrigeration, clean room conditions, aseptic processing, in-container sterilisation, the rheological mechanisms involved in the processing or handling of complex foods and in hygienic design. The use of CFD at the design stage can avoid the costly re-engineering of plant that can be required to solve uneven or inappropriate flows. CCFRA has also used the technique to assist companies in solving problems of uneven flow in existing equipment. For example the modelling of chocolate flow through a pipe manifold enabled a design to correct the uneven flow to be rapidly determined.

The importance of good hygienic design of both food processing equipment and the processing environment (e.g. walls, floors, drains) is recognised as a major factor in the hygienic processing of safe food and drink. It is also essential for achieving efficient and cost-effective processing. A problem facing both designers and purchasers of food equipment has been the lack of standards and guidelines. CCFRA has responded to this need and in collaboration with industry has produced a series of illustrated guidelines on hygenic design of equipment and processing areas, including a range of test procedures for assessing cleanability. Details of these and many other publications together with general activities of CCFRA can be obtained from the author or via the Association's web site (http://www.campden.co.uk).

GLOUCESTER PARK, LONDON

CALLING THEM SERVICED APARTMENTS IS AN UNDERSTATEMENT

If you are planning to stay in London for three months or more, consider Gloucester Park Apartments. Located in fashionable Kensington, they are the last word in luxury, sophistication and security.

Gloucester Park has an enviable reputation as the perfect base

for business or leisure. Facilities include a state-of-the-art gym, sauna, 24 hour concierge and porterage, full housekeeping and maintenance, private garaging and maid service.

The elegant air-conditioned apartments boast fully equipped Miele kitchens, bathrooms en-suite and balconies. Other thoughtful touches are multi-language cable television and two private telephone lines with voicemail.

For further information contact us at the address below.

GLOUCESTER PARK

Your home away from home

Gloucester Park Apartments, Ashburn Place, London SW7 4LL
Tel: +44 171 373 1444   Fax: +44 171 244 5050
e-mail: reservations@chevalgroup.com   web site: http://www.chevalgroup.com
THE CHEVAL GROUP OF SERVICED APARTMENTS

Dockspeed Limited

Dockspeed Limited was established in 1986 by Andrew Ingleston, armed with a Business Studies Degree, experience in the haulage industry from a family background, post graduate activity, a true entrepreneurial spirit and a start-up loan from The Princes Trust. From humble beginnings with only one vehicle, to the current "O" Licences for 60 vehicles, Dockspeed has expanded steadily and at a rate that has outstripped the stagnation encountered elsewhere within the haulage industry. From 1992 the Company targeted the refrigerated sector of the international freight business and in particular a niche market to supply groupage services for export consignments of food products applying the JIT concepts of the UK markets, to overnight deliveries between UK and Europe.

Dockspeed is focused on customer services and has an enviable reputation for achieving the delivery that other operators cannot, with the same cost and time. Its success has earned Dockspeed the accolade of International Operator of the Year in 1996 and 1998 and has been a finalist for the Motor Transport Award in 1995 and 1997. The appreciation of Dockspeed's quality of service and reputation amongst its peers is also reflected in the Award of Haulier of the Year 1998.

Today Dockspeed continues to supply haulage services that are targeted to markets that require:

• Temperature control of chilled frozen and/or ambient conditions

• Rapid running i.e. express services

• Time sensitive deliveries where short code and/or tight deadlines are involved

• Security and/or protection of high value and/or otherwise susceptible products

Arising from its international haulage operations, Dockspeed has developed services for groupage load consolidation, product storage and picking/packing in chilled frozen and ambient conditions, as well as order control and (lately) Supply Chain Management across European markets.

As part of its logical growth Dockspeed's services have been further developed and substantially enhanced with a £3.4 million investment in a new depot at their Lympne, Kent base. In addition to substantial chilled and frozen coldstores, this facility provides a new HQ Office, housing Dockspeed Operations and Communications Centre, and a vehicle centre providing cashless diesel refuelling and automated internal and external truck-washing facilities. The geographical position of this depot, about 5 km from the Channel Tunnel and witnin close proximity of cross channel ferry services, enables optimisation of drivers hours and holding of product at the most strategically beneficial place to support business between the UK and Europe.

Effective from Wednesday 5th August 1998 Dockspeed has been sold to Norfolk Line which is part of the Danish A.P. Moller Group, with Andrew Ingleston continuing as Managing Director. The acquisition by Norfolk Line will enable Dockspeed to sustain its development whilst forming a keystone within the strategic plan to develop Group business in the carriage of time sensitive products.

See how we bring you the most innovative communications solutions?

Behind Lucent Technologies is R&D engine Bell Labs. Home of 24,000 engineers and scientists in 17 countries around the world. (Nine facilities in Europe, five in the UK.)

The source of ideas and solutions to help you meet any/every complex communications need you face, today and tomorrow. Innovations from Bell Labs are helping reduce complexity, by integrating voice and data.

Our networking solutions are reducing congestion and dramatically increasing capacity. We've even developed new servers and software that are, right now, enabling true Internet Telephony.

We know what the network of the future looks like. We know how to take you there.

Find out now. Contact Lucent Technologies BCS.

Europa House,
Southwood Crescent,
Farnborough,
Hants. GU14 0NR.
Tel: (01252) 391600
Fax: (01252) 376966
www: http://www.lucentbcsuk.co.uk

Lucent Technologies
Bell Labs Innovations

Farnborough, UK
www.lucentbcsuk.co.uk

We make the things that make communications work.

Contents

Part 5 Business Locations in the UK

Part 6 Useful Addresses

The European Mosaic

Author: Steven Jagger, Managing Director of GfK Great Britain.

The fifteen nations that make up the European Union together make up the world's biggest consumer market in terms of expenditure. (Per capita GDP is $19,443, compared to $19,295 in NAFTA.) This market offers tremendous opportunities for American companies, provided they acknowledge certain key cultural and demographic differences. Many impediments to cross boarder transactions have been demolished and a shared currency, currently being adopted by 11 countries, will remove much of the uncertainty associated with multinational transaction. Still, the Union is by no means a 'Common Market'.

With all this talk of integration it is easy to over look basic differences between European countries. Europe is a mosaic - each country has its own language, its own customs, and its own culture and cuisine. (Even when two countries share the same language they have a different history.) It is important that that these differences are not overlooked. They explain why your product will sell in one country but not in another.

There are some overriding trends, such as an aging population, that are common to all European countries. However, variations in many other factors need to be considered before deciding how to launch your product or service in Europe. These variations include household size, income levels, spending patterns, women's role in society, and perceptions of advertising.

Four times as many Europeans live in the space occupied by one American. This number goes still higher in the affluent and highly educated northern countries such as Holland and Belgium. European houses are smaller and closer together. The roads are narrower, and a whole lot more crowded. As a result, automobiles, appliances, and packages need to be smaller.

Aging Population

The total population of Europe is not expected to grow very much between now and 2020, an extra 2% is all that is expected. At the same time people are growing older therefore we will experience an aging population.

Europe's Aging Population
Percentage change in the # 65 year olds from 1995 to 2020

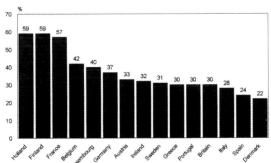

This population shift will generate demand for a new range of products and services designed to meet the entertainment needs of the swelling ranks of retirees. Additionally we will see a growing demand for products to meet the physical needs of an aging population; incontinence pads, stair lifts, sheltered housing, etc.

Household Size

Household size varies greatly between countries in the EU this is partially due to differences in each country's social security system but deeply ingrained cultural traditions also play a role. The result is varying size of appliances and packaging needs for each country.

The average European household consists of 2.54 persons but the differences around this average are enormous, 2.06 in Denmark to 3.26 in Spain. Half a person per household might not sound like much but this equates to significant differences in the composition of households. For example 36% of Danes live alone compared to only 13% of the Spanish population. Conversely 17% in Spain live in households composed of five or more members compared to five percent in Denmark.

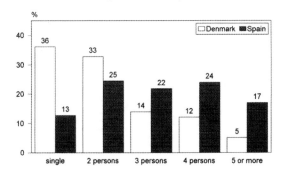

Single households are a phenomena of northern Europe, whilst southern Europeans tend to live in larger groups. Forty percent of Swedes live alone in single households whilst only 17% live in households of more than four people. In Spain the opposite is true, 41% live in large households and only 13% live alone

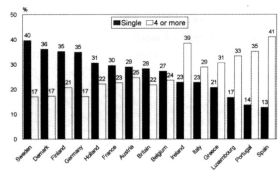

The reasons for this are mainly cultural, but also economic. A strong desire for independence is prevalent in the northern countries, whilst in the south, conviviality and extended family are stressed. A high level of youth unemployment in the southern countries serves to further limit the number of people living alone.

Marriage takes place at different ages in different countries. For example, Danes get married an average four years later than their Portuguese counterparts. This affects the purchase of major household appliances. When they come to marry, the average Dane has lived on his own, while the Portuguese has remained at home with his parents. It should come as no surprise, therefore, that purchases of appliances in Denmark are substantially higher than in Portugal.

Income and Expenditure patterns

Average, post tax, private income varies in Europe, from $12,802 per capita in Luxembourg to $4,627 in Greece.

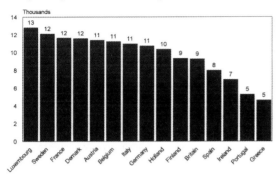

Differences in living costs reduce this income disparity. When this is taken into account, the picture changes. Italians have more disposable income than any other nationality and wealthy Swedes see a reduced purchasing power.

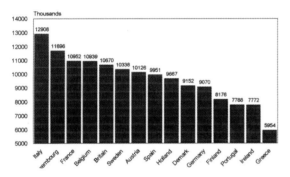

This, coupled with a strong cultural sense of style, explains why Italians spend roughly three times as much as Greeks on clothing. However, Austrians, who have substantially lower incomes than Italians, spend practically the same amount on clothing.

The Role of Women

Forty four percent of working age women in Europe have jobs, this varies greatly between countries (from 35% in Italy to 59% in Denmark). The level of female participation in the work force helps to explain differences in the average household income from country to country. This leads greater demands for childcare facilities and convenience food products in the countries where many women work.

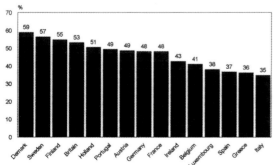

The number of single mothers is also an issue. Here the demarcation between north and south is also clear: 54% of the children born in Sweden in 1996 were outside marriage compared to only 3% in Greece.

Reactions to Advertising

The average European believes that there is too much advertising, that advertising temps people to buy things they don't need and makes things more expensive. This needs to be tempered by country differences the most pro advertising countries are Britain and Finland whilst the most anti are Germany and Spain. This is not linked to the amount of advertising that people see; yes Germans are exposed to more Advertising than the British or the Finns but the Spanish are exposed to even less. There is a very strong relationship between entertainment value and approval of advertising. Over and above this are differences in the type of advertising see in the different countries reflecting the local media market.

TV as % of ADv exp

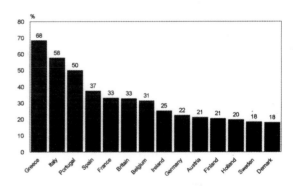

Cultural differences affect questionnaire responses

Asking purchase interest questions across Europe can be misleading, the same result from two countries will have a different meaning. You need to understand the cultural factors behind the questionnaire responses. These affect different types of questions differently. In southern Europe (Italy, Greece) there is a strong cultural desire for people to please the integrator by saying that they would do something in the future. In the extreme north people, (Sweden, Finland) people are more cautious and they tend to under claim their future actions. Questions about some non-personal aspect can produce similar results with the same meaning in both groups.

Looking East ñ The Future

The 217 million living to the east of the European Union should not be dismissed. They offer immense potential for the future. However, even with the current growth rates it will be a number of years before they achieve western European living standards.

Welcome to the world's biggest market.

Do you want to succeed in Europe?

Those who succeed are the best informed.

When it comes to testing products, concepts and advertising campaigns with real people, there's nobody better than GfK. We're Europe's leading market research company.

That's a position we've reached by providing an intelligent approach to testing, to reveal precisely how Europeans think and act.

We'll give you results which will make your business feel at home – in Europe and beyond.

So if you'd like your products and services examined, put us to the test – we speak your language.

GfK, revealing new answers

Call us today on
+44 171 872 4600.

INTRODUCTION OF THE EURO

The single currency is launched on 1 January 1999 and is likely to affect all businesses immediately, even though the UK will not be adopting it until 2002 at the earliest. Many businesses do not realise the impact that the introduction of the euro will have on them. It will not just affect those that buy and sell products and services in Europe. It is expected that the euro will become the most widely used foreign currency in the UK. It will certainly be used to conduct some business within the UK itself, particularly in supply chains involving large international and multinational companies.

The key message to businesses of all sizes is that many will be affected by the single currency and they must begin to plan now. Businesses will have to take strategic decisions before moving on to look at the operational changes that will follow on from them, including the impact on IT and accounting systems, treasury operations and human resources. And who better to help than a Chartered Accountant - a qualified professional who can give advice on all aspects of your business.

The Institute of Chartered Accountants in England and Wales has launched a series of guides to help all businesses deal with the introduction of the euro. For more information on the guides please contact Jacquie Parkins at the Institute, tel 0171 920 8623.

RUNCORN & WIDNES
• WHERE BUSINESS WORKS •

- Halton is a UK Intermediate area with European Objective 2 status.

- Situated between the conurbations of Liverpool and Greater Manchester, Halton has direct access to five million people within a twenty five mile radius.

- Halton can offer an unbeatable workforce, skilled, productive, adaptable and committed - fully supported by customised education and training facilities.

- Widnes and Runcorn can offer an impressive range and choice of land and premises in prime locations within the M62 and M56 corridors and within easy reach of Liverpool and Manchester airports and the Port of Liverpool.

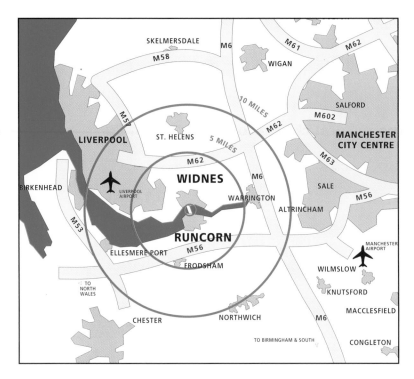

For more information concerning the opportunities for location and expansion in Halton contact the Economic Development Unit of Halton Borough Council on 0151 420 9428.

HALTON
BOROUGH COUNCIL
RUNCORN · WIDNES

• WHERE BUSINESS WORKS •

Foreword

The natural choice for investing in Europe

The UK attracts more foreign direct investment than any other developed country in the world apart from the US. Foreign investors mainly from North America, Europe and the Asia Pacific region produced an all time record of 618 projects last year. Britain also accounts for some 40 per cent of all US and Japanese investment in the EU and within the single market itself, cross-border investment is far higher into the UK than any other country. So why the popularity? It is a familiar story: a deregulated and flexible economy, low labour costs, tightly controlled inflation accompanied by rapid growth, low business and personal taxes – all backed by a hard-working, English-speaking workforce with a high level of skills. Couple these attractions with world-class business expertise; London's strength as a global financial centre; a strong commitment to the single European market; the right intellectual property rules; tax-free opportunities for research and development; the lack of foreign exchange controls or restrictions on repatriated profits, and you have a winning recipe for profitability.

It is the job of the UK's national inward investment agency, the Invest in Britain Bureau (IBB), to ensure companies worldwide know the reasons for this success and continue to locate in the UK when planning their international investments.

In all the major investment markets of the world, IBB advises companies on areas of the UK that best match their own requirements; provides initial information on costs, legal requirements and so on, and arranges visits that enable potential investors to view candidate sites at first hand.

IBB gives guidance on national, regional and local incentives where available to encourage investment in Britain. It also offers information on the necessary requirements for getting established, including issues such as work permits and immigration law. Contacts are supplied with key private sector companies and public sector organisations and advice is offered on worker availability and skills, component suppliers and sub-contractors.

Britain will continue to attract the interest of companies from all over the world as we further develop our research and development base and other business advantages for international investors in the European market. If you are not already in the UK or talking to British companies we would be happy to help you start.

Andrew Fraser
Chief Executive, Invest in Britain Bureau

Do you know what *your* employees think about health and safety?

Would you like to:

o **Raise the profile of health and safety in your organisation?**

o **Provide employee involvement in health and safety?**

o **Complement the active monitoring of your health and safety system?**

o **Develop cooperative solutions to health and safety problems with your employees?**

o **Complement health and safety audits?**

o **Set the agenda and focus for health and safety training and discussions?**

o **Provide a baseline for measuring the effect of initiatives?**

o **Benchmark your location against others in your organisation?**

o **Capture sensitive information from your employees in a confidential manner?**

The *Health and safety climate survey tool* can help you do all these.

This is a new product from the Health and Safety Executive, which gives organisations the means of collecting employees' views on some important health and safety related issues within their organisations.

The software package comes with a user manual which describes how to use the software, customise the questionnaire and analyse the data collected.

The guidelines highlight some important issues for organisations to consider within a framework process for planning and administering the survey, and taking the results forward. The emphasis is on transparency, visible management commitment and workforce involvement at all stages.

Employee involvement in health and safety is essential in effective occupational accident and ill-health prevention. The tool provides a direct way of involving the workforce. It can also give fresh impetus to the health and safety committee and safety representative systems by involving them in both planning and carrying out the survey, and in using the results to improve standards.

For more details or an information pack contact HSE Books:
Tel: 01787 881165
Fax: 01787 313995

HSE BOOKS

The Health and Safety Climate Survey Tool

A Message from the British-American Chamber of Commerce

Today, over 3,500 US companies are located in Britain, with a $78 billion stake in its economy. This figure reflects an increase of 30 per cent from five years ago, and now constitutes approximately 40 per cent of all US direct investment into the EU.

The British-American Chamber of Commerce, founded in 1920, exists to expand and sustain the partnership between the US and the U K. In recent years, the BACC has grown into an association of over 4,500 senior business executives in its offices in New York and London.

Both offices are members of the British American Business Council (BABC),the network of 34 British-American Business Associations throughout NorthAmerica and the UK. All BABC offices are engaged in senior level involvement with government on both sides of the Atlantic. The BACC London office acts as the BABC British administrative centre and assists in the development of new UK offices. As of 1998, it has four other English operations: Bristol, Birmingham, Manchester and Leeds. The British-American Business Council is today proud to call itself the premier forum for the exchange of information and the promotion of businesses actively engaged in transatlantic trade and investment.

The Chamber operates a trade information service for both members and non-members to assist them with any questions on doing business in either country. Specific company enquiries, lists of contacts and visa questions can all be handled by the in-house department. The service operates a Visa Exchange Programme - expedited processing of Jl and WP2 work permits – for member companies to transfer staff between Britain and America for training or work experience.

The Chamber publishes two quarterly magazines, *UK & USA*, and *Business Network* as well as a bilateral investment directory, available on CD-ROM, listing US and UK parent companies and their subsidiaries on both sides of the Atlantic. The Chamber also provides an annual membership directory and a newsletter, *The London-New York Briefing*. All publications are designed to showcase members, new business developments and promote the programmes in New York and London.

A varied events schedule includes seminars, briefings, speaker functions, networking receptions, lunches, dinners and sporting functions. Between 30 to 40 events are held each year. Special guests participating in the Chamber's events in the last six months in London include Lady Thatcher, the former prime minister, Gordon Brown, the UK Chancellor of the Exchequer, Arthur Levitt, the Chairman of the US Securities and Exchange Commission and Eddie George, the Governor of the Bank of England.

We would be delighted to assist any company wishing to set up operations in the UK, through any of our offices. Not only do we have the experienced staff but we have access to over 750 companies who can assist with the simplest to the most complicated operations.

The British-American Chamber of Commerce
8 Staple Inn
Holborn
London WC1V 7QH
Tel: +44 171 404 6400
Fax +44 171 404 6828
E-mail: pwaite@bacc.co.uk
Web site: http//www.bacc.org

The British-American Chamber of Commerce
32 Vanderbilt Avenue, 20th Floor
New York
NY 10017
Tel: +1 212 661 4060
Fax: +1 212 661 4074
E-mail: rfursland@bacc.org

The UK has long been described as the European Union's most attractive country for global corporations seeking a manufacturing presence. Today it is increasingly popular among those investing in research and development as well. And of course in the fields of banking and financial services, London's International pre-eminence continues whatever happens elsewhere in the world - Business Week stated recently that London is the global financial center for the 21st Century.

Most of the world's leading manufacturers have operations in Britain, whether in the automotive, electronics, pharmaceuticals, chemicals or other industries. Many have their European headquarters in the UK. Recent years have seen heavy foreign investment in British utilities and the country also has more customer communications centers and shared service centers than anywhere else in Europe. Recent investments by major North American corporations include Microsoft, Pfizer, Alcan, Abbot Laboratories and Capital One.

As British companies have been major investors in the US and Canada, North America corporations in particular have invested substantially in the united Kingdom. In fact, the UK is the world's second largest recipient of inward investment after the United States, claiming over 40% of US investment in the European Union and over 45% of Canadian. The UK is also a major recipient of cross-border investment within the EU, receiving more than any other member state.

So why the popularity? It is a virtuous circle. Success breeds success and well over half of the new investments tend to be expansions by companies already operating in the UK. Furthermore, almost a third of Britain's impressive growth in manufacturing productivity during the 1990s has been attributed to new production and management techniques introduced by overseas investors. Their influence in turn has brought new cost-control and self-improvement techniques to British-based suppliers. The Chairman of German car giant BMW, Bernd Pischetsrieder, has said: "Structural change has made Britain by far the most attractive place to invest in Europe."

As we approach the new millennium there are a number of reasons why the UK is clearly the most attractive all-round business environment of any large European economy. Not least is its global reputation for flexibility and competitiveness - factors at the heart of the Government's broad economic strategy, alongside its commitment to enhanced skills and opportunities for the national workforce.

The Government is determined to maintain stable economic conditions for business in Britain, wherever in the world investors are based. Corporation tax has been cut and investment incentives re-emphasized. A closer relationship with the rest of Europe and determination to complete the single market continue to underpin the UK's attractiveness.

What about the common European currency due to get started in 1999? Hasn't the UK refused to join it and won't that create barriers within the single European market, affecting investment prospects? The fact that long-term US and Canadian investments in Britain have shown no sign of slowing would appear to answer that, but the simple response is "no".

Britain has been holding the presidency of the European Union in the first half of 1998 during the most demanding period in its history - major decisions have been taken on monetary union. As well as offering strong and constructive support to Britain's European partners in helping to create more employment and prosperity across the continent, the UK Government has also declared support for the principle of monetary union, making clear and unambiguous economic benefit to the country the decisive test for membership.

The potential benefits of a successful Euro to Europe as a whole, including the UK, are obvious in terms of trade, transparency of costs and currency stability. However, business cycle conditions that differ from the rest of Europe do make it unrealistic for the UK to join in 1999 but if the right economic conditions are met and the British people give their assent, the country will adopt the European currency in a few years time.

In the meantime, Britain is actively involved with its partners in making arrangements for the new currency and UK-based business is being encouraged to prepare for the change. Membership of the single currency or not, all EU members will be co-operating well before individual national currencies disappear in 2002.

Internationally mobile investment requires an ever higher proportion of advanced skills in design, marketing, distribution and R&D as well as manufacturing. Government policies are directed towards providing those higher skills through greater investment in education at all levels as well as support for science and research.

After the US, no other developed country has Britain's combination of appeal to inward investors, profit from outward investment, and degree of innovation - technological change in the UK is inextricably bound up with the international economy. Where the British innovate, overseas investors are certain to profit.

Prime Minister Tony Blair has said: "We have an unrivaled track record. We were once the workshop of the world, leading the Industrial Revolution. Since then Britain can claim to be the birthplace of the majority of leading inventions of the last 100 years: the television, the computer, fiber optics, penicillin, the discovery of DNA, genetic fingerprinting, communication technology and the microwave oven. We have 90 Nobel Prizes for Science. Today we are leading the world in a creative revolution. Our design industry is worth £12 billion (nearly US $20 billion) a year and employs more than 300,000 people."

Add this innovation expertise to Britain's ever more sophisticated communications, its national infrastructure, culture and linguistic familiarity in a world where English is the standard language of international business, and you have a sure-fire recipe for continuing North American corporate success in Europe's most familiar investment location.

Tony Blair added: "We are committed to maintaining a business environment that provides every incentive for companies to grow, innovate and gain competitive advantage. You can plan corporate growth with confidence in the future.

"Nine out of ten Formula One cars are designed and built in Britain. We are world leaders in pharmaceuticals and telecommunications. We lead Europe in financial services with 560 overseas banks in London from 76 countries and a third of the world's foreign exchange business comes through London. We are the world center for creative advertising with £10 billion (US $16 billion) spent each year. Heathrow is the world's busiest airport for international passengers.

"Britain will continue to be the ideal base from which to operate internationally. If you have not already done so, now is the time to join us".

Est. 1921

A Message from the Canada-United Kingdom Chamber of Commerce

In 1921 a group of Canadian business people established 'the Canadian Chamber of Commerce in Great Britain Incorporated'. We have to presume that the objectives of that group, 77 years ago, were to co-ordinate the activities of Canadian companies wishing to export to the UK or to set up, or maybe even invest in the UK. Incorporated as a UK company in 1927, and changing its name to Canada-United Kingdom Chamber of Commerce in 1970, the Chamber has long since expanded its constituency to include UK companies in its membership.

For a great many years now, it has operated in the interests of companies from either side of the Atlantic, whether they be exporters or importers, inward or outward investors. The Chamber works very closely with all governments, national, federal or provincial. In the UK this is principally with the Department of Industry (DTI) and the Foreign and Commonwealth Office (FCO) in London and in the UK Consul-General offices in Canada. On the Canadian side, the contact is mainly with the High Commission representing the Federal Government of Canada (the Chamber is fortunate to operate from the High Commission offices in London's Grosvenor Square), and with provincial governments either direct, or through Agent General offices in London.

In response to member needs, the Chamber provides networking opportunities, information on economic and political situations and developments, and it endeavours to identify suitable contract opportunities for members and potential members. It sets out to achieve the position of 'foremost non-governmental authority on all aspects of two-way trade and investment between Canada, the United Kingdom and Europe'.

Through lunches, breakfast meetings, seminars, etc, the Chamber offers a first-class networking opportunity, one of the biggest lunches in its history being for the Prime Minister of Canada, the Hon Jean Chretien, when nearly 600 attended. Other major speakers have included a number of federal ministers and provincial premiers. The Chamber is always keen to give a platform to politicians and prominent business people from either Canada or the UK, and to guarantee a meaningful audience. The Chamber is also involved with exhibitions and missions.

Canada-United Kingdom Chamber of Commerce
38 Grosvenor Street London WIX 0DP
Tel: +44 171 259 6576
Fax: +44 171 259 6594

THERE'S MORE TO EUROPE THAN MEETS THE EYE

"Under the most vigorously controlled conditions of pressure, temperature, volume, humidity and other variables, the organism will do as it damn well pleases"

OLD HARVARD LAW

Research is a hydra-headed creature and the European species is large and mobile. Taming it will require concentration and consistency of effort, winning the contest by the ability to understand and subsequently influence behaviour.

If Europe is to perform for you as a market, thinking mainstream Europe and acting marginally local are the commands. This is our area of specialisation. We have the ability to help create universal standards that can be applied into local markets, then measured with practicality and intensity to change performance in a positive way.

The best-laid plans emanating from the centre of major organisations can be stifled at the surface by customer-facing staff. Performance research and measurement help your plans become achievements and not remain as spread sheets.

WHAT WE BELIEVE ABOUT RESEARCH

The Grass Roots Group approach to research is to concentrate on measuring what can be changed in the way staff and customers interact and behave. We view research as a performance measurement tool, not as a means of collecting interesting data. We distil actionable information from our findings and feed it back to those who can fastest and most effectively respond to a field issue.

They need to know quickly what we have discovered and what they should do about it. Not in days, weeks or months, but in minutes and hours. Our team uses the latest computer, Internet and telephone technology to observe field performance and record customer experiences for rapid reporting to the front-line troops. Like the man said…

"Computers are incredibly fast, accurate and stupid; humans are incredibly slow, inaccurate and brilliant; together they are powerful beyond imagination."
ALBERT EINSTEIN (1879-1955)

IN THE FACE OF SUCH ODDS, business needs sound market information before making critical moves. Europe as a market is a reality, and tackling it is an irresistible business challenge, but the requirement is for intelligence in both senses of the term.

THE EUROPEAN DIMENSION

We only have the choice between the changes that are imposed on us and those we desire and accomplish.
JEAN MONNET ('THE FATHER OF EUROPE')

In conjunction with Groupe Everest, France's leading business development and marketing consultancy, The Grass Roots Group has created InteResource to anticipate and respond to client demand for effective solutions to business challenges on an international scale.

Whilst its base is European, InteResource is a world-wide network represented in 70 countries where it is able to improve the business performance of organisations by making the most of their human assets. In co-founding InteResource we remain faithful to the belief that the quality of any organisation derives from the people who are its principal asset, but we share our knowledge, experience and methods with a wider audience.

InteResource brings together a group of companies experienced in performance improvement skills and techniques. By pooling their specialist knowledge and considerable resources, they are able to develop and implement effective solutions on a European and international basis, matching the scale of business opportunities.

WHAT WE PROVIDE

To say we just provide customer satisfaction research, Mystery Shopping and interactive surveys is like saying an Olympic marathon is a fun run.
Research is part of the solution, but only a base from which to start. Research in itself will not change the way things are done. We work in close partnership with our clients to define

the issues, providing a focus for the information we need and the changes we seek through the four proven catalysts for change:
Communication
Education
Measurement
Reward.
The types of projects that will be effected this way are, for example:

Customer focused
■ Performance measurement at the point of sale
■ Quality standards monitoring
■ Customer loyalty initiatives
■ Customer satisfaction outbound
■ Customer satisfaction inbound
■ Brand promotion and brand protection

Employee and channel focused
■ Skills evaluation and product training
■ Employee recognition and motivation
■ Employee communication
■ Channel communication
■ Trade improvement programmes
■ Team incentives

THE SPECIALIST TOOLS WE USE

Mystery Shopping allows the measurement of specific personal issues that customer surveys miss. It also provides highly effective, rapid and accurate feedback. Whether you are measuring the effectiveness of your staff training or running a service improvement programme, the sheer power and value of a structured Mystery Shopping programme must be seen to be believed. We provide an action replay, which can be viewed over and over again, to help your team improve.

Our fully trained Mystery Shoppers can cover an enormous range…
■ they can go through the process of selecting a new car;
■ they can ask detailed questions about a personal loan in a bank;
■ they can observe the length of queues in a fast-food outlet, then sample the product and report back (and we have been doing this in 18 countries).

Our Mystery Shopper database in the UK alone has over 16,000 individuals available for general assignments, whilst for more complex studies requiring expert evaluation we have some 1,500 skilled and experienced professionals.

Disabled Mystery Shoppers are a separate group of people all of whom have hearing, sight or physical impairments. They enable us to assist clients in complying with the requirements of the U.K. Disability Discrimination Act by assessing the service provided to people with disabilities.

Interactive Surveys allow our clients to act immediately on what their customers or staff are saying. Imagine the impact on service when a manager receives a fax or e-mail immediately reporting that day's measurement! Actual soundbites of direct customer comment can be available the same day, providing information to praise staff or to resolve customer problems fast - customer loyalty is created this way.

Interactive Voice Response allows us to automate large volumes of data, often making conventional techniques redundant. Why ask a customer to fill in a form and post it when they could pick up the 'phone and do the data entry for you? Their direct response will be faster and cheaper to process, and more credible when it arrives.

Internet Reporting is fast becoming a replacement for printed reports. Its ease of access and its flexibility dictate that in the future most actionable information will be transmitted in this way to remote office and field based staff. The real war on waste paper starts here.

Interactive Learning is our highly cost effective way of training thousands of people in product knowledge and service skills that are essential for your business and for dealing with your customers. Using latest technology, individuals work at their own pace and are recognised with certification and accreditation at various stages of their progress.

THE SERVICES WE OFFER

We provide a range of services and products enabling our clients to make the most of their human assets, whether defined as employees, third parties – such as dealers, networks or suppliers – or customers. These services and products fall into the four distinctive headings already mentioned.

Communication

Grass Roots provides a complete range of services to meet any communications need. Not everyone enjoys the written word; sometimes a visual image can convey a message just as powerfully. A clever combination of both can be infinitely more effective than the sum of the two parts. In the execution of the image we do not recognise conventional limitations of size, time, place or type of medium.

Good communications should keep people looking, reading, absorbing, responding and reacting. We wouldn't be happy with anything less.

Education

Having the right level of knowledge is the key to achieving optimum effectiveness. Knowing how to transform that knowledge into usable skills, then how to apply those skills in a more effective and productive way, is essential. After all, education is not just about what you learn, but how it is applied.

Measurement

Measurement both asks and answers the question "How am I doing?" The objective is action - the accurate and fair measurement of the quality and quantity of actions that can justify additional reward or recognition for effort.

We believe that performance improvement and achievement are motivation in themselves; and improved performance is prompted by timely and accurate measurement.

We don't rely on customer satisfaction surveys, because it's loyal not satisfied customers that drive a business. We'll research the service provided to existing customers by survey and discussion groups, and to prospective customers by Mystery Shopping. Using specifically designed questionnaires we are able to measure qualitative responses objectively.

Reward

To complement the end product of targeted research, effective measurement and monitoring, we provide the widest choice of cost-effective reward and recognition.

Our computer based stored value system provides account holders with security controlled access to check balances or place orders - either by fax, phone or post. Our award bank is open 24 hours a day 365 days a year for telephone banking, making the reward bank account the ideal tool for a staff incentive, trade incentive or customer loyalty programme.

Visit our Website on http://www.grg.co.uk

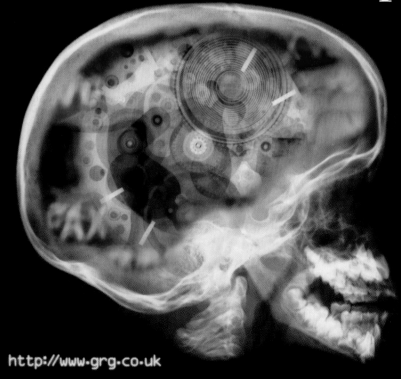

Find out what Europe is thinking

Since taking Europe by storm is no longer an option, the way to expand your presence is by capturing people's hearts and minds. To do that requires an understanding of the way Europe works and the way Europe thinks, because what you do not understand you cannot change.

Grass Roots brings you intelligence, in both senses of the term. We will obtain information, and we will help you make constructive use of it. We will deliver a solution, not a more rarefied definition of your problem.

We are radicals, not reactionaries, so do not expect too much respect for the status quo. Once we have helped you find out what Europe is thinking, we'll have some bright ideas for making it think differently about you and your company.

There's more to Europe than meets the eye

THE GRASS ROOTS GROUP PLC

PENNYROYAL COURT STATION ROAD
TRING HERTS HP23 5QZ UNITED KINGDOM
TELEPHONE:+44 (0)1442 829 400
FACSIMILE:+44 (0)1442 829 405
http://www.grg.co.uk

http://www.grg.co.uk

Part 1
The UK and Europe

1

An Historical and Cultural Overview

by Jonathan Reuvid

THE UK AND EUROPE

History has been unhelpful to the development of the UK's role in modern Europe. It encouraged the UK to cling for far too long to its 'island heritage' as an excuse for retaining a voyeuristic attitude towards mainland Europe and, at times, its European partners. The outlook today for the UK's constructive participation in the management and further development of the EU is brighter than at any time since it became a member of the European Community on 1 January 1973. However, it is important to understand why the UK was such a late entrant to the Community and the twists and turns of the UK's uneasy relationship with the Community in order to share the present mood of confidence.

From 1946 to 1973

While the Second World War changed the UK's global position both politically and economically for ever, its economic superiority in Europe, built upon its access to cheap raw materials from the British Empire, had been in decline since the end of the last century. By 1946 the US and Russia were the predominant World powers, with the US becoming pre-eminent both economically and militarily in the free world after its detente with the USSR in 1947 and the subsequent division of Europe from the Baltic to the Adriatic. Ravaged by war, the economies of Western Europe were rebuilt with the assistance of the European Recovery Program, introduced by US Secretary of State George Marshall in June 1947 under which the US generously poured $17 billion of grants into Western European states between 1948 and 1952. At the same time, the security of Europe against the threat of Russian aggression was ensured by the signing of the North Atlantic Pact which committed American troops to the defence of Western Europe under the North Atlantic Treaty Organization

(NATO) instituted in 1949. By these two acts, and its parallel involvement in the rehabilitation of the Japanese economy, the US assumed leadership of the capitalist world, unchallenged until the mid-sixties, except by France after the election of General Charles de Gaulle as President in 1958.

During this immediate post-war period, the UK began to come to terms with its diminished role in international affairs. The experience of the Second World War, in which the UK was the only European State not to be invaded, had reinforced the tendency of British politicians and policy-makers to consider the UK as still occupying a special position in world affairs. An adjustment might have been made after the First World War, if the US had not withdrawn from the international system, leaving a weakened UK to continue playing the role of world power. Even after the Second World War, the UK, unlike its European neighbours, continued to formulate its foreign policy in global terms, partly because it remained an imperial power and had assumed responsibilities under the Yalta Agreement for the colonial dependencies of defeated states which were not immediately able to take their independence. Therefore, British policy in the post-war 1940s and 1950s became framed in terms of three 'spheres' of influence, being first the special relationship with the US, second the Commonwealth and, definitely third, Europe. This policy was first articulated by Winston Churchill in opposition, but expressed the consensus view of both Conservative and Labour leaderships, as well as the Foreign Office. The need to maintain US engagement in Europe was perceived as paramount.

The concept of the 'special relationship' between the UK and the US was always, to some degree, the offspring of self-delusion by successive British governments. The presumption that America would need and accept guidance from another English-speaking nation in the management of its relations with other European States formed a psychological block to the

UK recognising the need to participate in the European Communities. Initially, the UK considered that the support of successive US Administrations for European unity was simply mistaken. Even after entry to the EC, until President Clinton, after taking office, expressed his preference for developing US relations with Germany, it was assumed by British governments that the special relationship constituted the natural communication link between the US and the EU.

In the 1950s there were practical commercial reasons as well as psychological factors why the UK placed the Commonwealth above Europe as a sphere of influence. In 1948 the UK sent 40 per cent of its exports and re-exports to the Commonwealth and this trading relationship would be jeopardised by any transfer to preferential trading with other European states. Indeed, sectors of the UK economy, supported by influential pressure groups, were wholly dependent on Commonwealth trade. In addition to the economic significance of the Commonwealth to the UK, there was a strong nostalgic link which found its expression in the popular sentiment that Commonwealth members were 'kith and kin' while continental Europeans were 'foreigners'. Finally, there was a belief, which has come to seem arrogant with the passing of the decades, that leadership of the Commonwealth gave the UK a louder voice than other Western European states.

These are the complementary factors, then, which led the UK to reject the French proposal for a customs union, first mooted in 1947 in response to the Marshall Plan at the Council for European Economic Cooperation (CEEC). Subsequent proposals, by the French, for a customs union as a 'third force' between the US and the USSR continued to be rebuffed by the UK. While the UK was content with the role of a political Robin to the US' Batman as a means of maintaining the security of Europe against the USSR, France nurtured the vision of leading a united Western Europe, an underlying tenet of the Fourth Republic and a fundamental theme of General de Gaulle's Presidency. Ironically, the US supported the idea of a customs union in 1947 and suggested subsequently that the UK should assume leadership of the West European movement for unity, a proposal rejected by the UK on the grounds of compromising British sovereignty and the Commonwealth economic link.

British unwillingness to become involved in Europe persisted through the introduction of the Schuman Plan for coal and steel, the Pleven Plan for the European Defence Community (EDC) and the formation of the European Economic Community (EEC). When the UK finally came to apply for membership of the European Communities in 1961, the factors driving the application were the successful economic performance of the six members of the EEC in comparison to that of the UK, the likelihood that the scope of the EEC would be extended to some form of political cooperation in the area of foreign policy and the implied threat to the UK's perceived relationship with the US. As students of this period of European history will recall, the 1961 application, encouraged by the Kennedy administration, was made by the Macmillan government with manifestly little enthusiasm. It was blocked in 1963 by a unilateral French veto, primarily on the grounds that the UK had not accepted a European vocation and of the UK's continued attachment to the US. The British Government's reaction to the veto was relaxed and a renewed application was made by the second Harold Wilson government in 1966 which was again blocked by de Gaulle, this time pre-empting any negotiation. The Labour Government left the application on the table in the knowledge that no progress could be made while de Gaulle remained in office. In 1969, shortly after President Pompidou's election as de Gaulle's successor, the Six agreed to proceed with negotiations for UK entry. Actual negotiation was conducted under the Heath Conservative Government which succeeded Labour in June 1970 and culminated in agreement one and a half years later. During this period the economic problems of deep recession, triggered by the first oil crisis, disrupted the smooth development of the EC, making it harder for the UK, which had been equally affected, to make a seamless entry in 1973.

From EC entry to the first Thatcher Government

Labour opposed the UK's entry to the EC on the terms negotiated by the Heath Government, which was the root cause of poor relations with the EC from the moment that the Wilson third government came to power in 1974. However, the UK had already established itself as an awkward partner, from the moment of entry, by its insistence that as many as possible of the Community's institutions should be located in Brussels, by pursuing its national objectives vigorously and by refusing to adapt to the established practice of the Six in linking issues together in package deals.

The Wilson Governments of 1974 to 1976 survived on the slimmest of Parliamentary majorities (no overall majority, in fact, until the second 1974 election and only three seats thereafter). It was plagued by domestic issues of which high inflation, unemployment and a record balance of payments deficit were the most serious. At this point, the EC was at the nadir of its popularity among the UK electorate, having been blamed somewhat unfairly for the UK's economic ills and being associated firmly in the public's mind with Heath and the discomforts of industrial unrest in the latter period of his government. Largely as a distraction from domestic ills, Wilson undertook to renegotiate the terms of UK entry to the EC on the basis that they had been disowned by the Labour Party at the February 1974 election and with the promise of an electoral vote on the revised terms. Although, in retrospect, the changes negotiated were relatively minor, Wilson was able to present the result as a triumph of negotiation and in 1975 proceeded to the referendum. Somewhat surprisingly, the result was a landslide in favour of remaining within the EC with a 67.2 per cent 'Yes' vote on a turnout of 64.6 per cent. The strength of the majority was attributed by observers at the time to the impressive line-up of establishment figures in favour of the Community, with divided Labour electors following their leader and a general bias in favour of the status quo.

If the Six had expected an improvement in the UK's behaviour after this impressive display of support, they were soon disappointed. During the remainder of Wilson's period in office until he stepped down in March 1976, a whole range of issues including pollution control, energy and the treatment of the UK's North Sea oil and the limitation of lorry drivers' hours came before the Council of Ministers on which the UK was

the persistent 'odd man out'. This legacy was inherited by Callaghan, Wilson's successor. Within weeks of his appointment, the UK was plunged into the sterling crisis which resulted in an initial standby credit from other Central Banks and subsequently a £3.9 billion loan from the IMF. The IMF conditions, which included major reductions in public spending plans for the budget years 1977–8 and 1978–9 and the sell-off of a major part of the Government's shares in British Petroleum, signalled the final retreat from Labour's 1974 manifesto commitments to an extensive social welfare programme. By now, with Liberal support, Callaghan was operating a minority Labour Government which perished in the winter of 1978 through its inability to hold down inflationary wage settlements during what came to be known as 'the winter of discontent'. In May 1979 the Conservative Party was returned to government under Margaret Thatcher.

Mrs Thatcher and the European Community

During the Callaghan Government the major issue which was to plague UK relationships with its European partners during the next twenty years, the European Monetary System (EMS), first came to the fore. The original EMS proposal originated from Germany, whose advocacy for 'a zone of monetary stability' was based on the adverse effects of the decline in value of the US dollar at that time on the German economy. The high incidence of speculative funds and the growing tendency to use the Deutschmark as a reserve currency were contributory factors. The German initiative was also intended to dampen inflation rates.

First, the issue of EC budget contributions became the battleground for Margaret Thatcher's running dispute with the UK's partners throughout the five-year period up to the June 1984 meeting of the Council of Ministers at Fontainebleau. By 1977 the UK had become the second biggest net contributor to the EC budget after Germany, and it was apparent that when the UK became a full member of the Community in 1980, after the transition period, it would be the largest net contributor with its 1977 deficit nearly doubling to about £800 million.

For the first three years of Mrs Thatcher's first government, the UK, in common with its European partners, faced a renewed world recession sparked off by the 1979 rise in oil prices. In the UK's case, the downturn was exaggerated by an increase in VAT from eight to fifteen per cent and interest rates of 12 to 14 per cent, rising to 17 per cent in November 1979. The battle on contributions to the EC budget must be viewed in the context of the UK Government's efforts to contain, if not reduce, public expenditure, which was a key plank in the Thatcher economic programme.

In January 1981, Ronald Reagan took office and the 'special relationship' was reborn, demonstrating that, so far as it exists, it resides in the personal rapport between individual leaders which has been established at intervals since Churchill and Roosevelt struck their first personal summit relationship in the dark days of World War Two.

The Reagan commitment to defence expenditure became the engine for a renaissance of American industry as leading edge technologies of telecommunications, computers, lasers and robotics were developed, first in the service of armaments and the space programme and subsequently for civilian applications. Thanks to this 'special relationship', the UK did not side with France and Germany to match the technological advances which the US had made. Instead the Thatcher Government set out to benefit directly from these developments by establishing the UK as a repository for foreign direct investment (FDI) from multinationals, especially Japanese and American and more recently Korean, who had acquired the new technologies and were seeking to establish subsidiaries and subcontractors within the European Community. The effectiveness of this strategy and the part which it has played in the economic revival of the UK is discussed further below.

Early skirmishes in the Thatcher crusade to reduce the UK's net EC budget contributions were inconclusive, although reductions for 1980 and 1981 were agreed with difficulty. Returned to popularity and power in 1983 after the Falklands conflict of 1982, Mrs Thatcher's Government enjoyed its most successful period in its second term of office, with reduced inflation, the rise in unemployment halted, increasing inward investment, a booming financial services sector and a general recovery from world recession which was more beneficial to the UK as an oil producer than to other European partners. During this period, Mrs Thatcher renewed her offensive against the restrictive practices of British Trade Unions, defeating the militant Miners Union at the conclusion of its protracted eleven month strike in February 1985.

In June 1983, the Genscher-Colombo Plan to 'relaunch' the Community raised the spectre of federalism through its references to EU, while the UK, at all times more concerned to remove barriers which still existed to the free working of the internal Community market, notably adverse effects on free trade in financial services, maintained its anti-federalist policy while advocating the creation of a genuine economic common market with the addition of cooperation on foreign policy.

There followed a series of disastrous meetings of the European Council of Ministers from December 1983 at which successive proposals for solving the issue of the UK's net contributions were rejected or sabotaged by threats and vetos. Finally, at the June Fontainebleau meeting of the Council of Ministers, the UK accepted a rebate of one billion ECU for 1984 and a limited formula for 1985 and 1986. The demand for an automatic and permanent formula for calculating rebates was abandoned. At the same time, small cuts in farm prices and dairy quotas encouraged the UK to believe that there was a firm intention to constrain CAP expenditure and to agree a rise in VAT revenues from 1.0 to 1.4 per cent.

Shortly after the Fontainebleau meeting, the Community was plunged into a budget crisis when the UK blocked the proposal for a 2 billion ECU supplementary budget for 1984, insisting on a programme of expenditure cuts and deferrals into 1985 with VAT increases to be brought forward from 1986 to 1985. In September, the UK relaxed its stance, agreeing to 1 billion ECU increase in the 1984 budget against a commitment to reach swift agreement on strict financial guidelines to control future budget growth, especially the CAP. At

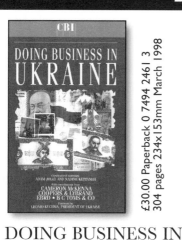

the next Council of Ministers meeting in Dublin in December, limited controlling procedures were agreed. At the same meeting, the accession of Spain and Portugal to the Community was approved.

After 1984 the focus of the UK's efforts within the Community shifted to freeing the internal market and drawing its partners away from unacceptable institutional reforms. On the world stage, the Group of Five declaration to take concerted action to bring down the value of the dollar was successful in causing a reduction from the March 1985 peak of 25 to 40 per cent against different OECD currencies. Similar action was agreed on interest rates and the Uruguay round of GATT negotiations followed in 1986 at which significant progress was made towards lowering trade barriers. By the end of 1986 oil prices had fallen some 40 per cent and the movement out of recession by the developed world enabled Western Europe to compete with the US for investment capital. Meanwhile, President Reagan's unilateral negotiations with President Gorbachev over NATO missile-reductions together with US foreign policy aggression in the Middle East (which had been fully supported by the UK but were much criticized by other EC members) helped to move defence up on the European political agenda.

The long battle over the UK's net budget contributions had been a distraction from the main debate between the partners over the development of the EC institutions. The basic UK position, as stated by Malcolm Rifkind in 1983, has hardly changed to this day:

> *To us, institutions must be subservient to policies. Closer co-operation should not be forced but must grow out of practical ways in which, as a Community, we can work together for our common good. Substance and reality must come before form.*

In the mid-1980s the institutional reform debate was focused on the need for more rapid decision-making goals and there was a majority proposal from the Dooge Committee in 1985 that the member states' veto should be abandoned in favour of majority voting, except for specific areas designated as being too sensitive to allow national interests to be over-ruled. The minority finding of the Committee members representing the UK, Denmark and Greece, with some backing from Ireland, was that the veto was an essential part of their terms of membership, but that its use should be constrained by a requirement for written justification whenever invoked. Likewise, the majority found in favour of an increase in the decision-making powers of the European Parliament while the minority advocated continuation of its consultative role. These and other matters were the subject of agreement at the December 1985 meeting of the Council of Ministers in Luxembourg in a revision to the Treaty of Rome which incorporated a statement that European union was the ultimate aim of the Community. The Single European Act, it was agreed, should include mention of the EMS and no major increase was proposed to the powers of the European Parliament. Majority voting would be limited to areas related to the freeing of the internal market, but taxation, free movement of persons, health controls and employee rights were excluded.

The UK's most positive contribution to the development of the Community in the second half of the 1980s was its successful drive towards the creation of a unified market starting with a proposal by the British Commissioner, Lord Cockfield, adopted in June 1985,of a timetable which comprised 300 specific proposals with target dates, including proposals for the harmonisation of VAT rates between member states. During the British Presidency of the Council of Ministers in 1986, a good start was made on carrying out the agreed programme with the endorsement of 47 measures relating to the internal market. The internal market was completed in all its essentials six years later, again under a British Presidency when a record number of 90 measures were agreed at the July 1992 Council of Ministers meeting.

In December 1986, the issue of a social dimension to the project to free the internal market surfaced for the first time and was translated in February 1987 by Jacques Delors, President of the Commission, into a package of 'social common market' measures, involving a considerable increase in EC funding, which was hotly debated over the next twelve months. Predictably, the UK took the stance that the Community should not be given more money until the detail of the limits on CAP expenditure had been firmly agreed. At an emergency Council of Ministers meeting in February 1988 a doubling of regional and social funds from 1992 was agreed in the context of increased funds availability to the Community, changes in the method of financing the EC budget, a continuation of the Fontainebleau rebate mechanism and tight and binding controls on the rate of increase of CAP expenditure.

The stage was now set for the next confrontation on what has proved to be the most genuinely contentious issue of the EU since the UK joined the community in 1976. For France and Germany the emergence of a single European currency is an essential accompaniment to a free internal market. At the June 1988 Hanover meeting of the Council of Ministers, they argued that the existing EMS needed to be strengthened by the creation of a European central bank and by moves to establish the ECU as the common currency. No one has been under any illusion that economic integration of the expanding Community could be accomplished without a common currency. Equally, it is clear that the adoption of a common currency entails loss of sovereignty and is a necessary precondition for advancing a federal Europe.

Predictably, the UK was once again isolated at the Hanover meeting. Mrs Thatcher had already clashed with her Chancellor, Nigel Lawson, over his willingness to commit the UK to 'shadow' the EMS by maintaining sterling within agreed margins, both in March 1988 when she judged that 'excessive intervention to support the pound' was incompatible with the fight against inflation, and again in May when sterling was next subjected to upward pressure. Although the brief given to the Delors Committee which followed was limited to the study of what steps were needed to strengthen EMS, Jacques Delors chose to use this study as a platform for a declaration that central decision-making and the 'social dimension' were corollaries to freeing the internal market. The Delors approach, later embodied in the Social Chapter of the Maastricht Treaty, was supported by Germany, Belgium, the Netherlands and Luxembourg in a joint declaration.

In 1989/90 the hand of history intervened directly with the collapse of Central and Eastern European communism. Leaders of most EC members, above all France, confronted by the emergence of a reunited Germany as a fait accompli, decided that there was an overriding need to accelerate towards political union in order to tie the new Germany into the Community. There was a fear that, without binding political links, Germany's inter-war alliances in Eastern Europe might be revived in a general drift towards the East. Even in the UK, the vision of a new Europe caught the imagination. A leader in the 5 December, 1989 edition of the *Independent* declared:

The events of our times call for both continued, perhaps even intensified effort of the twelve to integrate, and a role for the EC as a magnet that draws the forces of reform forward in Eastern Europe.

In the US, the Bush Presidency had begun in January 1989 and it soon became clear that its foreign policy would be driven by the need to reduce inherited budget and balance of payments deficits through savings.

Thus, when the European Bank for Reconstruction and Development (EBRD) was formed, 51 per cent of its capital was subscribed by the EC and member states with only 10 per cent provided by the US.

Throughout the remainder of the Thatcher Government, the UK continued to fight a rearguard action against the movement towards political union, in particular by opposing the proposed social charter and stages 2 and 3 of the Delors report on Monetary Union. At the June 1989 Madrid meeting, the UK softened its attitude towards the EMS by setting out its preconditions for UK entry and accepted Stage 1 of the Delors report (the clear coordination of national economic and monetary policies). At the April and June 1990 Council of Ministers meetings in Dublin, agreement was given to run an inter-governmental conference on political institutions in parallel with the monetary one approved previously. Only the UK voted against.

Ironically, at this time the UK and Denmark, the two member states with the strongest reservations about both monetary union and the reform of political institutions, had implemented more of the agreed 1992 legislation for completing the internal market than other members.

By mid-1990 the Labour Party was actively recommending entry to the exchange rate mechanism and on 5 October John Major, now Chancellor of the Exchequer, announced the UK's entry to EMS. At the end of that month at its Rome meeting, the European Council set a target date of 1 January 1994 for the start of the 2nd stage of the Delors Plan, again with only the UK in opposition. Mrs Thatcher's subsequent declaration to the House that there was little chance of the ECU being widely used in place of local currencies precipitated the resignation of her Foreign Secretary, Geoffrey Howe, whose critical resignation speech led to her own political fall.

1991–1997 The John Major Governments and Europe

The Government under John Major, which followed Mrs Thatcher's rejection as Leader, opened with a new start in relations with the rest of the Community but slid back to hostile relations after the Maastricht Treaty in December 1991. A combination of domestic politics, a paper-thin majority after the 1992 British election and a Conservative Party increasingly divided on Europe, and events in EC affairs, notably the collapse of the EMS and the drawn-out process of the Maastricht Treaty ratification, led to a retreat to a position of effective isolation and almost total lack of influence.

Perhaps the absence of a clear break with the previous Government's approach to Europe and the recent memory of Mrs Thatcher's confrontational style of trench warfare with the UK's partners were obstacles too difficult to surmount. Inevitably, the long years of continual dispute and blocking, with which Mr Major had himself been associated, had poisoned the well and were reflected in Mr Major's public bitterness latterly.

The Maastricht Treaty which was signed in December 1991 was initially rejected by Denmark in a referendum with a 50.7 per cent vote against and approved only narrowly in a French referendum by 50.6 per cent. Opt-out clauses for Denmark agreed under the British Presidency in 1992 enabled Denmark to achieve approval in a second referendum. In the UK's case, the Government decided against a referendum, having achieved the following:

- an opt-out clause, specific to the UK, on monetary union that either the national Parliament should be consulted or a referendum held before actually adopting a single currency;

- the replacement of the Social Chapter in the Treaty by a protocol signed by the other 11 members committing themselves to make progress on social issues. The UK is not committed beyond the Treaty of Rome and Single European Act obligations;

- the principle of subsidiarity written into the Treaty;

- decisions on foreign policy not subject to majority voting.

The Treaty was approved by the British Parliament on 3 November 1992 by a majority of only three votes. The Labour Party, which had expressed itself pro-EC, voted against on the grounds that the motion constituted a vote of confidence in the Government.

On 16 September 1992, the UK was forced out of the EMS through its inability to retain sterling parities under the pressure of concerted speculation, in spite of massive Bank of England open market operations. There were recriminations against the Bundesbank, which gave meagre support. The UK failed to negotiate a general realignment of currencies within the system and took the unilateral decision to withdraw. This event, more than any other in the last twenty years, affected Anglo-German relations adversely. It also destroyed the Conservative Party's reputation for prudent financial management and 'safe' government and was a root cause of its election disaster four and a half years later.

The final blow to the Conservative aspiration to be 'at the heart of Europe' was the 'mad cow disease' (BSE) issue which surfaced in March 1996 and led to bans across Europe on the import of British beef by member states. Although such unilateral action was illegal under the rules of the CAP, a ban was imposed by the European Commission. The subsequent argument fed the support of anti-marketeers in the Conservative Party, while the British Government's robust over-reaction inflicted severe damage on its reputation in the EU.

Back to the future

There are a variety of strands to the euphoria which greeted the election of New Labour to government in May 1997 and more specifically the appointment of Tony Blair as Prime Minister. The absence of a track record in government was not perceived as a deterrent to election by British voters; indeed the feat of making Labour electable seemed more of an accomplishment than the image of dreary, stale years in office which most of the Conservative front bench could offer.

The Conservative inheritance

The Thatcher revolution of the 1980s had certainly rolled back the frontiers of the welfare state through rigid expenditure control of the social services, the curtailment of trade union restrictive practices, reduction of the taxation burden on corporates and the better paid individual and the encouragement of small and medium-size industry in the service sectors and fields of innovative technology. These were the planks of Thatcherism which distinguished the economic, regulatory and fiscal climate in the UK from those of its EC partners and competitors.

In practical terms there are three British characteristics appealing to potential non-European investors seeking free access to the enlarging European Community:

- the anti-federalist stance of the British Government in the 1980s;

- its inherent antipathy to any social dimension in completing the internal Community market;

- its resistance to bureaucratic dirigisme from Brussels.

By offering a home for the advanced technologies of US, Japanese and Korean multinationals with investment incentives and regional aid, wherever available, instead of attempting to combine with European partners to set up in competition, the UK has garnered the lion's share of FDI in Europe with the added benefit that much of the new investment has been in the development areas, notably Wales and the North-East, where employment in the declining coal, steel and shipbuilding industries had been decimated.

The Conservative Government and local governments deserve due credit for this success as do the British managers, trade unions and workforces who have demonstrated great flexibility in retraining and a surprising willingness to adapt to new working practices, management methods and cultures. In 1996–97, the UK attracted 40 per cent of total US investment into the EU and more than 40 per cent of that from Japan and Asia's 'tiger' economies. Total inward investment was £9.3 billion of which other EU members, principally Germany, contributed £992 million.

UK inward investment may suffer in future years from alternatives in the central European countries as they join the EU. The Czech Republic, Poland and Hungary, in particular, have identified inward investment as the fast track to building their economies and offer low labour and site costs and highly attractive tax regimes. For the time being, however, the UK remains the most favoured destination for investment into Europe, as well as the Community. After inclusion of Poland, Russia, Hungary, the Czech Republic and all others in the European Top 12 by number of investment projects received in the first six months of 1997, the UK accounted for 34.5 per cent of the overall total. Another highlight in the UK's economic performance during the period of Conservative governments was Total Factor Productivity (TFP) Growth in the business sector, where the UK ranking among OECD countries rose from 11 in the period 1960 to 1973 to 4 in the period 1979 to 1995, exceeded only by Ireland, Finland and Spain.

The tough policies on public expenditure also bore fruit. Government current disbursements as a percentage of GDP had risen from an average of 31.8 per cent in the period 1960–1973 to 39.7 per cent in the period 1974–1979. However, Government Disbursements were held at 41.9 per cent of GDP over the period 1980–1989 and fell to 40.9 per cent in the period 1990–1995. Except for the Netherlands and Belgium, whose government disbursements fell rather more, all other OECD countries registered rises in the ratio of Disbursements to GDP between the latter two periods.

Finally, in the league table of comparative total compensation for manufacturing workers, the UK has maintained competitiveness. According to Price Waterhouse in *Plant Location International*, the UK average hourly rate was US$13.63 in 1996 compared with US$30.33 for Germany and US$18.85 for France. The UK ranked eighth lowest among the European countries surveyed; only Spain, Iceland, Greece and Portugal within the EU, and Poland, the Czech Republic, Hungary and Russia from outside the Union, registered lower hourly rates.

On the debit side, the social upheaval which the policies of the Thatcher governments generated had disagreeable consequences for those who failed to be upwardly mobile or, at least, to maintain their relative economic positions. Job security, where it still existed, was an anachronism. Ageism became acceptable. A new breed of para-entrepreneurs flourished, mainly in the service industries, for whom greed took precedence over social responsibility. Business ethics were too often flexible. Social service standards faltered, particularly in public education at primary and secondary school levels and in the National Health Service. In short, there was a growing awareness that the UK was no longer a caring society. As the 1990s unfolded, the grasping attitudes which had carried over from the 1980s became more repugnant and the electorate became monthly more disenchanted with a Government which no longer appeared competent and whose junior Ministers seemed particularly vulnerable to petty sleaze. In spite of solid achievements and a general respect for John Major as a decent man without style, the long period of Conservative government ended with a whimper in the landslide election victory of New Labour.

New lamps for old

The public had watched Tony Blair with fascination as he had set about completing the modernisation of the Labour Party, taming its unruly elements with unexpected communications skills and firmness and carving a new centre ground of Labour supporters from traditional Tory middle class and Home Counties territories. As the philosophy of New Labour emerged chrysalis-like from policy statements and platform speeches at Party Conferences, it became apparent that many of the sacred cows of socialism had been slain and that there would be no return to the policies of public ownership, collective wage bargaining and increased government spending on public services funded by high indirect taxation which had suffocated the UK economy in the past and deterred foreign investment in the '60s and '70s.

After its first twelve months in office, it seems clear that the UK economy is safe in the hands of a Chancellor who has demonstrated both fiscal rectitude and an openness to innovation. The early decisions to pass control of interest rates from the Treasury to the Bank of England and to remove from the Bank to a separate new authority its responsibility as watchdog

of City institutions were immediately reassuring. Tony Blair's charisma is undented and he retains an unusually high personal popularity, reinforced by his success as architect of the Northern Ireland Agreement. When he said, in a *Time* magazine interview after five months in office, that 'a new generation has come on that doesn't have the outdated attitudes of the past' and that 'there is a curious mixture of optimism about the future mixed with a realisation that the old British ways of getting things done are not going to be enough', it rang true. Just how the multi-cultural society which Mr Blair wants in which there are 'strong social bonds between people and where we recognise a sense of duty and obligation towards others' will evolve is still uncertain, but there is no doubting his sincerity.

There is more clarity in Tony Blair's explanation of the third way between US capitalism and the welfare states of Europe when he identifies the role of government to organise and secure provision – rather than fund it all. This is apparent both in the government's plans for pension reform, where people will be required to provide more of their own financial independence, and in the proposals for students to self-fund over time their contributions to the cost of their university education. These are the natural consequences of an enterprise culture where there is an emphasis on self-help by those who are fit and able.

In Europe, the Labour Government was greeted with relief and Tony Blair with modified rapture. The Government comes to the EU as committed Europeans with strong representation in the European Parliament. In contrast to the adversarial antics of previous UK Governments, the Labour Government is operating on a cordial level. Although Mr Blair has indicated acceptance of parts of the Social Chapter, he has also signalled that the UK will continue to exert pressure to restructure the CAP and to limit bureaucracy in the interests of the European consumer.

Only in the matter of the Monetary Union is there a significant divergence between the UK and its partners. It is now certain that the UK will not join the first wave of membership when the EMU starts on January 1999. The Blair Government has declared that it will not take a decision before the next UK election due in 2002. The reason given is that the UK economy is out of cycle with the other European economies and that convergence to the Maastricht criteria for entry would have required disruptive economic measures. While this is undoubtedly true, other members, not least France and Germany as well as Italy and Spain, have had to take exceptional measures to satisfy the convergence criteria and these may impose pressures after the start-up which would be difficult to manage. In fact, it would probably have been politically impossible for any

British Government to take the UK into EMU now after the expensive fiasco of the EMS and the degree of vocal opposition by the Eurosceptic wing of the Conservative Party and its supporters. It will most likely take three years of successful EMU operation and some positive public relations before the British electorate is reconciled to joining.

In the meantime, the UK will have to accept exclusion from some parts of the EMU club and its policy deliberations. For non-European corporates doing business with Europe, there may be some disadvantages in a UK base in the short-term in respect of fluctuating currency exchange rates and the mechanics of transactions within the internal EU market. However, with fewer European currencies in play, the settlement of international business transactions will in any case be simplified, provided that EMU operates smoothly. For the cautious, a seat on the sidelines in the UK with its strong economy during EMU's early stages may be even more attractive than before.

Part 2

Operating in the UK – An Overview from the DTI's Invest in Britain Bureau

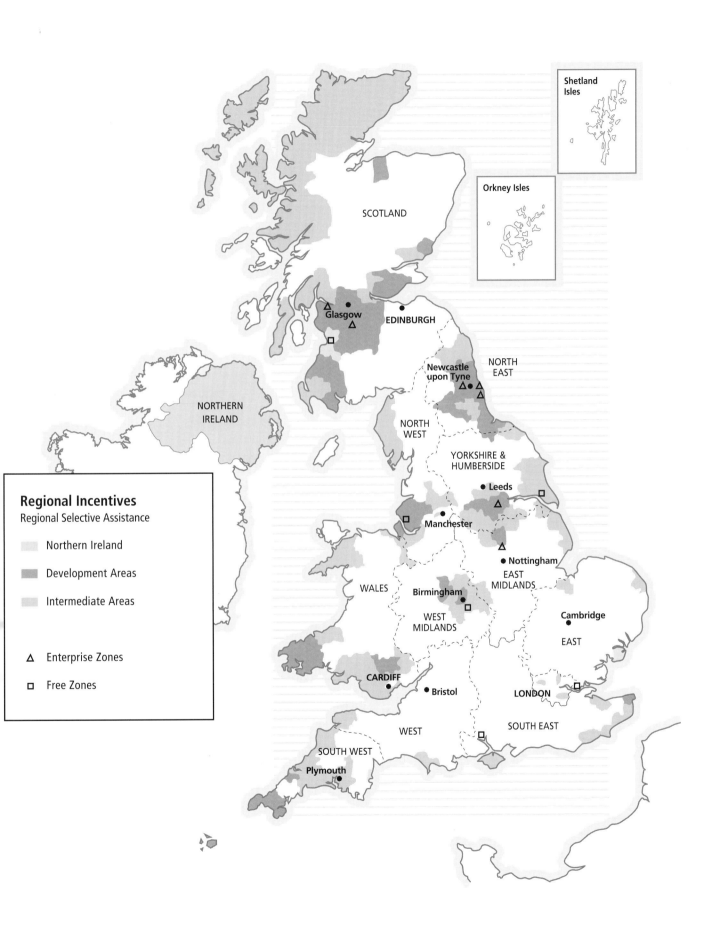

Regional Incentives

Regional Selective Assistance

Northern Ireland

Development Areas

Intermediate Areas

△ Enterprise Zones

□ Free Zones

SCOTLAND

Shetland Isles

Orkney Isles

NORTHERN IRELAND

Glasgow

EDINBURGH

Newcastle upon Tyne

NORTH EAST

NORTH WEST

YORKSHIRE & HUMBERSIDE

Leeds

Manchester

Nottingham

EAST MIDLANDS

WALES

Birmingham

WEST MIDLANDS

Cambridge

EAST

CARDIFF

Bristol

LONDON

SOUTH EAST

WEST

SOUTH WEST

Plymouth

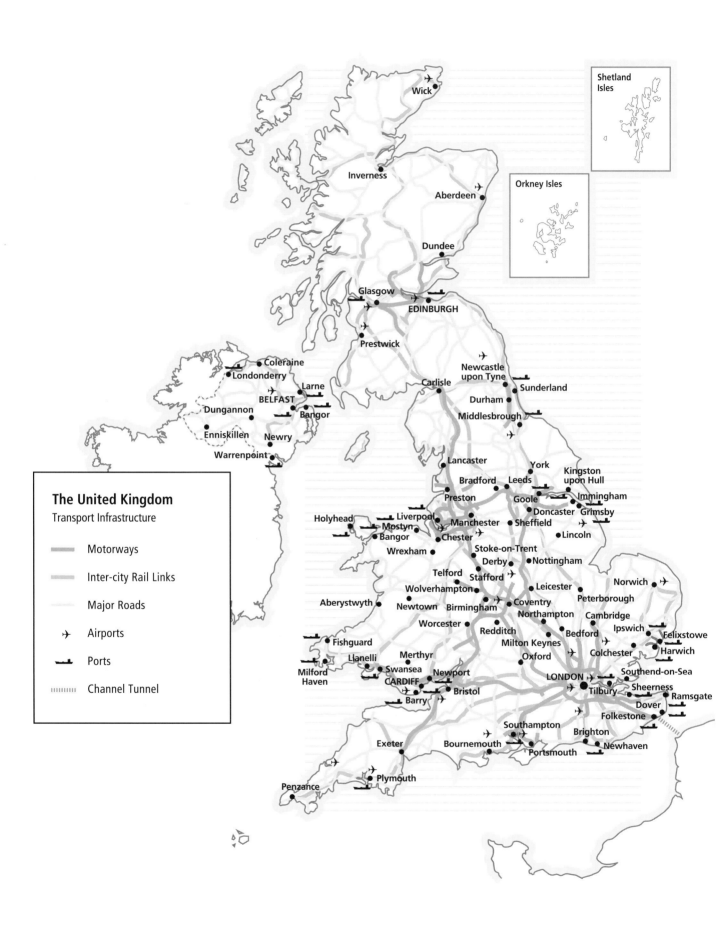

The United Kingdom
Transport Infrastructure

Motorways

Inter-city Rail Links

Major Roads

✈ Airports

⊥ Ports

Channel Tunnel

Shetland Isles

Orkney Isles

Wick

Inverness

Aberdeen

Dundee

Glasgow

EDINBURGH

Prestwick

Coleraine

Londonderry

Larne

BELFAST

Dungannon

Bangor

Enniskillen

Newry

Warrenpoint

Carlisle

Newcastle upon Tyne

Sunderland

Durham

Middlesbrough

Lancaster

York

Kingston upon Hull

Bradford

Leeds

Preston

Goole

Immingham

Holyhead

Liverpool

Manchester

Doncaster

Grimsby

Mostyn

Sheffield

Bangor

Chester

Lincoln

Wrexham

Stoke-on-Trent

Derby

Nottingham

Telford

Stafford

Newtown

Wolverhampton

Leicester

Norwich

Coventry

Peterborough

Aberystwyth

Birmingham

Northampton

Cambridge

Worcester

Redditch

Bedford

Ipswich

Milton Keynes

Felixstowe

Fishguard

Colchester

Harwich

Llanelli

Merthyr

Oxford

Southend-on-Sea

Milford Haven

Swansea

Newport

LONDON

Sheerness

CARDIFF

Bristol

Tilbury

Ramsgate

Barry

Dover

Folkestone

Southampton

Brighton

Exeter

Bournemouth

Newhaven

Portsmouth

Penzance

Plymouth

The European Market

EU Countries

EEA Countries (not in the EU)

Countries which applied to join the EU 1994-96

- - - Delivery zones from London

1 Same day delivery

2 Next day delivery

3 Delivery within 3 days

ICELAND
Reykjavik

SWEDEN

FINLAND

NORWAY

Helsinki

Oslo

Stockholm

ESTONIA

LATVIA

DENMARK

LITHUANIA

Copenhagen

Dublin

IRISH REPUBLIC

UK

NETHERLANDS

Berlin

POLAND

Amsterdam

London

Brussels

GERMANY

BELGIUM

Luxembourg

CZECH REP.

SLOVAKIA

Paris

Vienna

FRANCE

Berne

AUSTRIA

SWITZERLAND

SLOVENIA

HUNGARY

ROMANIA

ITALY

SPAIN

BULGARIA

PORTUGAL

Rome

Madrid

GREECE

Lisbon

Athens

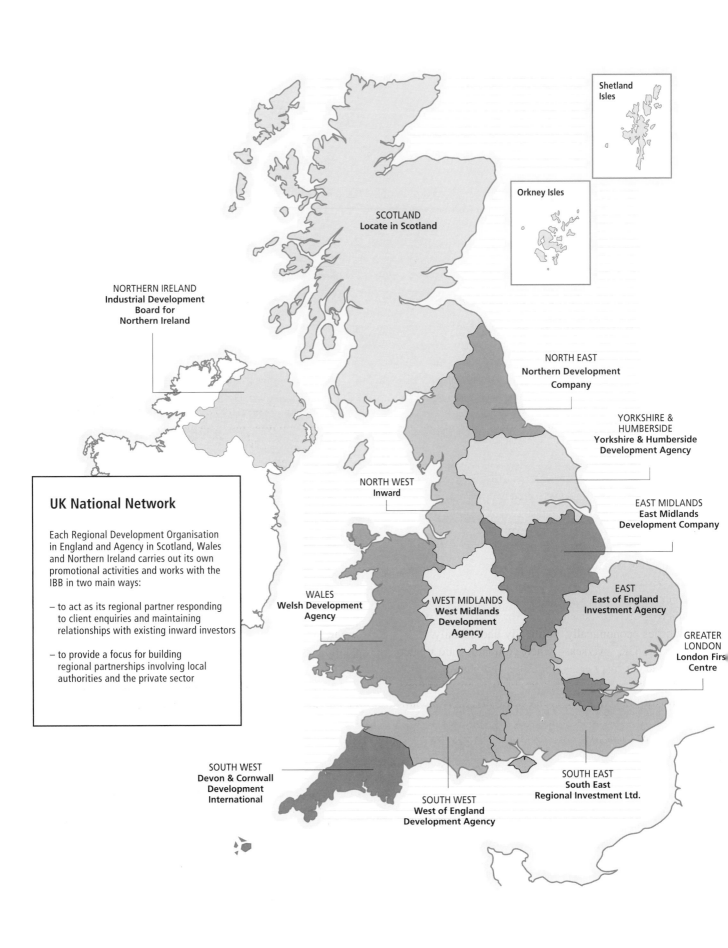

Shetland
Isles

Orkney Isles

SCOTLAND
Locate in Scotland

NORTHERN IRELAND
**Industrial Development
Board for
Northern Ireland**

NORTH EAST
**Northern Development
Company**

YORKSHIRE &
HUMBERSIDE
**Yorkshire & Humberside
Development Agency**

NORTH WEST
Inward

EAST MIDLANDS
**East Midlands
Development Company**

UK National Network

Each Regional Development Organisation
in England and Agency in Scotland, Wales
and Northern Ireland carries out its own
promotional activities and works with the
IBB in two main ways:

− to act as its regional partner responding
  to client enquiries and maintaining
  relationships with existing inward investors

− to provide a focus for building
  regional partnerships involving local
  authorities and the private sector

WALES
**Welsh Development
Agency**

WEST MIDLANDS
**West Midlands
Development
Agency**

EAST
**East of England
Investment Agency**

GREATER
LONDON
**London First
Centre**

SOUTH WEST
**Devon & Cornwall
Development
International**

SOUTH WEST
**West of England
Development Agency**

SOUTH EAST
**South East
Regional Investment Ltd.**

2

Operating in the UK and Marketing into Europe

by the Invest in Britain Bureau (DTI)

Thousands of international companies have chosen the UK as the place to locate their facilities, and profit from European and world markets. Why the UK?

The UK is one of the most vibrant and successful trading nations in the world. It has a highly developed infrastructure and fast, efficient links with other countries in the European Union and beyond, including the Middle East, Africa, North and South America and the Pacific Rim. It is also a world centre for financial and commodity markets.

The UK has a hard-working, educated population with an adaptable and motivated workforce, a strong science and technology base and a commitment to improving standards at every level. International companies have also found that the UK has the most competitive business environment of any country in the European Union and is a highly profitable base from which to operate. It is not only the easiest place in which to do business – it is one of the most stable countries economically, politically and socially.

In the UK, overseas-owned companies are treated in the same manner as domestic companies. Capital and profits can be remitted freely. It is not, therefore, surprising that the UK is the most favoured inward-investment location in Europe. It has attracted around 40 per cent of Japanese, US and Asian investment into the EU.

Britain today is very much a pro-business country, and that applies among other things to the level of taxation and the labour laws. We as a company find it especially beneficial to be able to operate our factories three shifts a day, seven days a week, basically around the clock, non-stop.

Jurgen Gehrets, Siemens UK chief executive

EUROPEAN OPPORTUNITIES

From the UK you can easily service the whole of the European market. The UK itself is a substantial market, with 58 million consumers, but it is just part of the world's largest free trade area – 377 million consumers in the European Economic Area (EEA) – the 15 European Union countries plus Iceland and Norway.

The UK is a leading player in Europe, working to create an environment in which wealth and job creation will flourish. It will work to promote labour flexibility and business success, and is committed to completing the single market and the continuing removal of trade barriers within the EEA.

FAST ACCESS TO MARKETS

Nine out of ten overseas companies in the UK export worldwide from the UK. UK-based companies are ideally positioned to do business with worldwide markets.

The UK's integrated transport network provides fast, low-cost delivery of raw materials and manufactured products throughout the EEA. A comprehensive toll-free motorway and road network joins all major UK cities and industrial centres to air and seaports.

Everywhere in the country is within 100 miles of a container port. Most of the UK's ports are privatised and equipped to handle high-volume roll-on roll-off container traffic. The UK's harbours handle over 500 million tonnes of freight each year, with more than 300 sailings per day to mainland Europe. The cost of shipments from the UK is between 25 and 35 per cent lower than from other European ports. Same-day delivery is standard from most of the UK to centres

The UK International Headquarters Company

by Martin Palmer, Jordans Limited

The UK constitutes one of the most attractive gateways for investment in Europe by non-EU entrepreneurs and multi-nationals. In fact the UK actively encourages foreign capital as evidenced by the statutory International Headquarters Company regime which is the prime focus of this article.

The UK International Headquarters Company (IHC) is a creation of the UK Finance Act 1994, and, in alliance with the concept of foreign income dividends, (also introduced by the 1994 Finance Act) the IHC is intended to make the UK a significant competitor for international investment as an international holding company location. The crucial benefit of the IHC is that it is exempt from paying advance corporation tax (ACT) when distributing a qualifying foreign income dividend (FID).

Although ACT will be abolished on 6 April 1999 (and therefore axiomatically the related concept of IHCs and FIDs will also be curtailed) an analysis of the IHC is appropriate because the regime is still current at the time of writing, and an explanation of the IHC regime will serve to illustrate some significant advantages of the UK tax system to the overseas investor, advantages which will continue to apply after the abolition of the IHC regime. This abolition is a relieving measure, because after 6 April 1999 all UK companies can function as IHCs, regardless of their ownership composition (IHC's must be owned predominantly by non-residents).

Prior to the IHC legislation, the UK was a particularly unfavourable location for multi-national companies generating substantial amounts of non-UK income. This was because of the UK tax regime's requirement that ACT should become due whenever a dividend was paid. In many cases zero or very low rates of UK corporation tax would be payable on the income of such companies, due to double taxation relief, and consequently the advance corporation tax became irrecoverable as there was no UK corporation tax payable against which to set off the ACT already paid. The IHC on the other hand, avoids this trap provided a foreign income dividend is distributed, because an IHC can distribute a foreign income dividend free of ACT.

At this juncture it is worth clarifying what a foreign income dividend is, because if the dividend distributed by the IHC does not qualify as a FID there will be no exemption from advance corporation tax.

The company distributing the FID must be able to establish that the dividend can be matched with distributable foreign profit. Only if this is established may the company elect FID treatment. The legislation defines distributable foreign profit as income or chargeable gain subject to UK corporation tax but in respect of which double taxation relief is afforded. The relief may be under a treaty, or may be under the UK's unilateral relief rule.

The company's distributable foreign profit is what is left of the foreign source profit after foreign tax has been paid.

If the foreign tax underlying the foreign profits received by the IHC exceed the UK corporation tax that would be payable on the same source of income then foreign tax credit relief will normally eliminate UK corporation tax altogether. Rates of foreign tax of less than 31% (currently the standard rate of corporation tax in the UK, although this will fall to 30% from 6 April 1999) will still be creditable against UK tax. Therefore the IHC regime is at its most effective where the IHC is the recipient of foreign profits which have been subject to rates of foreign corporate tax of 31% or more.

The UK IHC legislation creates interesting possibilities for offshore tax planning because, despite its appellation, no Headquarters Company functions need be provided by the IHC. In other words an IHC can be a pure holding company whose only manifestation, as far as the UK is concerned, is its UK tax residence. This can be achieved without expensive infrastructure. Clearly therefore the IHC is going to be uniquely placed to extract profits from many countries using the UK's double tax treaty network, or the EU Parent\Subsidiary Directive, to mitigate, or, eliminate the incidence of dividend withholding tax.

The scenario outlined in Diagram 1 is a vivid illustration of one of the important weaknesses of a pure offshore company which offers a zero tax base in its territory of incorporation. French law requires the French subsidiary to withhold tax of 25% of the gross dividend and pay it over to the French Fisc. The offshore company, without the protection of a double taxation treaty, must suffer the full rate of withholding tax, and of course this is the great weakness of the offshore company.

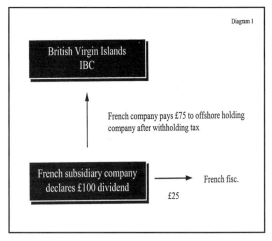

On the other hand, a UK company (whether or not qualifying as an IHC) can solve these withholding tax problems.

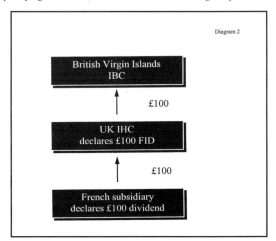

As a UK resident company, the IHC can qualify for the EU Parent\Subsidiary Directive and thus can receive the dividends free of French withholding tax.

The UK company can then receive the foreign income together with the accompanying foreign tax credit which will eliminate any UK corporation tax liability on the same income, and this enables the distribution of a FID by the UK company free of ACT, provided that at least 80% of the UK companyís ordinary share capital is ultimately owned by UK non-resident individuals (this is the fundamental requirement for qualification as an IHC).

An attractive feature of the UK tax regime for non-residents is that there is no form of dividend withholding tax on outward bound dividends to non-UK resident individuals or companies and therefore, in this scenario, the UK IHC can pay the foreign profits up to an offshore company free of all UK taxation consequences.

In relation to the EU Parent\Subsidiary Directive, this sort of structure will of course have to take account of any national anti-avoidance legislation applicable in the country of source of dividends.

To take two examples, Italy reserves the right not to apply the Parent\Subsidiary Directive and therefore to impose a withholding tax on dividend distributions if the structure involving the IHC has been established mainly to take advantage of the Directive. Therefore the existence of the UK company will need to be commercially justified.

The additional French domestic conditions for application of the Directive require that:

1) The UK company must have held at least 25% of the share capital of the French company for an uninterrupted period of at least two years prior to the payment of any dividend on which freedom from French withholding tax is sought.

   The Denkavit case of October 1996, decided by the European Court of Justice, establishes that any dividend withholding tax paid by the parent prior to the effluxion of the required two year period of ownership must be rebated to the company upon completion of this period of ownership.

2) The UK parent company must give evidence to the French distributing company or paying agent that the UK company is the beneficial owner of the dividend.

3) The UK parent company must not be controlled either directly or indirectly by one or more residents of non-EU countries unless the parent is able to show that the principal purpose, or one of the principal purposes of its participation in the French subsidiary is not to benefit from the exemption from French withholding tax.

   Non- EU investors planning to consolidate international intra-EU investments in one company have a valid commercial case for choosing the UK company as their holding vehicle, particularly if they are English speaking or have significant UK interests or UK professional advisors.

   Another approach to the third French domestic law condition for benefit under the directive (i.e. where the ultimate ownership of the UK parent company is held by non-EU parties) is to create two separate classes of shares in the UK parent company, concentrating all the voting rights and limited profit participation rights in one class of shares beneficially owned by UK or other EU resident individuals, and providing the substantial rights to profit participation by way of dividend to a second class of shares to be owned by the would be non-EU investors, this second class of shares carrying no voting rights. UK company law has the necessary flexibility to accommodate this sort of share capital arrangement.

Clearly, the ability of the UK company to benefit from the EU Parent\Subsidiary Directive, as well as the UK's large network of double tax treaties gives the UK important advantages as an International Holding Company location.

A rather unique feature of the IHC regime is that qualification for IHC status rests upon the ownership of the IHC, rather than its ownership of subsidiary companies.

In the light of the imminent abolition of the IHC it is not proposed to examine the qualification rules in detail, but it is sufficient to re-iterate that in broad terms, to qualify as an IHC, at least 80% of the ordinary share capital of the IHC must be beneficially owned by UK non-resident individuals.

The UK has many advantages over some of the better known holding company regimes:

● No capital duty.

● No minimum paid up share capital for private companies.

● The largest network of double tax treaties in the world normally with provisions as advantageous as those of other international holding company regimes, and in some cases with preferable treaties e.g. the UK treaty with the US has fewer anti-avoidance provisions than its Dutch and Swiss equivalents.

● Unlike Switzerland, the UK IHC can rely on the EU Parent\Subsidiary Directive.

● Unlike other holding company regimes such as Belgium's where a minimum percentage of dividend income is taxable to cover administration costs, the IHC does not need to pay any UK corporation tax. Of course it will report its foreign income but this will not normally be subject to UK corporation tax because of foreign tax credit relief.

● Unlike the participation exemption in the Netherlands where actual participation is required in the affairs of the subsidiary, an IHC does not need to participate in its subsidiaries affairs and activities. Indeed an IHC can trade in its own right through a foreign branch, distributing branch

profits as foreign income dividend.

The weakness of the IHC legislation is the lack of a Capital Gains Tax exemption for IHCs.

In some scenarios the weakness will not be relevant, either because investment is long term, or because a sale of the IHCs underlying assets is not contemplated.

But assuming the CGT problem is relevant to investors, how can this problem be resolved.

Indexation relief is currently available but this only reduces the scale of the problem without curing the problem itself. Planning solutions would include:

1) Selling the shares of the IHC rather than its underlying subsidiary or subsidiaries. Where the seller of the IHCs shares is UK non-resident there will be no liability to UK CGT on gains realised by the sale of those shares.

2) Alternatively; where the capital value of the subsidiary company is represented largely by retained earnings these can be dividended from the subsidiary to the IHC which can then declare them as FIDs in favour of the UK non-resident shareholders free of UK tax consequences.

3) Another solution would be to introduce an intermediate holding company with an exemption from CGT such as a Netherlands company between the UK company and its subsidiary in order to trap the gain.

This still leaves the problem that if the resulting cash rich Netherlands company were to dividend the profit to the IHC, these would not qualify as foreign income dividend because of the Netherlands "participation exemption" and would therefore attract UK corporation in full.

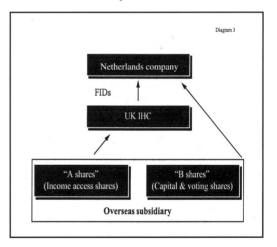

Diagram 3

Diagram 3 demonstrates one possible solution which is to create two classes of share capital in the trading subsidiary company so that the IHC owns one class of shares being income access shares and the IHC's Netherlands parent owns voting and capital growth shares. Thus capital gains on a sale of the subsidiary can be realised by the Netherlands company while income profits can be directed to the UK IHC and benefit from the UK's FID regime. From a UK taxation perspective there is no reason why a Bahamas or British Virgin Islands IBC could not be substituted for the Netherlands company to reduce costs.

In conclusion, the UK IHC regime offers an excellent platform for international tax planning and this platform will be even stronger after April 1999 when ACT is abolished and therefore every UK company can pay overseas dividend free of any form of withholding tax to offshore structures without the need to comply with any UK non-resident ownership qualifications.

Martin Palmer B.A. (Hons) Law,
International Corporate Services Devision
Director, Jordans Limited
21 St Thomas Street Bristol, BS1 6JS.
Tel: (0117) 918 1321 Fax: (0117) 923 0063

such as Amsterdam, Brussels, Paris and Hamburg. Next-day delivery is normal to cities such as Marseilles, Frankfurt and Milan. 'Our products can be with our customers across Europe within 24 hours,' (John Benningsen, managing director of Toshiba (UK) Ltd). Almost 20,000 UK-based haulage companies ensure that freight rates are very competitive. A range of UK-based national and pan-European operators offer value-added logistics services and European contract distribution.

The Channel Tunnel links the UK by road and rail to the rest of Europe. Paris and Brussels are each only three hours' journey from London by rail. London's Heathrow airport offers direct flights to over 100 European destinations, more than any other city in Europe. More than 20 regional airports serve all the major population centres in the UK. British airports also provide more international destinations than any other country in the EU. Many international courier companies such as UPS, DHL, Federal Express and Amtrak have significant operations in the UK.

A SKILLED AND ADAPTABLE WORKFORCE

The UK has the second-largest workforce in the EU, with 28 million skilled and adaptable workers, both full and part-time. Education in the UK is of a high standard with a strong emphasis on vocational education and training. This has been strongly reinforced by the UK Government.

The adoption of the latest working practices has resulted in a revolution in manufacturing skills and performance. 'Lean' manufacturing systems and a commitment to continuous improvement mean that the quality and productivity of the output from the UK factories now rival the best in the world – including Japan. Manufacturing productivity in the UK, measured by output per hour, rose by an average of 5.2 per cent a year between 1985 and 1995 – higher than the US, Germany, Japan or any other major developed economy.

The UK has few restrictions on working hours, over-time and holidays. A large number of companies setting up in the UK have negotiated single-union agreements. Many businesses operate shift work and 24-hour, seven-days-a-week schedules for both male and female employees, which give companies maximum return on capital. Terms of employment are generally agreed directly between companies and their employees. Labour relations in the UK are exceptionally good. Days lost through strikes are among the lowest in Europe, as are absences through vacations, public holidays and sickness. 'We looked at premises in Holland, Italy and France but the work environment in the UK focused our search here,' (Actron Electronics UK managing director James Hu). Staffing costs in the UK are highly competitive, because of the modest level of compulsory social costs on wages. As Bob Schwarz, vice president of world manufacturing for Black and Decker, says: 'Labour costs at our UK plant are about 50 per cent of what they were at our German plant and about 75 per cent of wages in Italy.'

LOW-COST UTILITIES

Deregulation and privatisation have contributed to the UK having the lowest utilities costs in the European Union. The UK is the only member of the European Union to be self-sufficient in energy, due to its North Sea oil and natural-gas reserves.

The UK's utilities, including electricity, gas and water, have been privatised – indeed a number of these are owned by overseas investors. Competition between regional suppliers of power gives industrial and commercial users opportunities to negotiate substantial price discounts. The UK's utilities are experienced at installing new facilities and negotiating for high volume industrial users.

The UK's telecommunications industry has led Europe in terms of liberalisation and offers companies a choice of suppliers. The UK is home to one of the most advanced telecommunications networks in the world and costs are highly competitive.

SETTING UP IN BUSINESS

High quality, modern industrial property is available throughout the UK together with green and brownfield sites. The UK also has a world-class construction and civil engineering industry, with an excellent record for building complex, large-scale industrial units quickly and to high standards. Many companies have been impressed by the speed and ease with which their custom-built facilities have been completed. It took only nine months from ground breaking for Seagate

Technology to have state-of-the-art clean-room facilities completed at their Northern Ireland plant.

If a company locates in one of seven Enterprise Zones (see page 25), it benefits from streamlined procedures for obtaining building permits, 100 per cent tax allowances on capital expenditure on commercial and industrial buildings and full exemption from local property taxes. Grants and other financial help may be available to businesses which generate local employment, in designated 'assisted' areas (see page 24). Investment incentives are especially generous in Northern Ireland (see page 33).

The UK has seven 'free zones' (see page 31), in which no taxes or charges are levied on goods from outside the European Union until these are released for free circulation. Among other benefits, the zones simplify customs procedures, add security and provide cash-flow benefits. Tax deductions for customs duties relating to the transshipment, handling and processing of goods for re-export are available throughout the UK.

WORLD-CLASS RESEARCH, DESIGN AND DEVELOPMENT

Many UK universities and scientific institutes are engaged in joint ventures designed to apply their academic findings to commercial projects. The UK Government encourages research and development which benefit industry – collaborative research programmes may qualify for UK and European Union financial support. Many overseas companies gain benefit from collaborative research with UK universities. For example, Microsoft Research has chosen the UK as the site of its first research laboratory outside the US because of Cambridge University's world-class reputation in computer science. The UK has more centres carrying out clinical research than any other European country, with over 170 contract research organisations.

EUROPE'S LEADING COMMUNICATIONS MARKET

The UK is a magnet for international call centres and home to almost half of all telebusiness agents in Europe.

The UK's telecommunications industry was deregulated far earlier than any other European country, and the UK is well ahead in its liberalisation policy. Over the last ten years, British Telecom (BT) has built up the most advanced telephone network in Europe and with CONCERT worldwide. BT leads Europe in telemarketing, sales, research, direct response, customer-help lines and customer services. Other major telecommunications companies such as Cable & Wireless and AT&T also offer national and international services from the UK. The UK also has one of the most competitive mobile communications markets in Europe. Prices are scheduled to go on falling in real terms. Competition between more than 150 licensed providers means that British telecommunication prices continue to fall. The UK also has one of the cheapest and most efficient international mail services in Europe.

The UK is increasingly the choice of multinational companies looking to set up worldwide or European headquarters and shared-service centres because of its high-quality telecommunications and low operating costs.

LANGUAGE

English is the world's business language. Far more people in the European Union speak English as a second language than any other, and nine out of ten Europeans consider it the most commercially useful. The UK is also home to speakers of over 190 languages and has a large pool of native and near-native multilingual people.

A LIBERAL TAX ENVIRONMENT

The UK offers your company low corporate and personal taxation, economic stability and a regulatory environment designed to encourage growth and profits. The UK has the lowest main corporation tax rate of any major industrialised country and has no additional local taxes on profits.

Although companies are taxed on an individual basis, the UK groups can offset tax losses made by one group company against profits made by another. Companies are granted full first-year write-off of the costs of offices or factories in any of the UK's seven enterprise zones. The UK's scientific research allowance (SRA) allows all R&D expenditure, including capital expenditure on buildings, plant and machinery, to be written off in full in the first year. Otherwise, investment in most plant and machinery qualifies for tax allowances at 25 per cent a year, on a reducing-balance basis.

The UK has no exchange controls and no restrictions on sending profits abroad. There are no withholding taxes on dividends paid overseas, and many double-taxation agreements also allow for interest to be paid free of withholding tax. The UK has the largest network of double-taxation agreements. The special rules for international headquarters companies enhance the UK's attractiveness as a location for group headquarters and holding companies.

EUROPE'S FINANCIAL SERVICES CAPITAL

London is Europe's business capital. Along with New York and Tokyo, the UK's capital is an essential component of the world's round-the-clock money and investment markets. The City of London has much the largest stock exchange, foreign exchange and international bond business of any European city. It is also a major centre for Eurocurrency trading, Eurobank transactions, insurance, futures and options, and fund management. Over 550 banks from 70 countries are located in London, against 280 in Paris and 250 in Frankfurt.

Strong financial service communities are also present in other UK cities, including Bristol, Edinburgh, Leeds and Manchester.

REGIONAL ASSISTANCE

The UK Government offers a wide range of assistance to overseas-owned, as well as domestic, companies locating in certain regions of the UK. The main aim of this policy is to encourage industrial investment.

Regional Selective Assistance (RSA)

This is available for projects in areas of the UK in need of investment to revitalise their economies. These regions – collectively known as 'Assisted Areas' – include those parts of England, Scotland and Wales designated as 'Development Areas' or 'Intermediate Areas'.

Project Grant is the main type of assistance. It is based on a project's capital expenditure costs and the number of jobs it is expected to create or safeguard – normally in the project's first three years. A grant is negotiated according to the amount considered necessary to enable the project to go ahead in the form proposed. Project Grant is normally paid in three instalments, linked to the creation of jobs, capital expenditure and to the project's progress. Eligible costs include:

- land purchase;
- site preparation and buildings;
- plant and machinery.

Other costs – such as patent rights, professional fees, installation and reinstallation of machinery – may also qualify.

A manufacturing or a service industry project may qualify for RSA if it:

- has a good chance of paying its way;
- will create or safeguard employment in the Assisted Areas;
- will benefit the regional and national economy;
- needs assistance to go ahead.

However, the majority of the finance for projects will be expected to come from private sector sources.

There are special arrangements with regard to financial assistance in Northern Ireland. (For more information see page 33.)

It is very difficult to establish the need for support if work on the project has already begun. Therefore, don't commit to a project until you have applied for assistance and received an offer.

Enterprise Zones

Enterprise Zones (EZs) are designated by the Government for a period of ten years. Zones usually comprise a number of sites with individual planning regimes: some are developed as business parks, others devoted to manufacturing, while others may have more varied uses. EZs are intended to encourage vigorous private sector activity by removing certain tax burdens and by relaxing or speeding up the application of some statutory or administrative controls. EZs are not directly connected with other existing policies such as those for inner cities or derelict land. The sites chosen can continue to benefit from whatever aid is available under other policies.

The order designating an EZ specifies a zone authority for each zone, such as the local council or development corporation. However, promotion of the zone may be undertaken by an agency, referred to below as the zone promoter, appointed by the zone authority.

The following benefits are available, for the period of designation of the zone, to both new and existing industrial and commercial enterprises in an EZ:

- 100 per cent allowances for corporation and income-tax purposes for capital expenditure on industrial and commercial buildings;
- exemption from the National Non-Domestic Rate (Uniform Business Rate) on industrial and commercial property;
- a greatly simplified planning regime; developments that conform with the published scheme for each zone do not require individual planning permission;

- those statutory controls remaining in force (eg planning) are administered more speedily;
- employers are exempt from industrial training levies and from the requirement to supply information to industrial training boards;
- applications from firms in EZs for certain customs facilities are processed as a matter of priority and certain criteria relaxed;
- government requests for statistical information are reduced.

Restricted Sectors

Certain businesses may be subject to European Community state-aid rules which restrict entitlement to state subsidies and may affect their ability to locate onto an EZ. The purpose of these rules is to ensure that aids to industry (like the EZ scheme) do not inhibit free and fair competition throughout the Community. Currently the Restricted Sectors include:

- synthetic fibres;
- motor vehicles;
- shipbuilding;
- coal and steel;
- metalworking;
- agriculture;
- food processing;
- fisheries.

Advice on which businesses may be affected, and how, can be obtained in the first instance from the zone authority or promoter.

More about the benefits

Rates

Industrial and commercial (including retail) property in EZs is exempt from the National Non-Domestic Rate (the Uniform Business Rate), but not from water and other service charges. Rates exemption is automatic, and, therefore, no special application or action is necessary to effect it.

Capital allowances

A special scheme, modelled on industrial building allowances, operates in EZs. There is an initial allowance for corporation or income-tax purposes of 100 per cent of capital expenditure on the construction, extension or improvement of industrial and commercial

IN EUROPE, START AT THE TOP.

Entering new markets can be both the biggest opportunity and the biggest threat for US companies, particularly when it is Europe that they have their sights on. Mature markets, but still very different, despite over 25 years of "unity", make Europe the place you would not want to take chances.

So when looking for the kind of Advertising Agency that can help them to get off the launchpad successfully, it is no surprise that most US multinationals choose to get close to the American agencies that have been in Europe for the longest and have developed the strongest networks.

Amongst those with long traditions in Europe, there is one agency that stands out as the best established and most successful: McCann-Erickson.

In main European centres since 1927, McCann is ranked No.1 on billings in Europe by AdAge and holds the leadership position in most, if not all, of the criteria for choice that marketers look for.

In terms of coverage, McCann not only covers Europe better than any other, but it also does it in greater strength. More McCann agencies are ranked by AdAge in the local top five than any other and if your aspirations extend to Africa or the Middle East, you will find McCann with more than double the strength of any other, US or European.

But dots on a map are one thing. Getting them all to work with the same understanding, in the responsive, results-oriented way you expect of your own organisation is quite another. That's why McCann owns controlling shares in more of its agencies.

It's that outstanding level of control which has enabled McCann to put in place a worldwide system of methodologies which ensure that marketers are met with the same disciplines and standards wherever they go. The McCann Road Map to Effective Advertising is the most comprehensive guide to how to develop local or international advertising you will find.

But if McCann stacks up well in theory, how well does it do in practice?

Over the last two years, McCann agencies have won, with their clients, more awards, far more, for advertising effectiveness in Europe, than anyone else. That includes successes for clients like GM, UPS, Black & Decker and RJR. Successes like that come from closeness to local consumers, welded to the ability to rise above local differences to produce outstanding creativity that crosses borders.

McCann's European client list reads like a who's who of top US businesses: Exxon, J&J, GM, Gillette, Coca-Cola, UPS, recently joined by the likes of Motorola, Gateway 2000 and Mastercard in the quest for new levels of success in Europe.

To service the wider communications needs of its multinational clients McCann WorldGroup has established parallel networks of specialist companies covering Relationship Marketing, Experiential (Events) Marketing, PR, Branding Consultancy, Online Marketing and Healthcare.

London is McCann's headquarters in Europe, but Paris, Frankfurt, Milan and Madrid are all major co-ordination centres. In fact wherever any marketer puts down his routes there is almost certain to be a McCann agency nearby that can key into the most powerful network in Europe.

WHERE WILL YOU FIND 'EUROPEAN AD AGENCY OF THE YEAR'?

(A CLUE).

You'll find us in New York. As well as in London, Paris, Frankfurt and 49

other cities in Europe. We won more European effectiveness awards

than any other agency last year. We've just been voted 'Most Admired

Agency in Europe' by senior marketing executives. And we won the M&M

'European Agency of the Year' last year. Call us. We speak your language.

Call Jim Heekin in London on 44 171 580 6690. McCANN-ERICKSON buildings. The initial allowance can be reduced to any amount the owner wishes, in which case the balance will be given in straight-line annual writing-down allowances of 25 per cent. For example, if 40 per cent is claimed initially, the writing-down allowances over three years will be 25 per cent, 25 per cent and 10 per cent respectively. If, in these cases, the building is brought into use in the same year as that in which the expenditure is incurred, an initial allowance and writing-down allowance will be given for that year.

Owners are eligible whether they occupy their buildings themselves or let them. The allowances apply to capital expenditure which is either:

- incurred within the zone's period of designation; or

- committed under a contract entered into within the zone's period of designation and incurred within 10 years of expiry of the zone.

The allowances apply to industrial buildings and qualifying hotels in place of the usual capital-allowances provisions. They also apply to all offices and to other commercial buildings used for trading or professional purposes (but not to dwelling houses) for which capital allowances are not normally available.

Where a building which qualifies for the allowance is sold unused, or within two years of being brought into use, then the purchaser can claim the relief. On any subsequent sale of the building within 25 years of its first having been brought into use, a balancing charge or allowance will be made in accordance with the normal industrial-building allowance rules. Relief is only available for construction costs: there is no relief for the underlying land (including the amount attributable to the land when an interest in land with a building on it is acquired).

Industrial Training Boards

Industrial Training Boards (ITBs) can normally impose a levy on employers and demand information from them. These powers do not apply to business establishments in EZs. Grants and advice on training may, however, still be available from ITBs.

Simplified Planning Regime

This is operated under a planning scheme prepared for each Zone. The scheme sets out the types of development for which planning permission is granted, without any individual application being required. Certain conditions governing development (for example, to ensure that health, safety, pollution and environmental standards are met) are built into each scheme and a limited number of matters can be reserved for approval by the zone authority. Any development proposal which does not conform with the conditions of the particular scheme will require individual planning permission in the normal way. Where such applications are needed, there are special arrangements to ensure that these are determined speedily.

As many forms of development in EZs are granted planning permission by the relevant scheme, it is expected that there will be less cause for appeals to the Secretary of State in EZs than elsewhere. However, where appeals do arise, the parties involved may obtain a copy of a note entitled 'Advice on the Enterprise Zone Planning System in England and Wales', from the Department of Environment, Transport and the Regions. (See below.)

Speedier administration

Every effort is made to ensure that administrative matters in EZs are handled as quickly as possible. Zone Authorities will deal with any residual planning applications and building-regulation approvals in as short a time as possible. The local authorities will deal with queries about land availability and release, highways access and public transport, etc, as a matter of priority. The suppliers of gas, electricity, water, sewerage and telecommunications services endeavour to deal quickly with connections for customers in EZs. A list of contacts for these services, together with notes on the adoption standards and other requirements to water and sewerage mains, can be obtained from the zone authority or promoter as listed below.

Customs facilities

Applications from firms within EZs for 'inward-processing relief' will be handled as a matter of priority. Inward-processing relief is an arrangement which allows goods to be imported for processing and subsequent export outside the European Union without payment of customs charges. Applications from firms which meet the conditions for authorisation to operate a customs warehouse will be processed rapidly. Authorisation to operate a customs warehouse allows an importer of non-Union goods to store those goods without payment of duty, VAT and other import charges. There are two categories of customs warehouse: the Public Warehouse for the use of any trader in the UK and the Private Warehouse which is reserved for the warehousing of goods by the warehouse keeper.

Further information on customs warehouses may be obtained from the local Excise and Inland Customs Advice Centre, whose address can be found in the local telephone directory.

RBLA – PROVIDING SECURITY SOLUTIONS INTO 2000 AND BEYOND

For over 70 years ROYAL BRITISH LEGION SECURITY have been providing the highest level of quality security and Managed Car Parking Services to diverse clientele from British Nuclear Fuels at Sellafield to the Harbour Commissionaires controlled Sea Port at Poole, from single plot car parks to high tech multi-levelled thousand vehicle operations.

Established in 1928 with our core employees emanating from the ranks of H M Armed Services the company has grown largely by recommendation and referral, into one of the most respected providers of Manned Security Services in the UK today.

Now operating out of nine regional branches, with a National Control Centre in London, we employ some 1600 highly trained and extremely well motivated, loyal personnel, we monitor CCTV Control Rooms (to Home Office approved standards) for Police and Local Authorities. We provide security trained and vetted reception staff of the highest calibre to enhance the corporate image of our clients.

Specialist control of access & egress points, coupled with electronically monitored foot patrols at Government and commercial buildings are only some of our varied activities in the security sector.

Our officer's also perform post room duties, issue identity cards, collect cash, act as approved key holders, and provide emergency, out of hours, responses to incidents on our clients behalf. We provide Security Courier services to many of our city based clients, and all our direct employed staff are in accordance with BSIA standards, which we are accredited to. Our sited officers generally operate as nominated First Aider's, being trained to Health & Safety approved levels. For the third year running we have achieved the RoSPA gold award.

We also provide for a further level of highly trained officers, operating strictly within the Aviation and Maritime Security Act (AMSA) and the National Aviation Security Programme (NASP) for various Aviation & Maritime assignments.

Matching our personnel to a clients needs has always been our forte. We actively encourage partnership principles with our clients, suppliers and employee alike. Continually building on our past to protect your future, let us provide your security solution into 2000 and beyond.

Royal British Legion, Attendants Co Ltd.,
Headquarters, Markham House,
33-39 Garstang Road, Preston,
Lancashire PR1 1JJ
Tel: 01772 250531 Fax: 01772 827633

Building on our past, to protect your future

British Security Services and
Car Park Management

Security Services/
- Professional Service Capacity
- Static Duties
- CCTV Monitoring
- Commissionnaires
- Mobile Patrols
- Key Holding and Alarm Response
- Security Receptionists

Car Park Management/
- On-Street Parking Enforcement and Control
- Off-Street Parking Enforcement and Control
- CCTV Monitoring
- Decriminalisation Parking Enforcement
- Cash Collection, Banking and Audit Control
- Traffic Management Information
- Traffic Flow Revision
- AA Gold Award Specialist

Aviation/
- Single source integrated Aviation Security Services.
- DETR and governmental agencies approved.
- From perimeter to R-Z – from baggage to aircraft clean and search.
- Employing CTC Vetted Ex-military personnel, trained to the highest AMSA standards.

Freephone/ 0800 731 9265

RBLS is a Division of The Royal British Legion Attendants Co. Ltd

Reduction in statistical requirements

Firms' activities within EZs are excluded from the scope of compulsory Government statistical requirements. The only exception is the Census of Employment. Normal administrative returns, such as those required for the collection of VAT, continue to be required.

Controls remaining in force

Unless it is stated elsewhere in this article that they have been lifted, assume that rules and regulations concerning industrial and commercial activity apply in EZs as they do in other areas. The relevant zone authority or promoter can advise on the applicability of individual controls.

Method and period of designation

Each EZ is designated by means of a Statutory Instrument and the period of designation, which so far has always been ten years, is specified in the Designation Order.

This section provides only a summary of information about Enterprise Zones in the UK as at 10 June 1997. Measures change from time to time and you should contact the information points listed below to confirm any item on which you intend to rely and to obtain any necessary further information.

Further information on enterprise zones

Invest in Britain Bureau
Department of Trade and Industry
1 Victoria Street
London
SW1H 0ET
Tel: +44 171 215 2501
Fax: +44 171 215 5651

For further information on Enterprise Zones in general, please contact:

Department of Environment,
Transport and the Regions
David Kincaid
Regeneration Division 3
4/E8
Bressenden Place
London SWIE 5DU
Tel: +44 171 890 3757
Fax: +44 171 890 3759

Current Enterprise Zones

Inverclyde EZ (expires 2 March 1999)
Bryce Boyd
Inverclyde District Council
6 Cathcart Square
Greenock PA15 1LS
Tel: +44 1475 882402
Fax: +44 1475 882468

Sunderland EZ No 1
Hylton Riverside/Southwick (expires 26 April 2000)
Andy James
Tyne & Wear Development Corporation
Bridge House
24 Bridge Street
Sunderland SR1 1TE
Tel: +44 191 553 1000
Fax: +44 191 553 1180

Sunderland EZ Nos. 2 & 3
Castletown & Doxford Park (expires 26 April 2000)
Mrs J Snaith
Sunderland City Council
PO Box 100
Civic Centre
Sunderland SR2 7DN
Tel: +44 191 553 1000
Fax: +44 191 553 1180

Deems Valley EZ Nos. 1–6 (expires 2 November 2005)
Peter Bright
Marketing Manager
Dearne Valley Partnership
Manvers House
PO Box 109
Wath-upon-Dearne
Rotherham S63 7YZ
Tel: +44 1709 760207
Fax: +44 1709 879199

East Durham EZ Nos. 1–6
(expires 28 November 2006)
Ken Greenfield
Chief Executive
East Durham Development Agency
4th Floor
Lee House
Peterlee
County Durham SR8 1DB
Tel: +44 191 586 3366
Fax: +44 191 518 0332

East Midlands EZ Nos. 1, 2 & 3
Holmewood (expires 2 November 2005)
Mel Pretious
Economic Development Unit
North East Derbyshire DC
Council House
Saltergate
Chesterfield
Derbyshire S40 1LF
Tel: +44 1246 212685
Fax: +44 1246 212620

East Midlands EZ No 4
Manton Wood (expires 16 November 2006)
Bob Dean
Local Plans Unit
Bassetlaw DC
Queens Buildings
Porter Street
Worksop
Nottinghamshire S80 2AH
Tel: +44 1909 533190
Fax: +44 1909 482622

East Midlands EZ Nos. 5 & 6
Crown Farm (expires 21 September 2005)
Steven Baker
Property Services
Mansfield DC
Civic Centre
Chesterfield Road South
Mansfield
Nottinghamshire NG17 7BH
Tel: +44 1623 656656
Fax: +44 1623 420197

East Midlands EZ No 7
Sherwood Business Park (expires 20 November 2005)
Peter Johnson
Economic Development
Ashfield DC
Urban Road
Kirkby-in-Ashfield
Nottinghamshire NG19 8DA
Tel: +44 1623 457352
Fax: +44 1623 457590

Lanarkshire EZ (expires 31 January 2003)
Steven Dickie
Lanarkshire Development Agency
New Lanarkshire House
Willow Drive
Strathclyde Business Park
Belishill
Lanarkshire ML4 3AD
Tel: +44 1698 745454
Fax: +44 1698 842211

Tyne Riverside EZ No 1 (expires 18 February 2006)
Tyne Riverside EZ Nos. 2–7 (expires 25 August 2006)
Tyne Riverside EZ Nos. 8–11 (expires 20 October 2006)
Ms Madeleine Rourke
Investment Officer
INTO
Howard House
Saville Street
North Shields
Tyne & Wear NE30 I NT
Tel: +44 191 200 6060
Fax: +44 191 200 6110

Free Zones

A Free Zone is an enclosed area in which non-Community goods are treated for import duties as outside the customs territory of the European Community. No customs duty, import VAT or other charges are due if the goods are not released for free circulation or entered under another customs procedure.

All imported goods, including EU goods which are free of duty, may be stored or processed in a Free Zone without payment of import VAT. The supply of goods or services to or within the zone is subject to the normal domestic VAT rules. The supply of imported goods in a Free Zone may be VAT zero-rated on condition that the recipient clears the goods for removal from the free zone to home use. Relief from excise duty is limited to the warehousing facilities available under existing legislation.

Those Free Zones now operating are:

- Birmingham Airport;
- Humberside;
- Liverpool;
- Port of Sheerness;
- Port of Tilbury;
- Prestwick Airport;
- Southampton.

Potential users of Free Zones should contact the appropriate free zone manager as listed below. Any person may apply for Free Zone designation.

Activities which may take place in a Free Zone include:

- loading, unloading and transshipment;
- storage, including stockholding pending the availability of quotas;

- handling operations carried out with a view to ensuring the preservation or improving the marketable quality of Free Zone goods, or preparing them for distribution or resale;

- processing of most third country goods for export outside the EU; and processing of community goods;

- destruction of, for example, unsaleable or surplus goods.

Benefits

Relief on customs duties relating to the transshipment, handling and processing of goods destined for re-export is already widely available throughout the UK. However, whilst the UK Free Zones do not offer any additional tariff advantages, they offer the following non-tariff advantages:

- simplified customs procedures;

- cash-flow benefit resulting from exemption of duty unless and until goods are exported or released into free circulation;

- security provided by a perimeter fence enclosing the Free Zone;

- economies of scale from the physical concentration of facilities;

- greater potential for improved marketing and presentation;

- greater flexibility in determining final destinations for goods subject to quota restrictions.

Further information on Free Zones

Please contact:
HM Customs & Excise Trade Policy Group Suspensory Reliefs Team
2nd Floor West CE Heath House
61 Victoria Avenue, Southend on Sea SS2 6EY
Tel: +44 1702 361775
Fax: +44 1702 361786

This section provides only a summary of information about Free Zones in the UK as at 7 April 1997. Measures change from time to time and you should contact the information points at the address shown above or those below to confirm any item on which you intend to rely and to obtain any necessary further information.

Free Zones: contacts list

Birmingham
Mr J Cooper
West Midlands Freeport Ltd
Birmingham International Airport
Birmingham B26 3AJ
Tel: +44 121 782 0100
Fax: +44 121 782 0119

Humberside
Mr TA Wilson
TDG Ltd Pinnacle Storage
West Carr Lane
Stoneferry, Hull HU8 0BS
Tel: +44 1482 839839
Fax: +44 1482 839565

Liverpool
Mr F Rowbottom
The Free Zone Manager
Liverpool Free Zone
Maritime Centre
Port of Liverpool L21 1LA
Tel: +44 151 949 6017
Fax: +44 151 949 6020

Port of Sheerness
Mr D Shoebridge
Medway Ports Limited
Sheerness Docks
Kent ME12 1RX
Tel: +44 1795 561234
Fax: +44 1795 668516

Prestwick Airport
The Freeport Manager
Freeport Scotland Ltd
Ayrshire, Scotland
Tel: +44 1292 281311
Fax: +44 1292 288417

Southampton
Mr G M Grainger, General Manager
Southampton Free Zone Ltd
Southampton SO1 0HJ
Tel: +44 1703 335995
Fax: +44 1703 335997

Tilbury
Free Zone Manager
Port of Tilbury London Ltd
Tilbury Dock
Essex RM18 7EJ
Tel: +44 1375 852200
Fax: +44 1375 855106

Incentives in Northern Ireland

Northern Ireland offers one of the most attractive investment packages in Europe, as many major multinational organisations have discovered. The Industrial Development Board for Northern Ireland (IDB), which has responsibility for assisting the profitable growth of Northern Ireland's manufacturing and tradeable service sectors and for promoting inward investment, offers a flexible package of assistance which can be tailored to a company's individual needs. The level of grant offered will vary according to the precise location within Northern Ireland. Assistance provided directly relates to the number of newly-created jobs in internationally mobile projects and/or those projects which will result in improved competitiveness and growth.

The cost of building a new factory in a high unemployment area, for example, can be reduced by 50 per cent, with similar grants being provided to meet machinery and equipment costs.

During the first three years, companies are likely to require the most help with the heavy demands made on both manpower expenditure and capital investment. This is where IDB incentives can be seen operating at their most effective. In addition to this, IDB can provide management incentive grants to help attract the top quality people needed to keep a new business on a progressive course. There is also a range of training grants available through the Training and Equipment Agency for blue-collar workers. Finally, tax rates on new investment in Northern Ireland, as with other parts of the UK, are very competitive. For instance, capital expenditure on plant and machinery, as well as construction costs for industrial buildings, including the total value of the IDB grant, can be written off at 25 per cent per annum for machinery and equipment and 4 per cent per annum for buildings.

A comprehensive list of the various forms of assistance is given below.

IDB incentives

Capital
Cash grants for buildings, machinery and equipment of up to 50 per cent may be available to internationally mobile projects locating in areas of high unemployment.

Revenue – grants toward start-up costs
Employment grants related to the number of newly-created jobs, designed to provide new projects with revenue inflow during the build-up period.

- **Interest relief grants:** Grants to reduce interest on loans from non-Government sources available for up to 7 years – 3 years at a broadly commercial rate followed by 4 years at 3 per cent.

- **Factory rents:** Rent grants up to 100 per cent of rental costs, for up to 5 years.

- **Marketing development grants (The 40/60 Scheme):** Up to 40 per cent of approved costs up to a maximum of £60,000 per year for up to three years, to help companies develop a strategic approach to their marketing activities.

Tax – depreciation allowances
Capital expenditure on machinery and equipment and construction costs of industrial buildings, including total value of IDB grant received (up to 45 per cent), can be written off at a rate of 25 per cent per year (reducing balance basis) for machinery and equipment, and 4 per cent per year (straight line basis) for buildings.

- **Industrial de-rating:** A further allowance, known as industrial de-rating consists of 100 per cent for manufacturing.

Finance – loans
The provision of Government loans may be considered in certain circumstances. Such loans will have regard to the total capital cost of the project, including working capital, and can include an interest-free period. Adequate security is required.

Share capital
Investment in the share capital of a company may be possible to suit the needs of a particular project.

Training & Employment Agency – company development programme
Up to 50 per cent of total net training and development costs, including wage costs, fees and travel.

Industrial Research & Technology Unit – research and development programmes compete
Support for market-driven product and process development. A project definition phase attracts assistance up to 50 per cent of eligible costs to a maximum grant of £15,000 ($24,750). A project-development phase attracts assistance up to 40 per cent of eligible costs (a 10 per cent Green bonus is available) to a maximum grant of £250,000 ($412,500).

Science and technology
Support for industrially relevant pre-competitive R&D undertaken collaboratively (university and industry) or

by industry alone. Assistance is available for up to 50 per cent of costs.

For further information, contact:

Industrial Development Board for Northern Ireland
IDB House
64 Chichester Street
Belfast BT1 4JX
Tel: +44 1232 233233
Fax: +44 1232 545000

This section provides only a summary of incentives in Northern Ireland as at 10 March 1997. Assistance levels and incentives change from time to time and you should contact the Industrial Development Board, at the address shown, to confirm any item on which you intend to rely or to obtain any necessary further information

RESEARCH AND DEVELOPMENT ASSISTANCE

Research assistance

Collaborative research programmes can qualify for selective financial support from the Department of Trade and Industry. Assistance is available under the following programmes:

- EUREKA
- LINK
- The EC Fourth Framework Programme for RTD
- SME programmes

EUREKA

EUREKA's main objective is the enhancement of Europe's productivity and competitiveness on the world market through market-oriented, industry-led collaborative research and development in any field of advanced technology. EUREKA has a network of National Project Co-ordinators which can bring project proposals to the attention of organisations in other member countries.

EUREKA membership currently includes 25 European countries plus the European Commission. Project participants are expected to arrange the necessary funding themselves for their EUREKA projects. However, the DTI may be able to assist with the project costs through non-repayable grants for consortium-building activities and research and development work.

For further information, contact:

Linda Prosper
EUREKA Unit 3.11
151 Buckingham Palace Road
London SW1W 9SS
Tel: +44 171 215 1618
Fax: +44 171 215 1700
E-Mail: linda.prosper@tidv.dti.gov.uk

LINK

The LINK initiative is a cross-government framework for collaborative research, first launched in 1986. It aims to promote partnership between the UK industry and the research base, thereby stimulating innovation and wealth creation. The research is pre-competitive and strategic and is undertaken within a well defined project management framework. LINK is managed through programmes covering discrete technology or generic product areas. Within each programme LINK supports a number of collaborative research projects involving academic and industrial partners. Programmes typically last for between four and six years.

There are currently 57 LINK programmes, of which 24 are open to new project proposals. Government departments and research councils provide up to 50 per cent of the total eligible costs of a LINK project, with the balance of funding coming from industry. The total value of projects underway or completed is approximately £430 million.

UK companies, both large and small, can take part. LINK actively encourages the involvement of small- and medium-sized enterprises. In addition, multinational companies are able to participate, provided that they have a significant manufacturing and research base in the UK, and the benefits of the research are used for wealth creation within the UK or European Union (EU). More than 1,300 companies and approximately 190 science-based institutions are involved in LINK projects.

For further information contact:

LINK Directorate
Office of Science and Technology
Department of Trade and Industry
1 Victoria Street
UG.A.35
London SW1H 0ET
Tel: +44 171 215 0053
Fax: +44 171 215 0054
E-mail: link.ost@gtnet.gov.uk

The EC Fourth Framework Programme for RTD

The European Community (EC) supports research and technological development (RTD) through the Fourth Framework Programme (FPIV), 1994–98. With a budget of over £10 billion, FPIV provides 50 per cent funding for collaborative research projects in a wide range of areas, from industrial and information technologies to life and social sciences. The projects are chosen through a process of competitive selection following evaluation by independent experts, with participation open to industry, universities and other research organisations.

There are also special measures to help small- and medium-sized enterprises participate. To be eligible, projects must be collaborative, ie, a UK organisation must work with at least one independent organisation from one of the other 14 EU Member States or from Norway, Iceland, Liechtenstein or Israel. In addition, the research undertaken must be broadly pre-competitive, that is, it should not be too near-market, though it should have excellent potential for eventual exploitation in the marketplace.

FPIV also places strong emphasis on the exploitation of the research results. In particular, the Dissemination and Exploitation of Results, or INNOVATION, programme supports measures aimed at facilitating the promotion of innovation, particularly through the exploitation of existing research results and technology transfer in collaboration with other Member States of the European Union. To carry out work in these areas, a network of 52 INNOVATION Relay Centres has been set up throughout the EU, including seven in the UK. Further details are available from the contact point below.

The DTI is keen to promote the potential benefits of FPIV and to help the UK organisations benefit through participation in FPIV projects. The EC R&D Team, which operates from the Office of Science and Technology, can provide general advice and information on FPIV, as well as contact names for more detailed information about the specific programmes.

For further information, contact:

EC R&D Team
Room 4/B
26–28 Old Queen Street
London SW1H 9HP
Tel: +44 171 271 6520 (EC R&D)
44 171 271 6525 (Innovation)
Fax: +44 171 271 6523

SME programmes

Assistance for small firms – Smart

Smart is a DTI scheme which provides support to small- and medium-sized enterprises in England. Smart was introduced on 1 April 1997 and includes key elements of the former SMART and SPUR schemes, and the innovation element of the regional enterprise grants.

Smart grants are awarded on a competitive basis to help with technical and commercial feasibility studies into innovative technology development, up to pre-production prototype, of new products or processes which demonstrate significant advances.

Feasibility studies

Funding at the rate of 75 per cent – up to £45,000 – against eligible project costs is available for individuals and businesses in England with fewer than 50 employees and turnover not exceeding ECU 7 million or an annual balance sheet total not exceeding ECU 5 million. Only feasibility studies greater than £30,000 are considered.

Development projects

Independent enterprises in England may compete for support for development projects. Winners receive a grant at the rate of 30 per cent up to a maximum of ECU 200,000. Enterprises must have fewer than 250 employees to qualify, and an annual RDA turnover not exceeding ECU 40 million or an annual balance sheet total not exceeding ECU 27 million. Only development projects in excess of ECU60,000 are considered.

Exceptional development projects

A very small number of exceptional development projects may receive a higher grant of up to ECU 600,000, at a variable rate up to a maximum of 30 per cent of total eligible costs.

Investing in the future

Smart reflects and supports the objectives of the Foresight Programme, which aims to accelerate and enhance the nation's prosperity and quality of life by recognising opportunities in markets and helping the development of new technologies. Foresight is spearheaded by 16 panels comprising representatives from industry, government and academia.

For further information, contact:

Phil Nash
Department of Trade and Industry
SME Technology Directorate
4.D.18
1 Victoria Street
London SW1H 0ET
Tel: +44 171 215 3821
Fax: +44 171 215 3932
E-mail: phil.nash@rsme.dti.gov.uk

For similar schemes in Scotland, Wales and Northern Ireland, contact:

Scottish Office Education and Industry Department
Tel: +44 141 242 5560

Welsh Office Industry and Training Department
Tel: +44 1222 825192

Department of Economic Development
(Northern Ireland)
Industrial Research and Technology Unit
Tel: +44 1232 529488

This section provides only a summary of research and development assistance as at 13 January 1998. Regulations change from time to time and you should contact the information points above to confirm any item on which you intend to rely, or to obtain any necessary further information.

Part 3
The UK as a Business Centre

3

Your Options for Entering the UK Market

by Allyson L Stewart-Allen, Director
International Marketing Partners Consultants

Given the variety of structural ways in which you may wish to grow your business within the UK market, how can you decide among these many options, each with their own inherent risks but unlimited rewards? Added to such choices, there are a number of management approaches to ensuring your UK growth is successful, each with varying costs, sometimes hidden, that go along with each.

Just how different the UK market is from your current business should not be underestimated despite a possibly similar language and culture. Statistically each year, hundreds of North American companies make the foray but soon return home empty-handed, having neglected some fundamental cultural and structural differences which could have saved them great amounts of time and money if only they'd been considered from the outset. Some considerations follow for you and your international team, to ensure your organisation is not one of these statistics:

STRUCTURAL ALTERNATIVES

One option I'll call 'go it alone', which basically means you put your own managers and staff on the ground in the UK and start up your office organically, as we call it in the consulting trade.

Another option is the 'alliance', also known as joint venture, joint marketing or strategic-alliance route, which means finding a mailorder bride and then gambling that the marriage is a long, faithful and rewarding one.

Then there's the 'virtual presence' option, which involves having some kind of presence in the market by way of a virtual office or staff who represent your interests in a more-or-less-permanent way.

There is also the 'hired taskforce' method, which involves paying a marketing consulting firm, contract sales force or marketing organisation for a fixed period who will go out and actively find leads for you and feed them back to your home base.

Last, but not least, you may want to 'acquire' a local company who already have a local presence in that UK or other European market, who have some goodwill established, and perhaps a reputation in the market that helps your own products or services.

Pros and cons of each

Let's look at what's involved by way of the pros and cons of each.

Go it alone

Let's start with the positive elements of this approach. Not only does the 'go it alone' method mean you have management control on the ground, but also first-hand local market intelligence and direct access to customers. On the down side, the learning curve for exceptional performance in that UK market will be long and steep. You will find you need to meet the financial costs up-front which will be high, and the risks – both of success and failure – are all yours.

Alliance

On the plus side, you have access to local market intelligence, access to customer bases through your partner, and shared risk and rewards with another organisation. You might even find the alliance nets you some benefits in your home market, by way of your partner reciprocally needing your help to develop their overseas business. Or, that the alliance gets you access to technologies you may not otherwise have.

On the other hand, with alliances, you tend to lose some control as far as marketing, information systems, human resources and financial decisions are concerned.

The learning curve is a little shorter than the 'go it alone' path, but still pretty significant. The other factor weighing against your alliance is that you are at the mercy of your partner's reputation and actions in the local market and what effects these will have on your brand, reputation and/or marketing strategy. Let's not also forget that the time involved in screening and then negotiating with the series of alliance partners you'll want to interview, is extensive. You ought to budget about 12 months for the entire process, from courtship to marriage.

Virtual presence

Not only is this a very affordable, 'instant' route to establishing your UK base, but it gives the right impression to those you are trying to do business with, in that you are taking the British market seriously enough to put a 'base' here. The costs, however, are not merely the office and answering service you hire, but the fact that you can't respond personally to your clients/customers who might need your help at short notice. Your control therefore over problem-solving is fairly limited. Not to mention, also, that your learning curve is even steeper than the 'go it alone' approach since you probably have no one from your team dedicated to feeding back market trends and intelligence.

Hired taskforce

By hiring a SWAT team in the UK, you are able to flatten your learning curve and cost-effectively and rapidly establish your base. Do, however, consider the fact that your ability to control the quality and speed of response of such experts might be limited by distance and time zones. Getting local market information may also be sporadic, as the team is focused on developing your business rather than providing you with market research, which is a different business activity. The trick here is managing these experts well, and defining in advance what you want from them over a realistic timeframe.

Acquire

Lastly, you have the option to buy that market share in the form of a competitor or supplier to you that is already in the UK. Not only does this get you instant presence, local market intelligence, access to customers and complete quality control, but a going concern whose infrastructure is already in place.

Against these benefits is the price tag of your target, which might be quite high against the real returns you actually achieve. The time involved, too, in identifying and researching these targets can be monumental, which often distracts your senior management to the detriment of your on-going home business.

INTERNATIONAL GROWTH MANAGEMENT ISSUES

As technology and the payoffs of international trade converge to draw ever more overseas firms into the European market, you are likely asking, 'How can I get a slice of the pie?' The answer, probably not exactly what you wanted to hear, is that expanding into foreign markets requires serious homework, deep commitment and patience. Is international marketing only for 'mega-companies' with deep pockets? Not if you follow some key steps and get the right people on the job, no matter what size of company you are.

Homework

The most important activity is doing your homework about your European market. Do these consumers/customers want what you have to offer? Are your retail and trade prices sustainable in that marketplace? What about the legal requirements for labelling, product liability or pollution control? Do the colours of your product range convey any unflattering attributes? What are your distributor channels? These and a host of other questions must be answered before *ever* putting your toe in a foreign market, even one as seemingly similar as the UK arena. Hundreds of companies make naïve mistakes in this game because they fail to carry out this up-front groundwork.

Let me give you an example. A well-known California soft drink tried to launch in Europe back in 1992, at the start of the New Age Beverage wave in the US. Having done almost nothing by way of consumer research in advance, the product was put into wholesale distribution in the UK first. Consumer enthusiasm was not overwhelming, and it was only after eight months that the marketing team started to learn why. Not only did the screw-top bottle – its shape and white plastic cap – convey to consumers this product was cheap and tacky, but the sweetness and flavour range was incompatible with local palates. Going back to the drawing board cost the company a significant amount of money, but the brand name was now tainted and would require a large PR and marketing communications budget to turn it around.

The contract

Another pitfall for you to note from this crash course is that getting the 'contract' agreed between your European marketing reps and the holders of the resources, usually HQ, is essential. If the organisation does not support the expansion, your reps aren't given the right quality or level of resources, and you don't have 'sponsors' in your company who want to see this international venture succeed, the probability is it won't.

A common scenario we see is that a rep in the UK or other parts of Europe, with minimal on-site support in terms of staff and/or budget, reports to home base in the US. Often the organisation structure to support the European efforts is inappropriate. The quality and frequency of communication across these regions may be poor. A good balance on the autonomy/control continuum between headquarters and UK pursuits is not struck. The reporting structure to enable the sharing of best marketing practice across several geographic boundaries doesn't happen.

Managing expectations

You will also find that unrealistic expectations can make or break an international venture. Questions about how quickly you can show a return on investment, how fast you can grow the customer base, how low the margins can be to distributors/wholesalers are usually only estimated (and not researched!) and then not very accurately.

Any significant profits from your UK activities – unless you're in bed with a key player in that market who can bring you up to speed quickly as discussed in the section above – expected in under 2 to 5 years are probably unrealistic. Also, don't expect that appreciating the local business customs, commercial pace, consumer tastes and lead times can be learned from a book. There is no such thing, for example, as a 'US of Europe', no homogeneous historical roots, consumer tastes, distribu-

tion chains, purchase behaviour, motivations or even common refrigerator sizes. Learning these subtleties takes time and on-the-ground experience and expertise.

Degree of localisation

Yet another challenge is deciding how much of the core product should be preserved, while making it appeal to 'local' tastes. Issues around a product's design, shape, size and government-imposed labelling requirements need to be taken into account. Take the example of refrigerators, where large side-by-side fridge/freezers generally cannot be accommodated in UK homes, which don't have the space. Another US company we've advised recently makes home-fitness equipment, the smaller versions of the weights and machines in your gym or hotel. After much research into why their UK sales were in decline ever since their launch on British shores, it emerged that not only did the average UK homeowner not have a large home that allowed for a room dedicated to exercising, but equally does not have the storage space for an exercise bike, treadmill or weight machines, unless they are collapsible.

So how have other North American companies – The Gap, Levi's, Sunkist, Microsoft, Kinko's – cracked the international marketing game? By preparing, preparing, preparing. All of these companies, large now but once quite small, study their target international market first, then write a plan which is tested in that market. As the landscape of the UK markets is different from those in North America much of the time, navigating without first learning how to read the map can be dangerous, expensive and irreparable.

Allyson L Stewart-Allen, Director of International Marketing Partners Consultants, is an American based in the UK helping US companies enter/grow in the UK and other European markets. She is a Registered Consultant with the Chartered Institute of Marketing.

4

The Accounting Profession Looks at British Company Law

by Desmond Wright, Deputy Technical Director, Institute of Chartered Accountants in England and Wales

INTRODUCTION

This chapter provides an overview of accounting in the UK. It looks at the structure of the accountancy profession, the relevant legal and regulatory framework for the profession and business entities, and at financial reporting and auditing requirements.

THE ACCOUNTANCY PROFESSION

There are six major accountancy bodies in the UK. They are independent, but coordinate for some purposes through the Consultative Committee of Accountancy Bodies (CCAB). Total membership exceeds 250,000. The largest body is the Institute of Chartered Accountants in England and Wales (ICAEW), with approximately 115,000 members at December 1997. Internationally it is the second largest accountancy body in the world after the American Institute of Certified Public Accountants.

Three main areas of accountants' activities in the UK are regulated by law:

- audit;

- insolvency;

- investment business.

These activities can only be undertaken by members of recognised professional bodies, which take responsibility for monitoring their members' compliance with the law. The tensions between acting as both a professional body and a regulator have caused difficulties, particularly after audit regulation was introduced at the beginning of the decade.

At the time of writing, the six members of the CCAB are working towards a new structure that would place some regulatory and related functions under a new and separate body. However, this has not yet been finally agreed. At the moment, therefore, the professional accountancy bodies themselves are responsible for ethical and disciplinary matters. The ICAEW sets high ethical standards for its members. The *Guide to Professional Ethics* sets out fundamental principles and elaborates on their application in practice. Failure to follow the guidelines can lead to disciplinary action against members or firms.

LEGAL FRAMEWORK

UK law comprises statutes and judicial decisions. The UK legal system is a common-law system, which establishes many legal principles through a developing body of case law. When adjudicating on statute law, the role of the courts is to interpret the statutes. A statute cannot be declared unconstitutional, as there is no written constitution. The European Union (EU) also has a law-making role, within the areas defined by the EU treaties. In general, EU member states are obliged to incorporate agreed European law within their domestic legal systems. Generally, European law overrides domestic law if the two are in conflict.

BUSINESS ENTITIES

There is a wide choice of business entity in the UK. Most foreign enterprises operate in the UK through the UK-incorporated subsidiary companies. Branch operations are also common. A branch may trade on its own account and carry on business for the overseas company. A 'place of business' may be established rather than a branch for activities that are only ancillary or incidental to the foreign business. In addition, other vehicles are available, including partnerships, joint ventures and sole proprietorships. This section concentrates primarily on the most common trading vehicle, the UK company.

COMPANY LAW

Although the law in Scotland is different in some respects from that in England and Wales, company law is the same throughout the UK (and Northern Ireland). The principal Act is the Companies Act 1985, as amended by the Companies Act 1989. UK company law incorporates the provisions of the relevant European company law Directives, and is therefore consistent with European law. However, the Directives allow a degree of flexibility, so that public reporting requirements, for example, may vary quite markedly between member states. UK reporting requirements generally are not dissimilar from those found in the US and Canada.

Company formation is straightforward in the UK and registration costs are small. 'Shelf' companies can be bought ready-made at short notice from formation agents or professional advisers. Changes to the name and other company statutes can be easily and quickly made. All limited companies (whether public or private) must file annual accounts with the Registrar of Companies, where they are available for public inspection. Small or medium-sized companies (as defined) may file abbreviated accounts which provide significantly less information than that provided by other companies (including all public limited companies). However, small and medium-sized companies must provide accounts for shareholders that contain all the information required by the Companies Act. Unlimited liability companies which are neither the subsidiary nor the parent of a limited liability company do not have to file accounts, but must still present them to members.

Audit requirements

Although there are now exemptions for very small companies (those with a turnover under £350,000), there is a general requirement for company accounts to be audited. This requirement includes unlimited liability companies. (However, sole traders and partnerships do not have to file accounts or have them audited.) The auditors are required to report to the members on every balance sheet and profit and loss account (income statement) laid before the company in general meetings. The auditors' report must state whether the accounts

have been properly prepared in accordance with the Companies Act 1985 and whether they show a true and fair view. In forming their opinion, auditors must consider whether the following conditions have been satisfied:

- proper accounting records have been kept;
- the accounts are in agreement with the accounting records; and
- the auditors have received all the information, explanations and returns necessary to form their opinion.

Company auditors must be members of a Recognised Supervisory Body (RSB) and authorised by it to audit. Although members of the ICAEW, for example, are entitled by statute to audit companies, the Institute in its role as an RSB imposes additional criteria for becoming a registered auditor. These deal principally with experience requirements, professional integrity, independence and the achievement of technical standards. It is a fundamental principle of the accountancy profession that auditors must be independent of their clients; they are therefore not allowed to have any financial interest in a client. However, as in North America, there is no bar to audit firms providing other services such as tax and consulting.

Auditing standards are set by the Auditing Practices Board, which has the overall role of advancing standards of auditing and associated review activities and of providing a framework for auditing practice. Although the APB is entirely funded by the CCAB, it has a great deal of independence. Its membership includes representatives from the business community and organisations outside the accountancy profession, and the professional bodies have no power to reject its pronouncements. In most cases, complying with auditing standards ensures compliance with International Standards of Auditing.

Accounting principles and practice

Every limited company must keep proper accounting records and file annual accounts that give a true and fair view of the state of the company's affairs and of its profit or loss for the year. The accounts must follow the format prescribed in the Companies Act 1985 and adhere to detailed disclosure requirements. These legal requirements are essentially the same throughout the European Union.

Accounting standards supplement the requirements of the Companies Act 1985 as to the form and content of the accounts. Since 1990, standards have been set by the Accounting Standards Board in the form of Financial Reporting Standards (FRS). The Board also adopted the Statements of Standard Accounting Practice (SSAPs) issued by its predecessor body. The Board is independent of the accountancy profession, which nevertheless continues to contribute to its funding jointly with other public and private sector bodies.

Accounting standards have authority in law. The directors of a company are required under the Companies Act 1985 to state whether the accounts have been prepared in accordance with applicable accounting standards and to explain with reasons any departure from either the law or standards. Accounting standards are mandatory on members of the UK accountancy profession. The auditors must refer in their report to any departure from accounting standards with which they do not concur.

In most cases, compliance with an accounting standard (SSAP or FRS) ensures compliance with the equivalent International Accounting Standard (IAS). Where certain standards diverge (for example, in relation to cash flow statements and accounting for goodwill), the domestic standards have precedence – there is no option to adopt the IAS. In contrast to some European countries, tax rules have little effect on accounting treatments adopted in the UK. Basically, profits for tax purposes are calculated by making a series of adjustments to the accounts drawn up according to generally accepted principles. For example, book depreciation of fixed assets is not accepted for tax purposes: statutory capital allowances must be used instead.

The financial statements

Annual accounts are the accounts of an individual company and any group accounts required by the Companies Act 1985. The assumptions underlying the accounts are laid down in the Act, which requires consistency, prudence, accrual accounting, the presumption of a going concern, and the separate determination and valuation of individual assets and liabilities. Financial statements are normally prepared on the historical cost basis. However, the Companies Act and accounting standards allow the revaluation of certain assets according to alternative accounting rules. The broad effect of these rules is to allow companies the option of adopting historical cost or current cost.

In addition there is a third option, the one adopted by many companies, which allows historical cost to be modified by stating certain tangible fixed assets (usually land and buildings) at market value.

The financial statements include the balance sheet of the company and a profit and loss account. A group must also include the group balance sheet, but can usually present the group profit and loss account instead of the holding company's individual profit and loss account. These statements are supplemented by notes, which must include a statement of accounting policies. Accounting standards require a cash flow statement, although this is not required by law and is subject to certain exemptions including an exemption for small companies. The annual accounts also include a statutory Directors' Report which provides a prescribed narrative supplement to the financial statements.

CONCLUSION

The spread of common law principles throughout the English-speaking world contrasts with the more prescriptive approach of the Code Napoleon, which forms the basis for the legal systems of many European countries. This contrast extends into accounting, where the principle of substance over form which underpins the concept of 'true and fair' reporting in the UK and the equivalent in North America, is not a feature of many continental systems. France, for example, has a *Plan Comptable* which sets out in detail the accounting model that must be followed. In Germany, although there is some allowance of substance over form, the accounting choices made by companies are often tax driven and thus can be at variance with best practice.

The audit tradition in the UK, with its history of highly developed capital markets, is also comparable with practice in the US and Canada. However, the audit requirement extends beyond public and listed companies to relatively small private companies that would not require an audit in North America.

These affinities in accounting and auditing between the UK and North America are mirrored in the structure and strength of the accountancy professions in the three countries. Accountants are generally businessmen and women first, rather than specialist technicians. This contrasts strongly with the small, closed professions of Europe.

5

SMEs and the Single Currency: Never Mind the Politics – When do we Feel the Impact?

Mark Henshaw, Partner, Grant Thornton

Gordon Brown's statement on 27 October 1997 clarifying the Government's position on Economic and Monetary Union (EMU) means that the UK is likely to join, but probably not in the first wave. Yet despite the claims and counter-claims which surround this issue, it is one which continues to cause great confusion for the owner-managers of Europe's small and medium-sized enterprises (SMEs). Mark Henshaw of Grant Thornton examines the practical issues involved.

According to Grant Thornton International's European Business Survey the vast majority of SMEs do not know what impact the introduction of the Euro will have on their business. UK SMEs were in the broadly pessimistic group of countries, together with Luxembourg (which is, paradoxically, the only country likely to meet all five criteria for convergence set out in the Maastricht Treaty), Turkey and Norway.

Until the Treasury released its 'Business Preparations for the Euro' pack in November 1997, little had been done by central Government to prepare UK business for the Euro. However, SMEs are not the only ones guilty of putting their heads in the sand. Many big businesses have also been slow in assessing, and preparing for, the impact of the Euro.

ACCOUNTANTS ARE WELL PLACED

Accountants in management are well placed to give the necessary advice to their boards on the practical business issues of the Euro, in addition to the accounting and financial reporting implications. They should be proactive in taking the lead to gather information about EMU and report to their boards on its implications. This can be done relatively quickly from reading articles, attending seminars or using the various checklists available.

Directors of SMEs cannot disregard EMU as an issue that can be dealt with solely by consultants – they must also ensure that they too keep abreast of developments. This is extremely important when they deal with shareholders, who will be keen to know how well prepared the business is. They should be aware of the practical business issues which can often be overlooked in the heat of political debate. For example, the level of training necessary for staff to cope with the change to a single currency is likely to be considerable.

It is also likely that organisations able to provide training will be at a premium. You should therefore decide as soon as possible how and when your staff will be trained in dealing with the new currency. Work will also have to be done to ensure computer and management information systems are able to cope with the additional 'Year 2000' problems looming. (At the 1997 CBI National Conference, Bernd Pischetsrieder, Chairman of BMW, estimated that their Euro conversion costs would be 60 million DM, and that their 'Year 2000' costs would be twice as large.) IT consultants will be at a premium, in terms of both availability and price. Other peripheral issues, such as the company's business stationery, will have to be considered. Order forms, invoices, etc will need to be changed to show the new currency. Of course for businesses that provide the necessary services – those involved in information technology, management consultants and suppliers of cash registers – the opportunities are enormous, and many of these are SMEs themselves.

CURRENCY RISKS REMAIN

Currency risks will remain whether we are inside or outside of EMU. When the UK eventually does join there is still a risk that the Euro will be a weak currency, or one which is subject to large fluctuations as it finds its market rate. This will especially be the case if the Maastricht convergence criteria are fudged when the first wave of countries join in 1999. These fluctuations will still have to be hedged against.

The UK has the largest percentage of SMEs in Europe exporting to the US and (with the exception of Denmark) to the Asia Pacific region (source: Grant Thornton and Business Strategies Limited European Business Survey). We would therefore potentially be at greater risk from a fluctuating Euro than our EU counterparts. In advance of the UK joining, the risks of currency fluctuations between the Euro and Sterling will need to be hedged against.

An issue which will affect SMEs is whether larger businesses based in the UK decide to invoice in, or only accept, Euros at the start of the changeover process, regardless of when the UK joins. One company has already written to its UK suppliers indicating that this will be the case. SMEs will need to assess whether they can afford to trade with such companies, who previously would have accepted an invoice in Sterling, and ensure their systems can cope. If they don't, they risk losing business. For many UK SMEs this may be the first time they have traded in a foreign currency and it is therefore an important consideration.

ACCOUNTING ISSUES

Accountants will primarily be faced with the accounting and financial reporting issues arising from EMU. The accounting issues expected are practical concerns; the financial reporting problems more esoteric and to a certain extent less certain and open to debate.

From an accounting and financial management systems perspective, the main issue faced by SMEs will be the timing of the changeover to a computer system that can cope with foreign currencies including the Euro. At some stage during the financial year in which we join EMU there will be a dual currency accounting system. For SMEs already exporting this is likely to be less of a problem. This may be solved by running a parallel company on the same system or taking the opportunity to purchase an entirely new system. This may best be done in conjunction with the resolution of any problems your computer system may have in coping with the year 2000.

Budgeting is also a potential problem. Many businesses have three- or five-year business plans and budgets. Urgent thought needs to be given to the date when these should reflect the new currency. Will this be:

- When the decision is taken to join?
- When the joining rate is fixed?
- Or the date that the UK joins?

The Euro is likely to become yet another unknown factor when preparing annual budgets.

FINANCIAL REPORTING ISSUES

The two principal financial reporting issues to be addressed are:

1. the restatement of assets and liabilities, on the basis that the local currency has ceased to exist; and

2. the realization of previously 'unrealized' exchange gains and losses.

The first issue, that of the restatement of assets and liabilities, is based on the premise that all past transactions would need to be restated as if the Euro had always been the currency. It is more likely, however, to be a simple matter that the values for assets and liabilities carried forward on the UK's entry date will be the old amounts, restated according to a fixed conversion factor (the rate at which the domestic currency is translated into Euros). This will also apply to historical profits and losses.

The second issue is that, as a result of adopting the Euro, the foreign exchange differences for countries within EMU may become realized when the UK joins. SSAP 20 Foreign Currency Translation – which determines the treatment of foreign exchange gains and losses – requires exchange gains and losses on both short- and long-term monetary assets and liabilities to be recognized when they arise. In the UK, therefore, it is unlikely that this will have any significant effect. No gains or losses between the participating countries would arise after exchange rates become fixed, unless EMU itself failed. There would of course continue to be exchange differences when trading with countries outside of EMU.

Other financial reporting issues to be considered are:

- the publication of financial statements in the Euro. The date from which this must happen has not yet been decided;

- readers of financial statements should be aware that once they are produced in Euros, interpreting accounts from different Member States may not be as easy as one might expect. Historical trading data will not necessarily be compatible, as although currencies were converging in the run up to EMU, there would still have been large differences in their values during that period;

- the carrying value of fixed assets which have to be replaced or altered as a result of EMU. For example, software or business equipment whose useful life will be shortened by the advent of the single currency (eg single currency tills), may have to be written down over a shorter period, once we join EMU and in the run up to entry;

- costs incurred in preparing for and converting to the Euro – training, consultancy time, etc – are unlikely to be viewed as exceptional. However, in the circumstances where such costs are considered exceptional, as they do not fall into one of the categories in paragraph 20 of FRS 3, they should be charged in arriving at operating profit.

CONCLUSION

The accounting and financial reporting problems are not necessarily the biggest headaches that SMEs face. Preparing for the practical everyday implications is much more likely to create problems for the management of a business in terms of both time and money. To reduce the burden of costs it may be possible to pool resources with other local businesses to organise training and to reconfigure accounting systems. There will, however, be no substitute for putting management time into ensuring your business is up to speed with the implications of the Euro.

Businesses cannot afford to put their heads in the sand. Regardless of the timing of the UK's entry, there will be implications and problems to be overcome. At the very least, SMEs should be appointing someone in their team to assess the potential impact of the Euro on their business and not wait until it is too late. The costs of making the necessary changes to existing systems will only increase as 1 January 1999 approaches.

6

A Business Checklist for the Euro: Fifty Questions to Help You Stay Ahead

by Grant Phillips, Communications Director, Business Banking Euro Programme

Whether or not Britain adopts the single currency, organisations that are able to make the necessary changes as speedily and as economically as possible will have a strong competitive advantage. Gaining this advantage will require forethought and advanced planning. It may call for a special task force to coordinate changes. You will need urgently to decide how EMU will impact your training, systems, marketing and stationery needs. You will also need to address the timescale of change during the implementation phase, costs of new systems and the procedures for evaluating developments. Recently a large corporate customer of Barclays Bank created a euro taskforce to identify every angle of the business that might be affected by EMU. Their operations division alone came up with 61 issues to be resolved.

To help your approach to 1999 and beyond, here are a few prompts. The list is by no means exhaustive, but by addressing these questions now you can ensure that your business is on the right track.

FIRST STEPS

1. Have you put the issue on your board/executive agenda?
2. Who has overall responsibility for EMU within your business?
3. Have you considered a 'euro taskforce' to review implications and timescales?
4. Are the necessary budget allocations established?
5. Is there a communications plan to raise in-house awareness?

STRATEGY

6. What assumptions are you making in your EMU planning?
7. What are the opportunities and threats arising from EMU for your business?
8. How will you protect your existing levels of business?
9. How can you develop your business further in the EMU environment?
10. What are the organisational implications of EMU for your business?
11. How much will EMU cost your business?

SALES

12. What are your customers' expectations of you?
13. What will your competitors be doing?
14. Are your marketing policies appropriate post-EMU?
15. Do you need new market research?
16. Will you continue to use the same delivery channels for your sales?
17. Will you achieve the same profit from your transactions?
18. Will you be affected by price-transparency across the euro-zone?
19. Does your pricing policy need reviewing? Will you need to adopt dual euro/£ pricing?
20. How will you establish terms of trade and security of payment from new customers?
21. What means of collecting monies due will you use (eg, plastic, electronic)?
22. Will your product literature need amending?

SUPPLIERS AND PURCHASING

23. Do you know how EMU may impact your suppliers' relationships with you?
24. Will your suppliers be invoicing you in euros? What methods of payment will you use?
25. Will you be able to benefit from pricing transparency across the euro-zone?

FINANCE AND TREASURY

26. How will your cashflow be affected?
27. How will you finance any costs arising from EMU implications?
28. How will you finance any planned growth arising from EMU?
29. Will you need euro bank accounts alongside/instead of your existing foreign currency and £ accounts?
30. Will you have surplus euro credit balances requiring investment?
31. What will be the currency of any borrowing requirement?
32. What will the balance be between euro income and expenditure?
33. What foreign exchange risks will you still have to manage?
34. Would the euro lead to a greater centralization of your finance functions?
35. Do you have any longer-term arrangements, eg, loans/foreign contracts extending post-EMU?

ACCOUNTING

36. If there is a delay in the UK participating in EMU, will you want to use euros before the UK joins?

37. What will you consider to be your main operating currency?
38. What will be your bank account and reconciliation requirements?
39. Will you be able to invoice and settle bills in euros?

SYSTEMS

40. What are your systems requirements for converting, reporting and information processing?
41. Will you have dual reporting requirements?
42. Are you bearing in mind Year 2000 compliance?
43. If your business deals in cash, could your machines/ systems cope with euros? During a transition period, could they handle both currencies?

ADMIN/PERSONNEL

44. How will you communicate the issues/raise awareness both internally and externally?
45. How will your staff react to this change?
46. What are the implications for training, recruitment, salary payments, and expenses?
47. Will your business stationery/documentation be euro-compliant?

LEGAL AND TAX

48. What legal and regulatory implications are there for your business?
49. Will your contract documentation need amending?
50. In the event of the issue of new notes and coins, will your systems/training mitigate any potential loss through fraud?

7

English Solicitors – First For International Business Law

by Rupert Winlaw, Law Society of England and Wales

Just as English has evolved into the recognised international language for commerce, so English law has long been regarded as the ideal legal basis for governing international transactions the world over.

Helped no doubt by the United Kingdom's historical position as a centre of world trade and finance, English law, and the solicitors who practise it, have for years been relied upon to regulate business contracts of every kind and in every corner of the globe.

The reputation of the English legal system has grown to such an extent that London firms – such as Clifford Chance or Cameron McKenna – which specialise in international transactions, now rank among the largest and most powerful legal firms in the world, with many having set up overseas branches in major foreign cities to cope with the demand. Business has become so brisk there are now almost 10,000 fee-earning solicitors based in and around London. In fact, in 80 per cent of cases before the Commercial Court in London, one or more of the litigants come from overseas.

The importance of English solicitors is also underlined in economic terms by the income they generate in exports for the UK. Last year this accounted for £511 million ($843 million), representing an impressive six per cent of the UK's total 'invisible earnings'. Indeed their earnings contribute so heavily to the UK service sector that this sector now generates more wealth than manufacturing. Despite this obvious success it would be misleading to suggest that English law is necessarily better than other national laws. Why then do so many companies from every corner of the globe rely so heavily on the English legal system to settle international disputes?

One major reason has to be that it is tried and trusted. Thanks to the UK's trading eminence last century and early this century, English law has become so well developed it is now considered to be extremely well suited for governing international contracts. Hand in hand with this, English solicitors are held in high regard among businessmen for their experience and for the expertise they can offer in all fields of commercial law.

History has blessed solicitors in other ways as well. For instance, there are strong legal ties between this country and the US, Canada, Australia, New Zealand and Hong Kong, among others, as a result of the former Empire. As such, English law and custom form the basis of common-law legal systems in former Commonwealth countries and the USA. It doesn't end there, however, as English solicitors also have other advantages on their side, the most obvious of which is that they speak English, the language used by the business community worldwide. However, for those who don't speak English, advice is still easily at hand as an increasing number of solicitors now speak a foreign language.

In addition, English solicitors have been able to benefit from the time-zone overlap which occurs thanks to the UK's central position between America and the Far East. This has been helpful in many ways and has helped London to become strong in many sectors of the legal market, particularly in maritime, insurance, reinsurance and commodities.

In addition, many firms now operate 24-hour practices to meet the immediate needs of clients anywhere in the world.

EUROPEAN UNION

A factor of increasing significance to businesspeople is the UK's membership of the European Union. For many countries, particularly those where English is spoken or who have the common law system, the UK is the gateway to the EU. This is particularly important as the EU is of growing significance in trade terms around the world, especially with the advent of the European Single Market.

European Union law is an integral part of UK law, which affects areas of concern to companies and businesses such as competition, employment, environmental protection and intellectual property. As such, English solicitors are an ideal source of advice for businesspeople from outside the EU, who are interested in finding out more on the new freedoms and business opportunities available.

In order to offer this service, solicitors have to ensure they are constantly up to date with the legislation coming from Brussels, the centre of the European Union, as well as decisions from the European Court in Luxembourg.

To achieve this, about 40 English solicitors' firms have set up offices in Brussels, while others have formed associations with lawyers in Belgium and other Member States.

The Law Society – the professional body which represents and regulates solicitors in England and Wales – also has an office in Brussels. This is part of a growing trend towards forming international networks of lawyers, not only within Europe, but around the world. The overall aim is to ensure that clients have access to legal advice when and where it is needed. All of this makes English solicitors ideally qualified to act as coordinators where legal advice covering different jurisdictions is required. It is because of this that businesspeople from around the world – and increasingly from the emerging markets in the Far East – turn to English solicitors, because they feel the law they practise is intrinsically the most appropriate system for their particular problem.

So for all your commercial needs, no matter where your business is based, it pays to seek advice from an English solicitor. Above all, you can be sure of cross-border advice which is second to none.

8

International Standards ISO 9000, ISO 14000

by the International Organisation for Standardisation

ISO: THE ORGANISATION BEHIND ISO 9000 AND ISO 14000

The ISO 9000 series of International Standards for quality management and quality assurance has been adopted in more than 90 countries and is being implemented by thousands of manufacturing or service organisations in both public and private sectors.

One of the most successful series of standards in the history of ISO (International Organisation for Standardisation), ISO 9000 has generated much publicity and made the name of ISO known to a wider business community than the specialists directly concerned with technical standards. The publication in September 1996 of the first standards in the ISO 14000 series on environmental management, and the speed with which they are being taken up by the business community, promise more publicity for the name 'ISO'. However, many members of the business community may have less of an idea of what the organisation behind ISO 9000 and ISO 14000 is and what it does.

MORE THAN ISO 9000 AND ISO 14000

ISO 9000 and ISO 14000 are two series among more than 11,000 International Standards published by ISO since it began operations in 1947. ISO develops standards for the following technical fields:

- mechanical engineering;
- basic chemicals;
- non-metallic materials;
- ores and metals;
- information processing, graphics and photography;
- agriculture;
- building;
- special technologies;
- health and medicine;
- basic subjects;
- environment;
- packaging and distribution of goods.

ISO's name

ISO is the International Organisation for Standardisation. 'ISO' is not an acronym, but a name, derived from the Greek word isos, meaning 'equal', which is the root of the prefix 'iso-' that occurs in a host of terms, such as 'isometric' (of equal measure or dimensions), and 'isonomy' (equality of laws, or of people before the law). From 'equal' to 'standard', the line of thinking that led to the choice of 'ISO' as the name of the organisation is easy to follow. In addition, the name ISO is used around the world to denote the organisation, thus avoiding a plethora of acronyms resulting from the translation of 'International Organisation for Standardisation' into the different national languages of members, eg IOS in English, OIN in French (from Organisation internationale de normalisation). Whatever the country, the short form of the Organisation's name is always ISO.

Non-governmental

ISO is a non-governmental organisation. It is not part of the United Nations Organisation (although it has strong links with nearly all bodies and specialised agencies of the UN family). Its membership, which is currently drawn from some 120 countries, is not composed of government delegations, but is made up of national standards institutes or organisations, on a one member organisation per country basis.

Voluntary

All the standards developed by ISO are voluntary. ISO has no power to enforce their implementation. A certain percentage of its standards, mainly those concerned with health, safety or the environment, has been adopted in some countries as part of their regulatory framework, or is referred to in legislation for which it serves as the technical basis. However, such adoptions are sovereign decisions by the regulatory authorities or governments of the countries concerned. ISO itself has no regulatory or legislative powers.

Consensus

ISO standards are market-driven. They are developed by international consensus among experts drawn from the industrial, technical or business sectors which have expressed the need for a particular standard. They may be joined by experts from government, regulatory authorities, testing bodies, academia, consumer groups or other organisations with relevant knowledge, or which have expressed a direct interest in the standard under development. Although ISO standards are voluntary, the fact that they are developed in response to market demand, and are based on consensus among the interested parties, ensures widespread use of the standards.

ISO's job

ISO develops worldwide technical agreements which are published as International Standards. This is a major operation. It is estimated that every working day of the year, there are 15 meetings around the world of ISO technical groups in which the standards-development work is actually carried out. In all, there are more than 2850 of these groups in which some 30,000 experts participate annually. This technical work is coordinated from ISO Central Secretariat in Geneva, which also publishes the standards.

Conforming to standards

It is not part of ISO's mission to verify that its standards are being implemented by users in conformity with the requirements of the standards. Conformity assessment, as this verification process is known, is a matter for suppliers and their clients in the private sector, and of regulatory bodies when ISO standards have been incorporated into public legislation.

In addition, there exist many testing laboratories and auditing bodies which offer independent (also known as 'third party') conformity assessment services to verify that products, services or systems measure up to ISO standards. Such organisations may perform these services under a mandate to a regulatory authority, or as a commercial activity of which the aim is to create confidence between suppliers and their clients. In some countries, ISO members carry out conformity assessment, either on behalf of their respective governments, or as a business operation. ISO itself, however, has no authority to control these activities.

What ISO does is develop in partnership with the IEC (International Electrotechnical Commission) ISO/IEC Guides covering various aspects of conformity assessment activities and the organisations that perform them. The voluntary criteria contained in these guides represent an international consensus on what constitutes acceptable practice. Their use contributes to the consistency and coherence of conformity assessment worldwide and so facilitates trade across borders.

ISO 9000 and ISO 14000 certification

As will be gathered from the above, ISO operates no system for verifying the conformance of organisations' quality systems with standards in the ISO 9000 series, or of environmental management systems against the ISO 14000 requirements. ISO itself does not carry out any ISO 9000 or ISO 14000 audits and does not award any certificates attesting to conformity with the standards commonly known as 'ISO 9000 certificates' or 'ISO 14000 certificates'. There is no such thing as 'ISO certification', whether in relation to ISO 9000, ISO 14000 or any other ISO standard.

A simple exercise to demonstrate why 'ISO certification' is a misleading abbreviation for 'ISO 9000 certification' or 'ISO 14000 certification' is to substitute the name of another institution for 'ISO'. For example, the phrase 'US Government certification' clearly gives the impression that it is the US Government which is carrying out the certification. This impression is wrong. ISO 9000 and ISO 14000 certification services are carried out in the US by independent certification bodies, not by the US Government. And not by ISO either, whether in the US or elsewhere, which is why 'ISO certification' is an unacceptable abbreviation for 'ISO 9000 certification' or 'ISO 14000 certification'.

ISO 9000 and ISO 14000 certificates are issued by certification bodies (in some countries, they are called 'registration' bodies) independently of ISO, even when a particular body may be part of a national standards organisation that is an ISO member. ISO has no authority to oversee the work of quality-management-system or environmental-management-system certification bodies. However, the relevant ISO/IEC Guides form a basis for acceptable practice by such bodies. A certification body's adherence, or the lack of it, to these guidelines may be used by a company as one of its criteria for choosing a certification body to audit its quality or environmental management system and issue an ISO 9000 or ISO 14000 certificate.

In a growing number of countries, accreditation bodies are being set up (sometimes, but not always, with a government mandate) to exercise a degree of control over the 'ISO 9000 and ISO 14000 certification industry'. Certification bodies which fulfil the criteria of the accreditation system are duly accredited, which can increase market confidence in the value of the ISO 9000 or ISO 14000 certificates issued by that registrar. The relevant ISO/IEC Guides (adopted by the EU as the EN 45000 series) are among the criteria applied by these accreditation bodies.

Therefore, while ISO does not perform ISO 9000 or ISO 14000 certification and exercises no authority over bodies that are engaged in these activities, its voluntary guidelines are widely used and help ensure good practice by those involved.

ISO 9000 FAMILY

The ISO 9000 family of standards represents an international consensus on good management practice. Its primary aim is to give organisations guidelines on what constitutes an effective quality-management system, which in turn can serve as a framework for continuous improvement. The standard ISO 9004–1 (and the other parts of ISO 9004) gives guidelines on the elements of quality management and a quality system.

The family also includes three quality assurance models ISO 9001, ISO 9002 and ISO 9003 against which the quality system can be audited to see that it complies with ISO 9000 requirements. The organisation should carry out this auditing itself to verify that it is managing its processes effectively. In addition, it may invite its clients to audit the quality system in order to give them confidence that the organisation is capable of delivering products or services that will meet their needs.

Lastly, the organisation may engage the services of an independent quality-system certification body to obtain an ISO 9000 certificate of conformity. This last option has proved extremely popular because of the perceived credibility of an independent verification. It may thus avoid multiple audits by the organisation's clients, or reduce the frequency or duration of client audits. The certificate can also help establish the organisation's credentials as a reliable business partner to potential clients, especially when supplier and customer are new to each other, or far removed geographically, as in an export context.

In some countries, government departments and public authorities are requiring companies bidding for procurement contracts to be ISO 9000 certificate holders. In some industrial sectors, major companies are requiring their suppliers to comply with ISO 9000. The client company may verify compliance itself, or may require the supplier to have an ISO 9000 certificate issued by an independent certification body.

ISO 14000 FAMILY

The ISO 14000 family, of which the first standards were published in September and October 1996, addresses various aspects of environmental management. The very first two standards, ISO 14004 and ISO 14001, deal with environmental management systems. These are management tools to enable an organisation of any size or type to control the impact of its activities, products or services on the environment. An environmental management system represents a structured approach to setting environmental objectives and targets, to achieving these and demonstrating that they have been achieved.

The standards do not specify levels of environmental performance, a fact which allows them to be implemented by a wide variety of organisations, whatever their current level of environmental maturity. However, a commitment to compliance with applicable environmental legislation and regulations is required, along with commitment to continual improvement for which the environmental management system provides the framework.

ISO 14004 provides guidelines on the elements of an environmental management system and its implementation and discusses principal issues involved.

ISO 14001 specifies the requirements for such an environmental management system. Fulfilling these requirements demands objective evidence which can be audited to demonstrate that the environmental management system is operating effectively in conformance with the standard. ISO 14001 can thus be used for internal purposes to provide assurance to the organisation's management and for external purposes to provide assurance to interested parties. In the external context, conformance to ISO 14001 can be used to support what an organisation claims about its own environmental policies and actions. It is suitable for both supplier's declarations of conformity, assessment of conformity by an external stakeholder such as a business client and for certification of conformity by an independent certification body.

Not product labels

ISO 9000 is not a product quality label or guarantee. ISO 14000 is not a 'green' or 'environmentally friendly' label for products. When an organisation has a management system certified to an ISO 9000 or ISO 14000 standard, this means that an independent auditor has checked that the processes influencing quality (ISO 9000), or the processes influencing the impact of the organisation's activities on the environment (ISO 14000), conform to the relevant standard's requirements. In plain language, ISO 9000 and ISO 14000 relate to the making of products. They are not product labels.

ISO's logo

The ISO logo is a registered trademark. ISO does not authorise its logo to be used, either by quality system or environmental management system certification bodies, or by the companies to which the latter issue ISO 9000 or ISO 14000 certificates. Allowing the ISO logo to be used would give the impression that ISO carries out certification activities, or has approved or authorised the organisation using its logo. Neither of these is the case.

ISO

To sum up, ISO (International Organisation for Standardisation) is a lot more than ISO 9000 and ISO 14000:

- ISO has developed more than 11,000 International Standards covering almost all technical fields;

- ISO is a non-governmental organisation with members from some 120 countries;

- ISO standards are voluntary and ISO has no authority to enforce their implementation;

- ISO does not carry out conformity assessment activities, although it develops guidelines for these which establish the foundations for good practice;

- ISO does not issue ISO 9000 or ISO 14000 certificates;

- 'ISO certification' does not exist, whether to ISO 9000, ISO 14000 or any other of the standards ISO has developed. The correct phrase is 'ISO 9000 certification' or 'ISO 14000 certification', which are performed independently of ISO;

- ISO 9000 and ISO 14000 are not product labels;

- The ISO logo is a registered trademark and ISO does not authorise its use in connection with ISO 9000 or ISO 14000 certification;

- ISO standards are market-driven. They are developed on the basis of international consensus among experts from the sector which has expressed a requirement for a particular standard;

In other words, ISO's standards are used to the extent that people find them useful. In cases like ISO 9000, which is the most visible current example, but not the only one, that can mean very useful!

For further information on ISO, ISO 9000 and ISO 14000, contact your national standards institute.

9

Britain's New Deal: Delivery Through Partnerships

by Leigh Lewis, Chief Executive, The Employment Service

Britain's Employment Service is rising to the challenge of delivering the government's New Deal programmes for young people aged 18–24 and those above that age who have been unemployed for more than two years. Once under way they will offer a new start and new hope to many of the country's long-term unemployed people.

Despite a buoyant UK economy and a steady decline in the overall level of unemployment, long-term unemployment remains unacceptably high, particularly for young people without skills and experience and for older people who have been unemployed for a very long time. The Employment Service was privileged to be asked immediately after the general election to coordinate the implementation of the government's New Deal programmes for these groups. As an executive agency of the Department for Education and Employment, we employ some 34,000 people, the great majority of whom work in more than 1000 Jobcentres nationwide. Our key priority is to help unemployed people back to work at the same time as helping the nation's employers fill jobs. To do so we now use some of the latest state-of-the-art technology.

SO WHAT IS THE NEW DEAL?

For young people who have been unemployed for six months or more it will offer four options, all of which will last for at least six months and include education or training towards an accredited qualification.

The first and perhaps most important step in their access to New Deal will be an initial 'Gateway' – an introductory advice and counselling period of up to four months during which a dedicated personal adviser will guide and support them through to their choice of a New Deal option. The Gateway is designed to meet individual needs and may include careers advice, help with basic skills, debt counselling and intensive job search. The Gateway will help the young person to choose one of the four options.

The employer option

Employers who offer jobs to young people on New Deal will receive a subsidy equal to £60 per week for up to six months for each young person they employ. A further £750 will be paid to help them meet the costs of providing the young person with training equivalent to one day per week working towards an accredited qualification.

The education and training option

This option will have a strong emphasis on meeting basic skills needs and will normally lead to a National Vocational Qualification. While on this option, the young person will receive an allowance equal to their Jobseeker's Allowance and will continue to receive any passported benefits. The option can last up to 12 months.

The environmental task force option

Young people who join this option will work for up to six months on a project which aims to improve the young person's employability whilst at the same time improving their own community's environment. Young people on this option may be paid a wage but, if not, will continue to receive an allowance equal to their Jobseeker's Allowance and will continue to receive any passported benefits and a grant of £400 paid in weekly instalments. Up to £750 towards providing training equivalent to one day per week will also be available to the provider.

The voluntary sector option

Under the voluntary sector option, participants will be offered the opportunity to work for up to six months with a voluntary organisation. Work done must provide benefit to the individual, the organisation, their clients and the wider community. Young people on this option can be paid a wage but, if not, will receive an allowance equal to their Jobseeker's Allowance and will continue to receive any passported benefits plus a grant of £400 paid in weekly instalments. Providers will receive up to £750 towards providing training equivalent to one day a week.

For job seekers over 25 who have been unemployed for two years or more, New Deal will offer help in the form of a £75 a week wage subsidy for up to six months, paid to employers who recruit them. For some job seekers in this group there will also be the opportunity to study full-time for up to a year while still receiving Jobseeker's Allowance.

I believe that the ultimate success of New Deal will depend on three main challenges:

- on the extent to which we can close the 'employability' gap experienced by many young people by offering them opportunities of genuine quality which will help them realise their employment ambitions;

- on our ability to meet the needs of all young people, particularly those who may be alienated and demotivated; and

- on the extent to which we can bring together a broad and inclusive group of partners who will work together to make New Deal a success.

Already, in this last respect, many important organisations all over Britain have agreed to join in partnership with us to make New Deal a success. They include local authorities, Training and Enterprise Councils, Careers Service companies, voluntary sector organisations, environmental groups, unemployed workers' groups and many others. But just as critical as any of these groups for New Deal's success will be employers. We need their support and participation not just to offer jobs to those on the New Deal but also to help us plan and deliver it. I am delighted to say that very large numbers of employers are already demonstrating their support and more are doing so every day. I will not be satisfied, however, until every employer in Britain knows about New Deal and is actively thinking about participating; not out of some vague notion of doing good but because they recognise that it will make good business sense both for them and for the communities in which they work.

For our part, as the Employment Service we are also mounting a major effort, based around a new set of values for our organisation, to ensure that we can help deliver the New Deal in a way which meets the expectations of the government, our partners and young people themselves. These values will underpin the change of focus we need to make to deliver New Deal successfully.

The proposed values on which we are consulting widely, both inside and outside of the Employment Service, are:

- Partnerships. The need for flexibility, local delivery, quality and individual solutions to problems are consistent messages received from a wide range of people consulted over the design of New Deal. Clearly, no single set of arrangements will work right across the country. Different elements of the New Deal will demand different delivery arrangements. It is essential that we harness the enthusiasm of all sectors of the community and not least at local level where many organisations have so much to offer.

- Service. Improving the service that the Employment Service gives to everyone we deal with is a key challenge, especially in the context of New Deal. We are continually striving to improve the quality of the service we deliver. To date over 100 Jobcentres are holders of the Charter Mark award, and more are striving to achieve it. But we know our service to both employers and job-seekers has to go on improving.

- Quality. Everything our agency does must focus on the paramount importance of quality. We are encouraging our regions to strive towards achieving Total Quality Management through the use of the Business Excellence Model developed by the British Quality Foundation. Using it has already helped us identify linkages and gaps between individual policies. It has also encouraged the use of business improvement techniques in Jobcentres as staff become more confident of their ability to change processes and show greater ownership of problems and problem solving.

- Results. The Employment Service is a performance-driven organisation. Our priorities are based on annual targets set as part of an Annual Performance Agreement. We know that we have no more right to exist than any other organisation, public or private. We must go on showing that the results we deliver are as good as anyone could reasonably expect with the resources at our disposal.

- Innovation. We need to keep pace with technological development and have a clear strategy for harnessing its potential. We need a constant search for ways to improve and streamline business procedures and practices, and we need to adopt a learning culture which will encourage our staff to approach change in an open and positive way.

- Ourselves. Our success is underpinned by the skills and abilities of our people. Our human resource strategies need to support and reinforce the rest of our work. We need to encourage our managers to lead by example, to invite open communication to encourage staff to share ideas and to seek constant improvement, not blame.

Our commitment to these values is evidence of our commitment to delivering New Deal. But we know we cannot succeed alone. We need the help of every employer and business organisation in the UK to help us accomplish this task. New Deal is too important to all of our futures for anything else.

Training and Enterprise Councils

by TEC National Council

Training and Enterprise Councils (TECs) are local employer-led strategic bodies, working in partnership to achieve sustainable economic growth ensuring increases in employment, prosperity and quality of life. Helping business to win in world markets is the priority. Competitiveness is the key, competitiveness of the economy as a whole, and of each individual and each business. As business-led strategic bodies, TECs have a vital role in continuing to develop and refine, with their partners, integrated local economic development strategies and practical working arrangements to drive competitiveness at the local level, and contribute to regional and national developments.

Their strategies help to:

- create and maintain dynamic local strategies with strategic partners, in particular local authorities;

- support competitive business, through effective investment in innovation and the development and management of people, and increase the use of business support services through the network of Business Links;

- build a world-class workforce and create a learning society with the skills essential to successful businesses and individuals.

TECs are independent companies formed by local people working for the benefit of their community under performance-related contracts with national government. There are 79 TECs covering England and Wales, of which a number have merged with their local Chamber of Commerce and are known as Chambers of Commerce, Training and Enterprise (CCTEs). TEC counterparts in Scotland are the 22 Local Enterprise Companies.

PARTNERS FOR PROSPERITY

As the key strategic body in the local business community, TECs work in close partnership with:

- national government;

- government offices for the regions;

- local government;

- European Commission;

- businesses and their representative bodies including local CBI and Chambers of Commerce;

- business sectoral bodies and trade associations;

- trades unions;

- education institutions at all levels – foundation, further education and higher education;

- individuals – all young people and adults, regardless of race, creed or gender;

- agencies in the education and training market;

- voluntary bodies whose work is relevant to TEC strategies;

- others with an interest in and capacity for furthering the competitiveness agenda.

As strategic organisations, TECs undertake local economic assessments of the needs of their local communities and work with other community agencies, particularly local authorities, to develop local economic development strategies to meet those needs. All the training and enterprise activities of the TECs and their local Business Link (see page 55) are designed to contribute to the achievement of those strategies.

TECs are not-for-profit companies incorporated under the Companies Acts and responsible for appointing their own Boards of Directors. Any surpluses or reserves must be re-invested in activities which support the development of the local economy. Enterprising and innovative organisations, TECs are committed to quality and continuous improvement to meet the evolving needs of their local economies and to secure the necessary resources.

TECs are employer-led organisations and provide the key private sector partner to local authorities. The eligibility requirements for Board membership are designed to ensure that they are of high standing and employer-led. Participation in their Board of others of like mind, especially from trade unions, local government, education and training, and the voluntary sectors, is an additional and vital ingredient.

TECs all display a number of common characteristics:

- local organisations, TECs are set up to devise local solutions to local needs;

- TECs work in partnership with others to be the key local private sector partners with all levels of government;

- TECs meet commercial contracts for clearly specified outcomes;

- TECs are performance-driven to deliver demanding results to high-quality standards;

- TECs are clear and transparent in financial accounting;

- TECs seek to be credible in their own community – open, honest and accountable;

- TECs seek to be impartial – the only lobby TECs pursue is the creation of wealth and prosperity for the good of the community and the individual;

- TECs are politically neutral, ready to work with any government or political party to further the sustainable development of their local communities;

- TECs are inclusive, reflecting the desire of their Directors to build a society which achieves 'a dynamic equilibrium between wealth creation on one side and social cohesion on the other'. (Prof Stephane Garelli, Director, World Competitiveness Report 1995);

- TECs work for the benefit of all regardless of race, gender, political persuasion or religious belief.

THE TEC VISION

Training and Enterprise Councils will assist the UK to become the most prosperous society in the European Community by placing education, training and enterprise in the broader context of economic and industrial development.

THE TEC MISSION

The purpose of TECs is to achieve sustainable economic growth and equity of opportunity in their local communities by stimulating the competitiveness of their businesses and maximising the skills and opportunities of their workforce. Their ultimate goal is a competitive society which has achieved a dynamic equilibrium between creation and social cohesion.

11

Business Link Helps Business Make the Right Connections

by Business Link

Business Link is a nationwide network of around 240 advice centres. It provides information and affordable advice to all businesses to help them develop and grow. Each Business Link has two core services, the information service and the advice service.

BUSINESS INFORMATION SERVICE

The information service provides a single, local point of access to information on any business query and access to the complete range of business advice delivered by organisations such as local authorities, Training and Enterprise Councils (TECs) and Chambers of Commerce, or provided by private organisations such as banks, marketing consultancies and accountants.

Previously, companies wanting business information or services in their area had to wade through a diverse number of channels. These sometimes overlapped, were often hard to find and almost always confusing. In the case of export advice, for example, a company would have had to decide whether to approach the local government office, the Chamber of Commerce, the TEC or a private consultancy specialising in the field. Now they can simply contact the local Business Link which will either answer the query itself or bring in the relevant partner organisation, whether public or private sector, or other appropriate outside body,

BUSINESS ADVICE SERVICE

The second main platform of the Business Link service is the provision of tailored, on-the-spot advice from a range of specialist advisers.

At the heart of the service is the Personal Business Adviser (PBA) who provides independent, affordable and long-term help, if necessary over several years.

This fulfils a fundamental gap in the market. Although there is plenty of short-term help available for small businesses, most companies need sustained support over a period of time in order to achieve significant change.

PBAs will help companies write a business strategy and implement it. In the process, they help overcome many of the classic cultural, organisational and financial barriers to growth. These range from a lack of strategic planning, because management is too busy fire-fighting daily operational pressures, to the need to create a management structure, motivate staff, control cashflow or benchmark against competitors. The PBA can also act as the channel through which other expert resources from the Business Link partnership can be accessed, with the Business Link bringing in the most appropriate partner or other service supplier.

Additionally, Business Links have expert advisers in key areas such as export, finance, innovation and technology, design, marketing and training. These advisers help with all aspects of their speciality and can cover everything from finding innovative sources of finance to new product development.

Cost

Pricing structures vary between Business Links but the fundamental premise is that they should be accessible and affordable, meeting the market need of SMEs (small and medium-size enterprises) unable to afford full market rates. Typically, a PBA might undertake an initial business review free of charge and then provide ongoing, subsidised consultancy.

Structure

All 89 Business Links are private-sector organisations comprising a number of partners which typically include TECs; Chambers of Commerce; local authorities; Enterprise Agencies; universities; banks and others. Each Business Link's board of directors is drawn from local businesses as well as from its partners. The 89 local partnerships have, between them, a total of around 240 outlets nationally.

Business Link Signpost Line

Businesses wanting to be directed to their nearest Business Link should call the Business Link Signpost Line on 0345 567 765 (from the UK). You will be asked for your postal code and will then be connected to the appropriate Business Link office.

KEY BUSINESS LINK SERVICES

- *Management Development* – help businesses devise business plans, manage strategic change, adopt competitive business practices and raise the quality of their management skills;

- *Export* – encourage businesses to develop an export strategy designed to increase the percentage of their turnover generated by export;

- *Finance* – Help businesses structure their finances more effectively, manage access to appropriate financial services and develop financial plans. Help with grants and other sources of finance.

- *Innovation* – help businesses look at the role of technology and design in their markets, products, corporate image and manufacturing and business processes to improve their market position;

- *Marketing* – help businesses develop a coherent marketing strategy and programme that positions them and the demand for their products and services against the competition;

- *Training* – provide information, advice and access to services to help businesses with employment and training issues;

- *Information* – help businesses and their advisers to access accurate, relevant and timely information covering areas such as market intelligence, company and product sourcing, grants and finance and regulatory issues.

IMPACT OF BUSINESS LINK

By December 1997:

- nearly 1.3 million businesses were registered on the databases of operational Business Links;

- more than 107,000 businesses in total used Business Links in the latest quarter;

- over 8 per cent of all businesses in England with one or more employees used Business Links as did 18 per cent of all businesses with 10–49 employees and 41 per cent of those with 50–199 employees.

- 57 per cent of businesses using Business Links had under 10 employees;

- over 18,000 businesses were advised by personal business advisers;

- over 23,000 businesses had received counselling;

- a recent MORI Baseline tracking survey showed a 70 per cent customer satisfaction rate with Business Links;

- 100 per cent of VAT-registered businesses were covered by operational Business Links;

- now complete, the network had 89 partnerships;

- all 200 towns and cities with over 50,000 population were covered by Business Links;

- around 700 personal business advisers were in place;

- all businesses had access to the innovation & technology and design counselling services;

- 82 export development counsellors were in place;

- 70 per cent of Business Links had financial packaging counsellors.

12

Investors in People – the Key Facts

by Investors in People

Over 30 per cent of the UK workforce, some 6.9 million employees, are now benefiting from the Investors in People Standard, the national standard which links people development to the achievement of business goals. Take up of the Standard has been fast, with more than 30,000 organisations now involved. This growth means Investors in People is set to achieve its targets of Investors in People recognition for 70 per cent of all organisations employing 200 or more, and 35 per cent of medium-sized organisations, by the year 2000.

The Investors in People Standard was developed in 1990 in collaboration with the UK's leading businesses, both large and small, and a review was also carried out in 1995. Extensive research among employers and other relevant organisations resulted in an overwhelming endorsement of the Standard. It is designed as a tool to improve business performance and competitiveness, by providing a framework for best practice in human-resource development. Employers use it to review and improve the performance of their employees against specified corporate aims in order to improve the organisation's overall effectiveness.

The benefits of Investors in People can be measured. Independent research into investors in people companies has shown that two thirds of them will attribute improvements in their performance directly to the fact that they have adopted the Investors Standard.

Below are some of the proven bottom-line business benefits:

- improved profitability: the Cumberland Hotel has increased its revenue by 50 per cent; TNT has doubled its turnover in the last five years; F.I. Group has seen pre-tax profit grow by 40 per cent over the last four years; DeVere Hotels have increased profit by 51.4 per cent;

- improved productivity: British Steel quadrupled productivity;

- business performance: Chessington World of Adventures exceeded admission targets by 10 per cent;

- improvements: Hotpoint has seen annual cost savings of £163.2 million ($269 million) in its Peterborough factory through team working;

- improvements motivation: Nationwide Building Society has increased employee satisfaction from 59 per cent to 64 per cent; Waterfields Bakery reduced staff turnover by 44 per cent; and Kwik-Fit reduced staff turnover by 30 per cent;

- public recognition: becoming an Investor in People helps both recruit and keep the best people.

Companies which have achieved the Standard have gone through a process based on four principles:

- commitment to develop all employees to achieve business goals and targets;

- regularly reviewing training and development needs in the context of the business;

- taking relevant action to meet training and development throughout people's employment;

- evaluating outcomes of training and development for individuals and the organisation as a basis for continuous improvement.

Becoming an Investor in People involves a number of key steps:

- understanding the Standard and its strategic implications;

- diagnosing the gaps between current practice and the Standard;

- making the commitment to achieve the Standard;

- communicating that to staff planning;

- taking action to bring about change;

- bringing together evidence for assessment (this can be as simple as showing human resource strategy in the business plan);

- recognition and working to keep the culture of continuous improvement alive.

Once organisations are assessed and have met the Standard, they can be publicly recognised as an Investor in People. Accreditation lasts for three years, after which time organisations are reassessed to ensure the Standard is being maintained. The only direct cost is that of assessment and the length of time leading up to assessment usually ranges between six and eighteen months.

The Investors in People Standard is led by Investors in People UK, a non-profit making organisation, part funded by the Department of Employment and Education. The organisation has responsibility for setting the Standard, driving forward its progress through national promotion, monitoring for quality and ensuring its continued relevance.

The actual delivery of Investors in People is through the Training and Enterprise Councils (TECs) in England and Wales (see page 53), the Local Enterprise Companies (LECs) in Scotland, and the Training and Employment Agency Northern Ireland. All these agencies provide support to the organisations in their local area. Sector specific support is available through Industry Training Organisations. Small firms may approach their local Business Link for advice (see page 55).

As the UK organisations of all sectors and sizes begin to recognise that the creativity, skills and learning potential of employees provide the key to success, Investors in People is becoming an integral part of management thinking in order to ensure competitive success. Already, almost half of the 29,500 organisations involved with the Standard employ fewer than 50 people, highlighting the Standard's flexibility for any type or size of business.

13

Business Excellence in Europe

*by Tony Mosely, Visiting Fellow in Service Excellence,
Manchester Business School*

W Edwards Deming made such a profound impact on Japanese industry that he is credited with having introduced 'quality' into everyone's business agenda. The Malcolm Baldrige National Quality Award in the US set the scene for a quality revolution that has had repercussions in Europe as well. The EFQM (European Foundation for Quality Management) quality model is very similar to the Malcolm Baldrige model. It was launched in 1992 and has now been copied by many of the countries in Europe for their own national quality awards. Some regions within countries have launched similar awards. For example, 'Excellence North West' was formed in the UK. It was co-sponsored by Manchester Business School in 1994 and presented its first series of awards in 1995 based on the EFQM model. This 'European Quality Model' has now been renamed as the 'European Business Excellence Model'.

In 1998, Manchester Business School decided that the UK executives could learn a lot from the various companies that had won quality awards in different parts of Europe. Having established an excellent reputation for its study tours of world-class service companies, it chose the study tour route to bring this home to people. Senior executives are sometimes reluctant to spend their valuable time at conferences, but many 'Service Excellence Experience' study tours have proved not only popular but also effective at inspiring some of the UK's business leaders. Professor John A Murphy (Abbey National Visiting Professor in Service Quality at Manchester Business School) assembled a group of twelve outstanding winning companies (two from each of six countries) that were happy to share their secrets with a group of the UK executives on a six-day study tour in June 1998. This is called 'Europe's BEST' (Business Excellence Study Tour). To meet the tight timescale required to fit in all the visits, an aircraft is chartered to make all the hops between cities. This limits the size of the group to eighteen but provides the flexibility that is necessary. Consultants 'Achieve Global' sponsor the tour and accompany the group to provide guidance where necessary.

It is interesting to note that while the approaches to business management are becoming more uniform across Europe, it is the UK which is showing the greatest interest in improvement. Although membership of the EFQM covers all the European countries, the number of UK companies which are members outweighs that from other nations. Indeed the publishers of the *European Quality Journal* find themselves with a preponderance of articles from UK organisations.

It is clear that when a whole nation gears up its business to rival the Japanese on quality issues, that nation will play a pivotal role in shaping any inward investment. The UK is in a position to become such a nation. There is a growing number of UK business leaders who understand the issues of service and business excellence on the world stage.

The idea of study tours as a way of learning about customer-service issues was conceived by Professor Brian Moores in 1990. His first tour for Manchester Business School took place to the US in June of that year. With financial support from the Scottish Development Agency, this first tour visited 27 companies over a period of 19 days. The 19 people who participated were so enthralled by what they learnt that future tours were assured by the referrals which resulted. Every year since then a group of very senior executives have been captivated by some of the remarkably innovative solutions to management that they have seen. The real benefit from the tour is that it provides a chance to see, relate to and challenge the people who have originated outstanding reputations.

Some commercial organisations have attempted to emulate such tours but have failed to make a business out of it. The key to success comes from the academic credentials of the Business School that open doors to some exceptional companies. The success of the North American tours has since been mirrored by an annual study tour of impressive UK companies called 'Best of British Service'. Some of the notable visits have been to winners of the BQF (British Quality Foundation) quality awards. It is easy to find good exemplars from such winners. This has encouraged Manchester Business School to mount the first study tour in Europe to winners of the EFQM Awards.

Service quality is not the only thing which lends itself to learning from study tours. The Marketing Council in the UK commissioned Manchester Business School in 1997 to lead a group of CEOs on a study tour of prime exponents of what they call 'Pan-Company Marketing'. The implication of this philosophy is that everyone in the organisation should be facing the customer. The Marketing Council is keen that marketing should not be seen as a function in an organisation but as a way of life for all employees. The first study tour established some basic principles that have led to the creation of a model against which companies can judge themselves. Further tours are planned to validate this model and publish a definitive book on the subject. Involving senior people in the UK firms not only adds credibility to the exercise but also spreads the gospel on this important area of management.

14

Intellectual Property

by The Chartered Institute of Patent Agents

Intellectual property in all its forms, patents, trade marks, designs and copyright, forms an important and often neglected asset for many companies.

PATENTS

Patents protect inventions by giving the owner of the patent the right to stop anyone from making or using the invention. This right to stop others is limited in time, usually for up to 20 years. In other words a patent is a right to stop competition for the invention for a limited period. This right to stop competition exists only in the country for which a patent has been granted. Thus, a German patent will only enable the owner to stop competition in Germany, a UK patent can stop competition in the UK and so on. Generally speaking patents are used to protect the markets in which an invention is to be exploited.

Key patent points to remember:

- don't make the details of your invention public before you file a patent application;

- to get a patent, your invention must not have been disclosed publicly anywhere in the world before you apply – even by yourself;

- patents are not kept secret – they are published, usually 18 months after application;

- ignorance that you are infringing someone else's patent is no defence.

TRADE MARKS

Trade marks are signs which are used to distinguish the goods or services of one trader from those of another. In this context, the word 'sign' is used very broadly. Although most trade marks are words or logos or combinations of the two, other forms such as three dimensional shapes, combinations of colours and even sounds can be, and indeed are, used as trade marks.

Trade marks can be considered as essentially indications of the origin of a particular product or service. The formulation or make-up of many products sold under a particular trade mark may well vary as time goes by, but the trade mark will remain unchanged. For example, the compositions of most well known washing powders have been changed many times over the years but they are still sold under the same trade mark. Trade marks are therefore a most important means of protecting the reputation and goodwill that a trader has built up. Trade mark registration gives you the best protection from unfair competition.

Generally speaking, the protection afforded to industrial designs under European law is for the 'new' features of shape, configuration, form, patterns or ornament of an industrial product which convey an aesthetic effect. In other words there must be some appeal to the eye in the design for which protection is sought. In this context, the term 'new' means it has not been made available or disclosed to the public in the state in question before the date on which the application to register the design was filed.

COPYRIGHT

Copyright is a right associated with a particular 'copyright work' such as books, films, music, computer programmes etc. It is easiest thought of as a right to stop people copying the work, either in the same form, or in some other form without permission.

The Chartered Institute of Patent Agents

For most companies, the decision to apply for patent, trade mark or design protection outside of their own country is one which is taken after a good deal of thought and discussion. For example, the inventions for which a company seeks overseas protection will usually have been the result of considerable research and development. Often they will be regarded as a company's investment in the future. It makes obvious sense therefore to ensure that these inventions have the best protection that can be obtained in the important markets of the world.

For many inventions, Western Europe, with a population well in excess of 350 million, is clearly such a market. With the European Patent Office offering the opportunity of obtaining patent protection in up to 18 states by means of a single application, it is easy to see why the input to the European Patent Office is increasing all the time. You need, however, to make sure that you get the best possible advice and service when you apply for a European patent. This is where the Chartered Institute of Patent Agents comes in.

Founded in 1882 and incorporated by Royal Charter in 1891, the Chartered Institute of Patent Agents has been at the forefront of intellectual property for more than a century. The Institute's reputation throughout the world has led to its members being in great demand. A major factor in establishing this reputation is the extensive experience and comprehensive examination requirements necessary before anyone can become a member. UK candidates consistently have the highest pass rate in the European Patent Attorneys qualifying examination. An additional factor in making members of the Institute particularly effective within Europe is the long established adversarial legal system in the UK which forms the basis for success in hearings before the European Patent Office. Members of the Chartered Institute of Patent Agents are not only fully qualified European Patent Attorneys, they also deal with related areas of law such as designs, copyright and trade marks, including representation before the European Community Trade Mark Office.

Whilst members of the Institute are spread throughout the UK, many have their offices close to the Institute, which is right in the heart of legal London. One great advantage of this location is the fact that the Filing Office for European and UK applications is only 100 metres away. With its helpful staff and on-line search facilities, this Filing Office is equivalent to having a branch of the European Patent Office right on the doorstep.

Within the context of the European scene, the fact that English is overwhelmingly the most commonly used of the three official languages gives the British Patent Agents the advantage of working in their mother tongue. The deep understanding of a language in all its subtleties by the person drafting a patent application can sometimes make a crucial difference in the protection afforded by the patent when it is finally granted. The Chartered Institute of Patent Agents' influence is felt on a number of law-making bodies both in the United Kingdom and in Europe.

So, whatever the field of technology of your invention, the nature of your trade mark or your design, you will find that there are members of the Chartered Institute of Patent Agents who are ideally equipped to assist you in obtaining strong intellectual property protection in Europe. For well over 100 years the Institutes' members' unique qualifications, professionalism and unrivalled expertise have benefited companies throughout the world.

For further information and a geographically arranged directory contact the Chartered Institute of Patent Agents.

15

Effects on UK Business of Harmonisation of European Trade Marks

by Christopher Cook, Partner and Senior Trade Mark Attorney,
Forrester Ketley & Co

For many UK businesses the introduction of the Community Trade Mark (the CTM) in April 1996 was eagerly anticipated. Spain was given the location of the Community Trade Marks Office (OHIM) and the Spanish government opted to site the office in Alicante in South Eastern Spain. While seeming to many an unusual choice, Alicante is in Valencia, an area in which the Spanish government wishes to encourage employment and growth.

Before the Community Trade Mark, the trade mark laws and practice of the individual member states of the EU were not consistent and the CTM was seen to be a real opportunity for harmony and consistency of approach with respect to trade mark protection.

The system has now been in place for nearly two years and initially proved to be a victim of its own success. In the first 18 months in excess of 60,000 Community applications were filed at OHIM, far more than had originally been anticipated, leading to delays in processing applications. Procedures are, however, beginning to improve and applicants can expect to secure protection for their trade marks more quickly from now on.

Many UK businesses have already taken advantage of the Community system, reaping the benefit of reduced filing fees compared with separate national filings in the member states of the EU. The general prosecution costs of a CTM are also far lower than might be anticipated for equivalent national applications. The prosecution can be carried on in English and can be dealt with by a UK trade mark attorney.

Another valid long-term advantage for UK businesses, particularly those with large trade mark portfolios, is that once a CTM is in place there is only one registration to administer and to renew. Many businesses have existing national trade marks in place,

but this in itself need not prevent the filing of a CTM application. In fact it is possible to claim 'seniority' from earlier national Marks.

No proof of use is required on renewal (every ten years) and use in only one EU country will suffice to maintain a CTM throughout the entire Union against an attack on the grounds of non-use. Thus, as long as a Mark is used in at least one country, subsequent use may take place in other countries at the convenience of the owner. There exists, therefore, the possibility of registering and then 'reserving' a Mark for future use in the various countries of the EU.

However, it is only fair to point out that there are also disadvantages to any UK enterprise contemplating seeking a CTM registration. The most obvious is that if the trade mark is for one reason or another not available for registration in any one country of the Union then the application will fail. Although conversion to national applications is a possibility, there are attendant costs. The CTM system is very much 'all or nothing' and there may be some difficulties in attempting to select a Mark that is available for use and registration in all countries of the EU.

The risk of encountering opposition under the Community system is therefore reasonably high, and this can give rise to significant additional expense. Not only may the applicant have to defend opposition proceedings but it may also be necessary to translate documents and evidence into another official language of the Community office. The system has, however, a two month 'cooling off' period once any opposition has been filed, during which an applicant may decide to withdraw voluntarily his application without incurring the cost of fighting the opposition.

A major effect for UK companies is that the Community system has opened a 'back door' into this country for foreign-owned trade marks. The mere existence of earlier marks entered in the UK Register will not prevent the same or a confusingly similar Community Mark becoming registered with effect in the UK unless some positive action is taken by the owner of the earlier UK right.

OHIM does not have the power to reject a CTM on the basis of a prior national registration in the UK (or indeed in any other member state of the EU). Only the owners of prior UK registrations can prevent registration by taking action themselves. It is important, therefore, that owners of national UK rights should subscribe to a service which can monitor published Community applications and also conduct an 'early warning' watch on more recently filed applications. More proactively, any business with an interest in Europe would be well advised to file its own Community application. As indicated, use in the UK would be sufficient to maintain a Community Trade Mark against a non-use attack and so a business would not be obliged to extend its commercial activities throughout the whole of the European Community.

The effect of trade mark harmonisation in Europe on UK business cannot be undervalued. All businesses should give serious and detailed consideration to their trade mark portfolios and attempt to plug any gaps by making sure that their rights are protected throughout the EU. They should also bear in mind that they need to maintain vigilance should other parties seek to obtain Community-wide rights which might impinge adversely on their existing national registrations.

Forrester Ketley & Co was established in 1884 and has substantial expertise in all areas of intellectual property, providing advice on securing patent, trade mark, design and copyright protection in the UK and throughout the world. The firm has offices in London and Birmingham with associated firms in Germany and Eastern Europe.

16

A Short Guide To UK Immigration

by Sanwar Ali, Managing Partner, BCL Immigration Services

As the UK is part of the European Union (EU), a UK citizen, like citizens of the other EU countries, has the right to live and work in any of the other EU countries. Also, non-EU dependants of EU nationals have an automatic right to gain entry to an EU country to join their EU national relative. A further benefit is that after becoming a UK citizen, one may keep one's other nationality/ies.

IMMIGRATION RULES

UK immigration and nationality law is amongst the most complex in the world. We always advise that one seeks the best possible professional advice before applying under any of the categories. In addition, due to complexities, this is not an exhaustive list and does not go into every conceivable detail on the requirements for a particular immigration category. In general, the business, investor and employment-related categories lead to permanent residence after four years and would eventually lead to UK citizenship.

BUSINESS INVESTMENT

This application is usually made from abroad and is likely to take at least a few months. It is strongly recommended that unless one has very good reasons, an application is not made from within the UK. One is initially granted twelve months entry as a business-person. The investment requirement is at least £200,000 in the UK and must create employment for at least two members of the resident job market. One should have comprehensive plans with regard to the investment requirements for the new business in the first twelve months, which can be incorporated into a business plan. The investment can be made partly from borrowed money and in the form of, for example, plant and equipment.

If the investment is considerably greater than the minimum £200,000 the Home Office is likely to look more favourably on applications that may be weaker in other respects. It is normally expected that the full investment is made and the jobs are created by the end of the first year. After this first period of time, assuming that the business is profitable or will eventually be profitable, a three-year extension to stay in the UK is granted. If one wishes to enter the UK to join as a partner in an existing business, the requirements are quite similar.

Exemption from investment and employment-creation requirements

It should be noted that overseas lawyers, writers and artists who are self-employed are exempt from the investment and employment-creation requirements of the business rules. This is also true for nationals of Hungary, Poland, Bulgaria, the Czech Republic, Romania or Slovakia, who wish to set up any type of business in the UK.

Sole representative

It is possible to apply as the representative of an overseas firm that has no branch, subsidiary or other representative in the UK. Once the application has been made from abroad, entry into the UK for a period of one year is usually granted. After one year an extension of three years is normally granted. The application is usually granted within one or two weeks but in difficult cases can take months. It must be stated that the overseas firm must be a legitimate trading organisation. If a business is run by one person who if he were to enter the UK on this basis would leave no one to run the business back in the firm's country of origin, the application will not be granted. This must be primarily for the benefit of the overseas firm and not as a matter of convenience for the person concerned. You are only allowed up to a minority share in the business.

PERMITS

Full work permit

Application is made to the Department for Education and Employment in the UK and the permit is granted for a period up to four years depending on the circumstances. The application, depending on the type of permit, takes between two weeks and two months to process. It must be stressed that it is the employer who applies for the permit and not the prospective employee. The work permit is granted for a particular employer which obviously means that one may not work for more than one employer at the same time. After the permit is granted, one should enter the UK with the permit rather than apply whilst still in the UK to stay on this basis.

The ease of obtaining work permits varies with the prevalent economic situation in the UK. It is easier to obtain a permit during a period of high economic growth than a recession. The full work permit is usually granted to employ someone who has high skill levels which are not readily available in the UK and the EC. It is easier to obtain a work permit to employ someone who is transferring employment from an overseas subsidiary to a UK subsidiary of the same company. It is also permitted to employ, for example, high ranking personnel at management and director level who may be earning in excess of £50,000.

Other work permits

Entertainers, sports people and models come under different rules. Depending on the circumstances, it may not even be necessary to apply for a permit, especially if entering for a period limited to six months as a visitor. Obviously as most people in this category work on an international level, they would not normally wish to make their permanent home in the UK. A permit may be granted for the hotel and catering industry. This is normally granted to hotel/restaurant managers, head chefs, highly skilled waiting staff and senior hotel receptionists. It is normal to be granted up to three years on this basis.

Training permit

Entry into the UK is for up to three years under the training permit scheme. This scheme is similar to the work-permit scheme in that it is the employer who applies and the application is made to the Department for Education and Employment in the UK. The main purpose of this scheme is to enable people to enter the UK to receive training which is not readily available to them in their own country.

The experience should be of a type that is not readily available in one's home country but will be of use there. One must have the necessary educational or professional qualifications and demonstrate the ability to benefit from the training. The work must be for a minimum of 30 hours per week. One must be 18 years and over and be near the start of one's career to qualify. The employer must be able to give the proposed training, be registered with the appropriate professional institute if training leads to a professional qualification, give a fixed time for the duration of the training and provide a detailed programme including dates. The wages and other conditions must be equivalent to those offered in other on-the-job training in the area.

Work experience scheme

For the work experience scheme entry will normally be granted for one year. However, under exceptional circumstances this may be increased to two years. In other respects the above first and second paragraphs relating to training permits apply. The experience should be of a type that is not readily available in the home country but will be of use there.

One must have the necessary educational, professional or job experience to be able to benefit from the work experience. The work must be for a minimum of 30 hours a week. One must be between 18 and 35 years of age and be near the start of one's career to qualify. The employer must be able to give the proposed work experience, give a fixed time for the duration of the experience, provide a detailed programme including dates and state the purpose of the experience. The employment should be surplus to the usual needs of the employer and only pocket money or a maintenance allowance can be paid. If there is a head-for-head exchange between the UK employer and an overseas employer these conditions do not apply. These conditions also do not apply if one is presently working for the same employer abroad or is being paid by the employer from abroad.

UK ANCESTRY

A commonwealth national with a grandparent who was born in the UK may enter the UK for a period of four years to work here. It is normally also possible to apply whilst in the UK to switch from another immigration category to this one. After four years in the UK one is normally granted permanent residence.

Permanent residence and UK nationality

In the above employment, business and investor-related categories, permanent residence is usually granted after four years. Further, those who have spent ten years legally in the UK in any category whatsoever are usually granted permanent residence. The main benefit is for those who are in an immigration category that does not normally lead to permanent residence. It frequently occurs, for example, that if one has been a student for many years in the UK, which does not in itself lead to permanent residence, one can take advantage of this. For example, someone who has been a student for eight years who then remained for a further two years on a training permit would normally gain permanent residence. Once permanent residence has been granted, there are no longer any restrictions on the work or business one may do in the UK and no time limits on stay in the UK. In addition can apply for parents and other relatives to enter the UK if they are dependants. After being granted permanent residence, one may apply for UK citizenship after a further period of one year. There are many other aspects pertaining to immigration beyond the scope of this article, such as marriage and UK ancestry.

Section 4

The UK's World-class Capabilities

17

UK Consultants – A Source of International Expertise

*by Brian O'Rorke, Former Executive Director,
Management Consultancies Association*

The role of management consultants is often misunderstood. Too often they are perceived as advisers to management concerned with the reorganisation of a company's structure – a euphemism for 'downsizing'. It is not surprising that as a result they are denigrated, being seen as exponents of job losses with all the human emotions that that involves. All this is a pity, for management consultants' major role is that of providing business solutions. In short, they are an investment made by clients in their future, as well as being the means by which new ideas, new skills and new technology are spread, not only through organisations but the economy itself.

UK management consultants hold a peer position within the EU. Its management consultancy market is not only the most mature and developed, but also, as the figure below shows, proportionately the largest when taking into consideration the size of UK GDP compared with that of the whole of the EU.

The fact that the UK also has the greatest concentration of international management consultancy practices within its shores also demonstrates that, globally, its consultancy market stands on a par with the City of London's financial expertise as a major world centre.

It is not surprising, therefore, that UK management consultants play a major role not only in ensuring that Europe as one of the world's three major business markets is competitive, forward-looking and innovative, but are also seen as an authoritative source of knowledge on both inward investment into the EU and on global export markets. The concentration within the UK of international consultancy practices has another great advantage in that it means that UK-based firms have an unrivalled worldwide networking system, which helps ensure not only the availability of intimate knowledge of foreign markets for organisations seeking to export, but also support on inward investment.

Management consultants are both catalysts and multipliers. An example of the latter can best be demonstrated by the deregulation initiatives of the Thatcher period of UK government. In assisting the UK public sector to privatise large areas of its nationalised

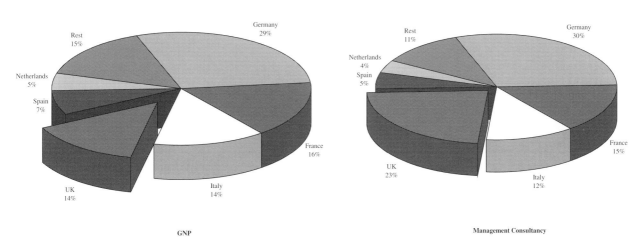

Figure 17.1 *The UK's proportion of European Union management consultancy*

industries and to restructure the manner in which central and local government operated, UK management consultants built up an unrivalled knowledge and skill in this sector. The result has been that the UK has been able to export this knowledge internationally, with our management consultants playing a major role in assisting foreign governments implement similar policies. Deutsche Telekom and the Australian Government are two examples of major clients in this sphere.

In 1997, nearly 15 per cent of the total income of the Management Consultancies Association (MCA) (the trade association for leading management consultancy practices in the UK) came from overseas earnings, the largest percentage for an EU country. Management consultancies are invaluable 'pathfinders' acting worldwide, as UK consultants do, in undertaking feasibility studies of local and national projects. A knowledge of these projects ensures that they are in a position not only to give advice, but to propose solutions involving complete international assistance. Both Indonesia and China have benefited largely from this assistance.

In the world of change in which we now live, the need for consultants is becoming increasingly important. To meet these client demands, UK management consultancies have become increasingly sector-oriented. Sectors are either market-oriented (for example retail, travel and tourism, telecommunications) or process-knowledge centred (eg risk management, accountancy systems), or domain-focused (eg Information Technology, Human Resources). The MCA in London is in a position to advise inward investors and potential management consultancy clients on the specialisation of each firm, thereby saving overseas organisations considerable time and expense. The MCA, whose details are given elsewhere, provides this assistance on both a confidential and free basis.

A lack of knowledge of market conditions can often be a recipe for disaster. Organisations such as the MCA provide an element of security, in that an overseas client employing a member firm of the MCA is protected by that organisation's Code of Professional Practice. This ensures that not only is the consultancy expressly forbidden from seeking work for which it is not qualified, but the work itself has to meet standards set by the MCA – failure to meet these can mean the organisation could be subject to disciplinary action.

The introduction of the European Monetary Union provides considerable scope for firms wishing to enter the European market. Price transparency is likely to mean lower prices and much tighter margins. As firms respond to fierce new competitiveness pressures, they will restructure, rationalise and merge to compete more cost-effectively. This will lead to lean and more efficient organisations, though initially in continental Europe, as opposed to the UK, which is delaying entry. It will also mean a substantial loss of jobs. The debate among European business leaders has moved on from the need to reform labour markets and welfare systems, so obvious that it has become truism. The current discussions in the business community are how to foster entrepreneurism in Europe, how to speed up the formation of small companies which, as the US has shown, are responsible for most of the new employment. In the establishment of this new order, UK management consultants will have a major part to play in the support not only of firms already based in Europe, but those seeking entry to exploit the competitive advantages that will be created by the introduction of the Euro.

Management consultancy today is very much part of the fabric of business and, as such, few organisations nowadays can afford not to use them when undertaking a policy of change. Often their importance in economic terms is ignored by governments, but as you will read elsewhere in this book, their role in support of governments and of private sector clients is inestimable. That over 95 per cent of the top 100 public companies in the UK use management consultancies of the MCA on a regular basis, demonstrates their value and importance.

18

What Makes London Such An Attractive Source Of Finance?

by Tim Sweeney, Director General, British Bankers' Association

INTERNATIONAL STATURE

London is the premier international financial centre in the world, because more international financial business happens here than in any other financial centre worldwide. While the financial markets in Tokyo and New York thrive thanks to the strength of their local economies, the opposite is the case in London. If UK financial markets traded on the strength of the domestic economy alone they would not have the capacity to be world players.

London's success stems from the fact that for its financial community in the City of London, the global economy is its local economy. It is hard to make this claim for any other financial centre in the world, and it is this international dimension which attracts the several hundred foreign banks which are based in London, supporting the many thousands of international businesses that seek financial services here.

CONCENTRATED RESOURCES

London's financial community, known collectively (if not quite accurately) as 'The City', occupies an area of about two square kilometres on the north bank of the River Thames by London Bridge, and Docklands, a new development area a short distance downriver. The City's modern dynamism derives from the markets that have and continue to evolve, and which the City has helped create, since the '50s and '60s. Many of the institutions and products that predominate today barely existed ten or fifteen years ago.

The City houses the head offices of most British banks, the Lloyd's of London insurance market, over five hundred foreign banks, the commodity markets, the Stock Exchange, derivatives markets, the discount houses and the investment banks.

AN EFFICIENT BANKING INFRASTRUCTURE

The core of any banking system is money transmission. In the UK, the national settlement system is now 'real time' – that is, accounts are settled at the precise moment when customers instruct their banks to make the payments, rather than waiting to the end of the working day for net credits or debits to be calculated. The new system also settles 'gross': debits and credits are actioned instantly and separately. The introduction of 'real time gross settlement' is an example of the role of the central national bank, the Bank of England, in working to keep the UK banking system competitive and efficient.

WHOLESALE MONEY MARKETS

Just as money transmission is a basic function of a bank's daily operation, the money markets are equally key in supporting a bank's wholesale activity. The money markets allocate credit, redistribute reserves and determine short-run sterling (UK currency) interest rates. While the sterling money markets are not the prime concern of international banks, the efficiency of the domestic money market is a useful source of reassurance to overseas banks and corporates.

The sterling market acts as a balancing mechanism for UK retail banks, investment banks, discount houses, large corporations and local authorities. The market is used either for placing surplus funds overnight, or for placing funds for a longer period. Most transactions are for a period of up to three months and deals are struck for a fixed period. The market is telephone-based, and business is often conducted between brokers. The sterling money markets are similar to the Euro-currency markets which also evolved in the 1960s.

EUROCURRENCY

'Eurocurrency' is simply a term for any currency deposits or loans held outside the EU country to which the currency refers. The Eurocurrency markets are London's largest capital markets and naturally attract the custom of international banks as the major players, though the depth of the markets, and the keen pricing that this brings, also attract multinationals and large corporates, foreign central banks and international monetary agencies.

The Euromarkets have run historically as professional, interbank markets without a central exchange or strict regulatory control. They are in fact, international markets rather than European markets, most of whose business has been conducted out of London. There are two types of Euromarkets:

- banking markets – deposits and loans in European currency, and banks' external liabilities and assets in domestic currency;

- capital markets – Eurobonds and Euro Commercial Paper, and bonds issued by foreign organisations on domestic capital markets.

STRENGTH IN EUROBONDS AND SWAPS

London is also the world centre for Eurobond trading, with 75 per cent of all global secondary market trading in dollar-denominated Eurobonds taking place over here. Over 60 per cent of all dollar and yen Eurobond issuance also takes place in London. A related, 'parallel swaps' market enables modifications to the terms and currency of bond issues. The swaps market in general is also huge. Only New York and London count as players in this business, and it is estimated that London has between 30 to 40 per cent of the global swaps business.

LENDING WORLDWIDE

The figures for international bank lending from London are also exceedingly large. At $1,704 billion annually, more than 18 per cent of the world market of international lending is carried out by banks operating out of the UK. $1,239 billion, or nearly three-quarters of the total figure annually, consists of foreign currency loans to overseas residents.

A COSMOPOLITAN MARKETPLACE

Markets are not the only aspect of banking, nor the only attraction for corporates to come to the City. An important part of banking is client relationships, and foreign banks are present in the City because their corporate clients already want to do business in the UK. Since the early 1980s, the City has increasingly helped the UK to become the gateway to Europe for major companies from around the world.

London continues to be host to the largest number of foreign banks of any city in the world and this number is set to increase over the next few years. With economic change and development in many of the world's emerging markets including Latin America and Eastern Europe, more banks in these regions are realising international ambitions. For them, London is a natural first port of call. US, Japanese and other East Asian companies have consistently sought to invest money in the UK, attracted by the English language, labour flexibility, good labour relations, low rates of taxation, government grants and access to a huge European single market of over three hundred million potential consumers. It makes sound business sense for banks to be present in a regional market where their corporate clients are operating, and it is proven that companies prefer to deal with the same bank wherever they are doing business. Practically, this often means a bank from the company's home country: 'If your clients are over here, so should you be.'

A EUROPEAN BRIDGEHEAD

The EU gives many new opportunities to foreign banks, and London is increasingly becoming the European centre of choice, particularly in investment banking. If a bank is incorporated within an EU country it now has the automatic right of authorisation in any of the other fourteen markets. If a bank's country of origin is outside the EU, establishing an incorporated subsidiary company in London provides the same rights of access to these other markets.

This European dimension will increasingly be a factor in the years ahead. For US investment banks, London has always been the entrance into Europe. Firms such as Goldman Sachs and Morgan Stanley have run the majority of their operations out of London, with only smaller offices in the other European financial centres such as Paris and Frankfurt. The dominance of London has been further consolidated by the strategic decisions of several of the largest German banks in

Singer & Friedlander

Specialists in UK corporate finance

Singer & Friedlander is an independent, established UK investment banking group quoted on the London Stock Exchange. Singer & Friedlander provides a full range of corporate finance services including:

Mergers and acquisitions

Flotations / IPO's

Raising capital

Independent financial advice

Management buyouts / buyins

We specialise in the provision of corporate finance advice to growing, publicly quoted companies in the UK. We also act as nominated adviser to companies quoted on the Alternative Investment Market (AIM).

We have the capability to initiate and advise upon cross border mergers and acquisitions, particularly in Europe, to offer overseas acquisitions opportunities to UK companies and to advise overseas companies wishing to acquire businesses in the UK.

In addition we provide advice to private companies, particularly those wishing to achieve a listing on the London Stock Exchange or a trade sale.

For further information on Singer & Friedlander Corporate Finance, please contact:
Marc Cramsie, Ian Dighé, Brendan Russell, Giles Elliott or Graham Hall
21 New Street
Bishopsgate
London EC2M 4HR
Tel: 0171 623 3000   Fax: 0171 929 5338

Singer & Friedlander Limited is regulated by the SFA

recent years. Major German banks including Deutsche Bank and Dresdner Bank have now decided to focus most of their investment banking activities in London.

PLATFORM FOR REMOTE TRADING

Contemporary developments such as 'remote trading', which are enabled by the newly introduced Investment Service Directive, increase the attraction of operating out of a single centre. Remote trading gives banks the facility to trade on any of the European bourses from their London base. They do not have to be concerned with becoming members of the local exchanges, or to staff operations at that centre. Therefore, for foreign banks wishing to establish a foothold in the financial markets of the EU, the best place to begin would be London, where volumes of market activity drive keen pricing.

FOREIGN EXCHANGE

The trend towards increasing market concentration in a few financial centres of choice can also be seen in the foreign exchange market. Here again London is the world's leading centre for trading, with, at 30 per cent of world market share, a larger volume of this activity than New York and Tokyo put together. London's daily average turnover in foreign exchange exceeds $500 billion. London's foreign exchange market is clearly a major attraction for foreign banks, with nine out of ten foreign banks based in London participating in the market. Increasingly, London is proving to be the centre of first choice for foreign banks entering this market.

PREPARING FOR EURO CURRENCY

For some time now it has been apparent to bankers that the major companies active in the UK have accepted some need for banking services denominated in euros, and some companies have already announced moves towards a full conversion to euro-denominated accounting. As suppliers to corporates, banks in the UK are already marketing a range of euro-denominated services. The advent of the euro is not expected to present a barrier to continuing trading through London, where the sheer volume of business activity has always delivered keen pricing – an obvious attraction.

As London is one of the world's three leading money markets, there is a clear incentive for banks to open dealing lines for euro business. For the finance directors of international companies, there is a clear continuing appeal in the range and depth of treasury services which exist only in the UK markets, whether they simply want hedging through currency purchase or forward-rate agreements, or more exotic fare such as barrier options.

In addressing the market for corporate euro services, banks in the UK are simply extending and redenominating the services which they already know well. The detailed workings of this shift have been (and continue to be) the subject of an enormous amount of work by many associations and markets in the City. The net result is to produce the continuity of services which all businesses look for in a mature market. So, for example, the member banks of the British Bankers' Association (BBA), numbering more than 300 banks from 60 countries worldwide and representing perhaps 95 per cent of banking activity in the UK, are building on work in the City. These banks will be prepared for operation of euro services in financial markets (foreign exchange, money markets, derivatives, bonds and shares) and corporate banking (cash management, treasury, raising capital, trade services).

At an industry level, the BBA has worked extensively with others in the city to resolve the technical wrinkles which inevitably accompany any redenomination, for example:

- market continuity – many financial instruments, such as bonds, most loans, futures and options, may have a lifespan of three years or more and so may straddle the date for the first wave of EMU convergence. It is vital for the banking community that the arrival of EMU is not seen to create any 'basis risk', whereby the originally recognised value of a financial instrument is suddenly called into question. Newly created market conventions will now recognise the value and set the transfer pricing of any contracts which are still outstanding at the date of the currency change.

- market hours and bank holidays – whether you represent an international corporate or a bank, you need liquidity, access to finance at reasonable prices without delay. If we were to incorporate all the European public holidays into the London financial markets' trading calendar this would have resulted in the loss of more than 50 trading days, reducing local liquidity and seriously compromising a global competitive advantage. The solution now agreed is to have a standard market year based on trading on all but the universal public holidays of Christmas Day and New Year's Day.

STRUCTURAL STRENGTH

London's market position is buttressed by four structural factors:

- the participation of financial service practitioners in developing new regulation;

- as a link between Far Eastern and US time zones;

- use of English as its language of business;

- the large presence of foreign banks, perpetuating the size, dynamism and keen pricing of financial markets.

The continuing inherent dynamism of the London market as a banking centre can be seen despite the fact that sterling has long been replaced by the dollar as the world's international currency, and that today sterling business accounts for a small portion of the total volume of the market. In due course, we may expect the euro to take its place alongside the dollar as a major currency for world trade, with London continuing to facilitate access to the currency. Foreign exchange dealing is increasingly associated with other financial transactions such as derivatives and money market instruments, and London's strength in these latter markets serves to underpin its competitive position in the former.

FACILITATING CAPITAL EVENTS

For international corporates seeking to raise capital share issue, the changes instituted by 'Big-Bang' deregulation in the 1980s have helped the London Stock Exchange to maintain a keen competitive edge. London dominates global turnover in international equities, with two-thirds of global cross-exchange trading and 90 per cent of cross-exchange trading in Europe.

DERIVATIVES

Cash markets are often overshadowed by the derivatives markets – both in terms of news-media hype, and in the dynamism and growth of the markets and of new products. London is home to the leading financial futures and commodities exchanges in Europe, with the largest derivatives exchange (LIFFE – the London International Financial Futures Exchange). Like many of the other London exchanges, it is globally unique in that it has an international rather than domestic franchise. Even more competitive on the global stage are London's commodities futures exchanges. The London Metal Exchange has 50 per cent of the world turnover in metals futures, while the International Petroleum Exchange has 20 per cent of the share in energy products. All these exchanges have a very international clientele, with 97 per cent of the turnover on the LME assignable to international houses.

HUMAN RESOURCES

Thanks partly to London's depth of activity in financial-service markets, partly to the opportunities for 'financial engineering' and market innovation, the City continues to attract a pool of highly qualified labour, including traders, managers and settlements staff. There is also high-quality expertise available in associated areas, such as risk management and control and the advanced information-technology systems that support contemporary dealing floors.

The City houses many different markets and professional support services with world-class skills, producing a competitive advantage based not just on leadership in any given market, but on a comprehensive package. Without robust legal and accounting professions none of the financial business transacted in London could be conceivable in its current scale or scope: the most important associated professional services, law and accountancy, are present in great strength and generally within a ten-minute walk of any institution.

LEGISLATIVE AND REGULATORY FRAMEWORK

Just as high quality professional advisers are essential to the success of London as a financial centre, a similarly well regarded regulatory and legislative framework is fundamental. Under the new Labour government there is now recognition of the move toward a new structure for the banking industry, characterised by an ending of traditional demarcation lines between types of business. As the Chancellor, Gordon Brown, put it in his announcement of 20 May 1997, 'the distinctions between different types of financial institutions – banks, securities firms, and insurance companies – are becoming increasingly blurred'.

If the emergence of a new financial-services industry and the ending of traditional banking is one factor driving regulatory change, then the second major factor is the globalisation of financial markets and the increasingly international operation of many of the major players. To understand risk within a business, regulators will increasingly focus, not only on legal entities, but on business entities, many of which bear little surface resemblance to their underlying legal structures. Having accepted the case for change, the new Labour government is opting for radical change, rather than incremental reform. There is little doubt that the new Financial Services Authority will facilitate trade in financial services and agreement about such matters such as consolidated supervision.

MONETARY CONTROLS

That the Government has chosen to give operational independence to the Bank of England in the setting of interest rates has broadly been welcomed in the City. In principle the Bank of England's Monetary Policy Committee can control rates without reference to the exigencies of a particular electoral situation and can take firmer counter-inflationary action sooner. This will help reinforce the structural changes in the UK which have occurred since 1979 and which have led to a low inflation economy.

CONCLUSION

The key to the success of the London markets is their openness. They are open both in terms of the range and diversity of market participants, and in terms of the state or bureaucratic control that is exercised on the markets. Many of the markets that have developed in the past two decades in London have done so because they were seeking to escape restrictive regulations elsewhere.

This openness has given London its key distinguishing feature: its internationalism. The international bias of the London markets is self evident from the composition of the market players in the City. The British Bankers' Association for example, has over 300 member banks whose headquarters are based in over 60 different countries. Its members cover most of the globe. Within the British Bankers' Association, foreign banks have the same privileges and rights as do domestic banks. A seat at the table of our most senior executive committee is reserved for a representative of the foreign banks in London. The openness of our membership structure is a reflection of a fundamental operating characteristic of the London markets. London is an open market and, indeed, the only way it can maintain its global pre-eminence is to maintain and cherish this openness.

The UK's conspicuous international success in financial markets is not simply a product of tradition; rather, it is about the City's resource of creativity in devising and marketing the financial services which the world's corporate customers need. As in other successful business sectors where 'creative capital' is a prime asset, banking makes a strong contribution to the national economy, consistently more than four per cent of our national product. This creativity is a durable asset unlikely to be dented by the impact of EMU or other evolutions.

19

Factoring in the European Context

Ted Ettershank, Chairman, The Factors and Discounters Association

During 1996 the factoring industry continued to prosper in the UK. Invoice discounting grew at 25.4 per cent and factoring by 12.7 per cent. The confidential nature of some forms of invoice discounting was a contributory factor here. The use of the bank overdraft declined by 5.1 per cent, and term loans by 2.3 per cent. The major users of factoring and invoice discounting continued to be manufacturers, mainly in the engineering, electronics, metals, chemicals and plastics industries. This is perhaps only to be expected in view of their heavy requirement for working capital to finance raw materials and work in progress, in addition to finished goods inventories and accounts receivable.

As more authoritative sources praise the virtues of asset-based finance, so companies became better disposed towards invoice factoring and discounting. This trend was undoubtedly assisted by the generally jaundiced disillusionment of business with the merits of the conventional bank overdraft as a form of *long-term* working capital finance. In Europe the UK is exceptional in placing so much reliance on the bank overdraft. The fact that it is temporary and repayable on demand had been somewhat overlooked, especially by those companies that had enjoyed such a facility with the same bank for many years.

In the 1990s, the total factoring and discounting market has grown by 20 per cent compound per annum and in 1996 the total annual factoring volume reached £40 billion, with over 19,000 firms using factoring and discounting. The factoring industry financed some £2 billion of overseas trade, where growth amounted to 23 per cent. Domestic invoice discounting continued to dominate the market, amounting to 68 per cent of the total. Domestic factoring amounted to 27 per cent and international business 5 per cent. The growth of international business is impressive: in 1996 export factoring grew by 16.5 per cent, import factoring by 19.6 per cent and export invoice discounting by 32.5 per cent (see Figure 19.1).

	1992	1993	1994	1995	1996
Export factoring	316.2	433.2	469.3	594.0	692.0
Import factoring	326.6	342.0	373.2	536.0	641.0
Export invoice discounting				529.0	701.0
Total	**642.8**	**775.2**	**842.5**	**1659.0**	**2034.0**

Figure 19.1 *Export and import factoring (£m) 1992–1996*

The market sectors served by the industry are heavily biased towards manufacturing, which alone accounts for 49 per cent of total business. Distribution accounts for 29 per cent, services 17 per cent and transport 5 per cent (see Figure 19.2). The industry is constantly reviewing and revising its offerings to increase their appeal. A new trend in 1997 has been for a combination of finance to be offered in a single package. This system was pioneered by amongst others, TSB Commercial Finance and called by them 'Packaged finance'. Advances are now more frequently made against inventories and fixed assets such as plant and machinery. Land and buildings can also come into the equation.

Industry sector	£m	%
Manufacturing	20,185	50.0
Distribution	11,138	27.6
Services	7,003	17.3
Transport	2,060	5.1
Total	**40,386**	**100.0**

Figure 19.2 *Factoring and invoice discounting business by industry sector (£m and per cent) 1996*

It seems highly likely that the industry will continue to enjoy its current rapid rate of growth for the foreseeable future. The potential market is enormous, since at present the industry supplies less than 3 per cent of the total working capital requirement in the UK. The increasing support for the suitability of the industry's wares by professional intermediaries, especially accountants, is also helping the image of the industry to improve. There is still an over-reliance on the bank overdraft, even in highly unsuitable circumstances. However, the vulnerability that this causes is becoming better understood as time passes.

The past year has seen a major development in the structure of the industry's associations. Until recently there were no less than three bodies involved: the Association of British Factors and Discounters, the Association of Invoice Factors, and the European Chapter of the Commercial Finance Association. Now there is one: the Factors and Discounters Association. The spirit of cooperation has enabled the industry to clarify its position greatly in the financial world by speaking with one voice. The Association helps raise awareness of the flexible funding options that are increasingly available to growing businesses and represents their interests on such issues as late payment of invoices and improving cashflow. Members of the Factors and Discounters Association all provide flexible forms of finance and have demonstrated that they have strong balance sheets to support their activities.

20

Raising Private Equity

by Norman Murray, Chairman of the British Venture Capital Association and Chief Executive of Morgan Grenfell Development Capital

The US has been vital to the development and success of the UK private equity market,[1] not only by providing a role model, but also money. In 1997 more funds than ever before were raised by UK private equity firms. Although the precise details are not yet known, a considerable amount will again have come from institutional investors based in the US. In 1996, 34 per cent of funds raised by UK private equity firms came from US investors, with only 57 per cent coming from domestic investors. Partly as a result of this input, a strong London Stock Exchange and good investment opportunities available in the UK, the UK market now accounts for nearly 50 per cent of total annual European private equity investment. The UK market is second only in the world in size and importance to the US market. In 1996, relative to GDP, the UK invested about the same amount in early stage-to-expanding companies as the US. Although the US economy is some seven times the size of the UK's, the UK market made just over half as many investments as the US.[2]

The first few UK private equity funds were raised in the early to mid-1980s. Since then UK firms have proved they have the experience and knowledge to not only invest successfully in the UK, but into Europe and throughout the world. As a result, as was particularly evident in 1997, a few firms raised the first $1 billion funds and even the first £1 billion fund was raised. Most of these are to be focused on investing in large management buy-outs (MBOs) in Europe.

The record amounts raised last year can be attributed to market maturity, the experience of the UK private equity managers and the demonstration of their success through the latest performance figures announced in May 1997. On a one, three, five and ten-year basis, private equity funds were shown to have out-performed all the FTSE indices and all other significant asset classes held by the UK pension funds in The WM Company/British Venture Capital Association (BVCA) 1996 Performance Measurement Survey.[3] Had UK pension funds invested a larger amount in a diversified portfolio of private equity funds, they would have achieved higher returns overall.

Private equity has a role in any balanced portfolio. Investment into this sector adds valuable diversity to a portfolio and, with the right spread of funds, investors will have the opportunity to benefit from the excellent returns being produced by the private equity industry.

UK private equity funds produced a one-year return to 31 December 1996 of 42.9 per cent, which compares with 29.7 per cent achieved by US private equity funds and 10.7 per cent by UK pension funds as a whole. On a three and five-year basis, UK private equity fund returns were 26.6 per cent and 25.7 per cent respectively, compared with 8.2 per cent and 14 per cent for UK pension funds. These good aggregate return figures include a wide spread of returns between the various funds. By the end of 1996, of the £3.4 billion of funds raised by the more mature funds between 1980 and 1992, 132 per cent had already been returned to investors. The funds still retain a conservatively valued 39 per cent of their original commitments in companies which are yet to be realised.

---

1. 'Private equity' in Europe is synonymous with the term 'private equity' as it is used in the US – equity investments in unquoted companies in start-up to management buy-out companies. To prevent confusion in this article, the term 'private equity' has been used. When we refer to 'management buy-outs' or 'MBOs', these are where the incumbent management of a company raises finance to buy the business they manage from the parent company.
2. Comparing BVCA investment figures with those of VentureOne.
3. This was the third 'Performance Measurement Survey' commissioned by the British Venture Capital Association and was for the first time produced by The WM Company, the world's leading independent performance measurer.

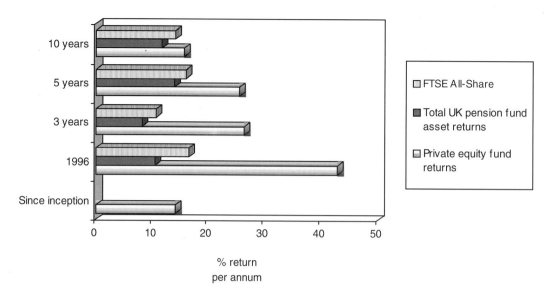

Source: The WM Company/BVCA

NB: The returns shown are net of all costs and include interim valuations that have proven historically to be conservative.

Figure 20.1 *UK private equity, pension fund assets and FTSE all-share returns*

INVESTING IN THE COMPANIES OF TOMORROW

As many US investors know, private equity investment through funds managed by experienced firms enables them to invest in a range of carefully selected, ambitious, quality, high-growth companies before they realise their full potential, become well-known, or float on a stock exchange. It allows investors to participate in the MBOs of divisions of well established and famous companies and to benefit from the revitalisation of businesses. Each year around 40 per cent of trading company flotations on the Official List of the London Stock Exchange are private equity-backed companies. Following flotation, the majority of the private equity-backed companies have been shown to outperform other types of flotations[4] and private-equity-backed MBO flotations capitalised at over £25 million have consistently out-performed the FTSE All-Share index.[5]

Companies such as Golden Wonder (the snacks), Tetley (the teabags), Hamleys (the toy shop) and Compass Group plc (one of the world's largest contract catering companies), are just a few of the better known companies to have benefited from private equity provided to finance their MBOs since the late 1980s.

Many well known companies and consumer brands in the UK have been started up and/or developed with private equity backing, such as British Biotech Group plc, Hodder Headline, the publishers, Phileas Fogg snacks (formerly owned by Derwent Valley Holdings and subsequently sold to United Biscuits), Denplan (the dental insurance company, finally sold to PPP) and New Covent Garden Soup Company, just a few of the names with which many people in the UK will be familiar.

The UK market is probably about a decade behind that in the US in terms of development. The US market has a number of advantages over the UK; it has a much larger, homogeneous market place than is present in the UK and Europe; it has a more developed 'entrepreneurial' culture; the industry has benefited from much greater government investment over 15 years; private equity is recognised as an asset class; and it has the NASDAQ stock market, which is well supported by investors and analysts who invest more readily in early-stage, non-profit making, smaller companies than investors in the UK. Such is the strength of NASDAQ, many international UK companies have floated on the exchange and yet have had to wait some years before they could float (if at all) on the London Stock Exchange. The recognition of private equity as

---

4. *Source:* BVCA research from 1 June 1992 to 31 December 1996.

5. *Source:* HSBC James Capel research by Sally Collier in 1997 of MBOs capitalised over £25 million with a 'significant' stake held by a private equity firm.

an asset class in the UK has meant that in the US pension funds invest on average five per cent[6] of their portfolios in 'alternative assets' which is practically synonymous with private equity. In the UK, less than 1 per cent[7] of pension fund assets are invested in private equity.

The situation in the UK has changed dramatically over the past 10 years. The Thatcher years brought in a stronger entrepreneurial and commercial culture that provided more attractive investment opportunities for the UK private equity firms. Legislative change allowed the structuring of MBOs and the setting up of on-shore private equity funds. Various other tax incentives encouraged business angels and entrepreneurs. The Stock Exchange listing rules changed to allow more biotechnology companies to float at an earlier stage in their development. The UK now has the Alternative Investment Market (AIM), which is proving an additional exit route for private equity firms' investments and EASDAQ is slowly growing in importance. These are just a few of the higher profile changes that occurred and have resulted in the UK market becoming a role model, not just for other European countries, but for many other countries world-wide.

Why should business people consider raising private equity and what do investors look for in a company and its management team?

Private equity provides long-term, committed, risk-sharing capital, which helps unquoted companies grow and compete. The ability to provide capital and experience and contacts, sets private equity apart from other sources of business capital. Although private equity requires the management to sell some shares and at times to give the private equity investor a non-executive board position, it seeks to increase value to the management, without taking management control. The private equity investor makes returns from the growth and profitability of the business, whereas lenders have a legal right to interest on a loan and its repayment, irrespective of its success or failure.

Ideally, private equity investors look for a company with a good commercial product or service, with an excellent potential for high growth. It is essential to have a strong management team with direct experience of the product and its market, who can demonstrate real commitment and ambition to turn their business plan into reality.

Private equity helps UK companies to grow and succeed faster than others

Almost 90 per cent of private equity-backed companies in a BVCA/Coopers & Lybrand report said they would not have existed, or would have grown less rapidly, without private equity. This contribution to growth was clearly quantified by the survey. On average, private equity-backed companies' sales rose by 34 per cent per annum (or five times faster than FTSE 100 companies), exports grew by 29 per cent per annum and investment increased by 28 per cent per annum.

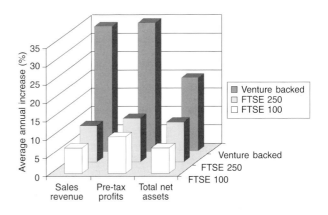

Figure 20.2 *Private equity helps companies out-perform others*

The scope of private equity's involvement in UK companies is significant. One million people in the UK are estimated to be employed by companies currently in receipt of private equity – representing five per cent of private sector employment. Over the four years to 1994/5, the number of people employed in private equity-backed companies increased by 15 per cent per annum, against a national growth rate of less than one per cent per annum.

While the growth and success of these firms owe much to private equity investment, the non-financial input by the private equity firms is also a very important contributor. Of the private equity-backed companies analysed in the survey, 88 per cent said they had benefited from their private equity backers providing more

6. *Source:* Goldman Sachs & Co./Frank Russell Capital Inc. 1995 and 1997 Survey of Alternative Investing.
7. *Source:* National Association of Pension Funds 1995 and The WM Company 1998.

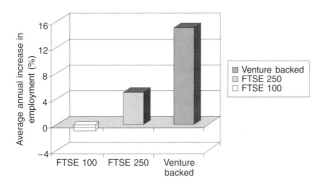

Figure 20.3 *Private equity backed companies create more new jobs more rapidly than others*

than just money. In particular, they highly rated private equity firms' advice and guidance on strategic matters, financial advice, their 'challenging the status quo', and acting as a 'sounding board for ideas'. Most private equity investors have a wide range of experience. Many have worked in industry, others have a financial background, but most importantly, all have the specialist experience of funding and assisting companies at a time of rapid development and growth.

The outlook

The UK private equity industry is now benefiting from the maturity and experience it has gained over the past 15 years. The UK private equity managers are well positioned to offer investors their experience in investing in European unquoted companies. This has enabled UK managers to raise record amounts from institutional investors and offers UK and continental European companies a better availability of private equity than ever before. The UK industry will continue to change, develop and build on its experience, to ensure that it remains at the forefront of the world private equity market.

The British Venture Capital Association (BVCA) represents virtually every major source of private equity in the UK, accounting for over 95 per cent of annual private equity investment. It is dedicated to promoting the private equity industry for the benefit of entrepreneurs, investors, private equity practitioners and the economy as a whole. It undertakes a wide range of research and produces a number of useful publications which are available to callers.

21

The Heart of World Advertising

by Nick Phillips, Director General, Institute of Practitioners in Advertising

Overall the advertising sector is worth around £13 billion ($21.5 billion) or 1.1 per cent of gross domestic product. All of the larger agencies are members of the Institute of Practitioners in Advertising (IPA). 13,000 people are employed directly in IPA agencies but the sector also gives associated employment to other marketing services industries (eg market research) and outside production services (eg producers, film crews, directors, post-production).

The industry is heavily concentrated in London, where over three-quarters of agency staff are employed (although there are also large and successful agencies in other centres such as Manchester, Leeds, Birmingham, Glasgow, Edinburgh, Newcastle and Belfast). London is acknowledged alongside New York as one of the two world centres of creative advertising. UK agencies occupy the top four positions in the international league table of Cannes Award winners in the last five years (1993–97).

In terms of world-wide agency structure the major international agencies (some two dozen) tend to manage their businesses for their clients in three geographical areas – the Americas; Europe, Middle East and Africa; and Asia Pacific. As far as Europe is concerned, in the majority of cases (some two thirds) the international European headquarters are in London.

The ultimate ownership of the major international agencies is US, British, French or Japanese. Five of the international agencies are British-owned and head-quartered in London. English is overwhelmingly the language of business within the international agency networks.

Michael Porter, of Harvard University, in his seminal work *The Competitive Advantage of Nations*, nominates advertising as one of the areas in which the UK has a competitive advantage world-wide.

For an overseas marketing company wishing to expand in Europe, the UK is the most appropriate gateway in terms of size, expertise, organisation and common language. In addition to the two dozen international agencies, there are also some 18 independent agencies who are affiliated to agencies in other European countries and used to managing international campaigns on a co-operative basis. The agency that the marketing company selects would, if one of the larger agencies, international agencies, or 'internationally-affiliated' agencies, be a member of the IPA. So the marketing company would indirectly be a beneficiary of the IPA's services.

THE IPA

The IPA is in many respects the model for other trade bodies around the world. The IPA's Advertising Effectiveness Awards, founded in 1980 and held every two years, have been taken up by many other countries including Australia, Canada, New Zealand, South Africa, Ireland and Sweden. Their excellence has long been recognised: head and shoulders above all other UK industry awards in terms of awareness and appreciation among clients, and long heralded by other countries as the most rigorous awards in the world.

The key objectives of the IPA effectiveness awards are:

- to demonstrate that advertising is both a serious commercial investment and a contributor to profit, not just cost;

- to improve understanding of the crucial role advertising plays in brand marketing and marketing communications generally;

- to encourage new and improved methods of evaluation and thereby to promote advertising accountability and continuous improvement in professional standards.

Over the years some 600 submissions have been written – case histories of famous brands and famous advertising eg Barclaycard, British Airways, BMW, BT,

Daewoo, De Beers, Levi's, Orange, Reebok, Renault Clio. These are all available for study in the IPA's own databank that has been classified on over 30 criteria. They are also a major component of the Internet-based World Advertising Research Center (WARC), started in 1998.

Increasingly the emphasis of this awards programme is on 'learning' rather than 'winning': learning how advertising not only has a direct effect on sales (and therefore corporate profitability) but also has other effects. There is the long term impact of advertising on brand value or the ability of advertising to affect an organisation's culture, promote the corporate brand, win trust and respect among trade partners and suppliers or create goodwill among investors and legislators.

It is not only in the IPA's Advertising Effectiveness awards that the UK leads the world. The discipline of account planning (the linking of sensitive consumer understanding with creative strategy, development and evaluation) started in the UK some thirty years ago and has spread around the world.

The IPA has a major programme of training (both residential and shorter skills enhancement courses) and has set up an agency trainer network to facilitate best practice in training among member agencies. It is at the centre of setting the standards for media research (television viewing, radio listening, readership research) which are adapted in other countries. Advertising freedoms are underpinned by responsible self-regulation, where once again the UK model has been taken up by others.

The IPA has, in conjunction with clients and now supported by other bodies, developed a best practice guide for clients seeking a new agency through a pitching process. Again in conjunction with client organisations, it is developing a model business contract (suggested terms and conditions for agency client agreements) and other examples of best practice, eg in print production.

All of these factors combine to make the UK the natural start-point for an overseas investor in the European market who is looking for strategic advice on marketing communication and the creation and placing of advertising.

The marketer will benefit from:

- an acknowledged centre of world advertising;

- the home of Europe's top creative award winners;

- the organisational centre of European advertising, whose common language is English;

- the choice of international agencies or 'internationally-affiliated' agencies;

- agencies in membership of the IPA, which is a model for trade bodies around the world, leading the way on advertising effectiveness, planning, training, media research, self-regulation and other examples of best practice.

As each advertisement for the UK National Lottery (which had an incredibly successful launch) concludes:

'It could be you'

22

Trends in UK Advertising Media

Bob Wootton, Director of Media Services, The Incorporated Society of British Advertisers Ltd

OVERVIEW

As elsewhere in business, the underlying trend in the UK media scene is towards rationalisation, synergy and the resultant economies of scale. Bigger media companies are getting bigger, absorbing others so as to be ready for a time when six or seven players are expected to lead the global media industry, though the debate continues to rage over whether our current regulatory regime prevents indigenous media companies from achieving sufficient critical mass to compete on the world stage.

This process of consolidation is already accelerating in anticipation of the Broadcasting Act, which got on to the statute books in late 1996, and whose provisions pave the way for some further shakedown of ownership of the media. Advertising and media-buying agencies are also consolidating, with over 80 per cent of all television advertising bookings now being placed through the top 25 buying points.

Advertisers are clear in their desire for a vibrant media scene, offering strength and diversity of communication channels through which they can reach their target customers, but are also keen that the market continues to be well-regulated, as past evidence suggests that media companies can be quick to overexploit strong trading positions.

OVERALL TRENDS

Figures 22.1 and 22.2 show trends in UK media spends over the last five years, with projections for the next five. In broad terms, broadcast continues to grow at the expense of graphic media. Television now accounts for 33 per cent of all adspend and is set to grow further as digital technology allows many new channels to air, providing both new targeting and entry opportunities for advertisers.

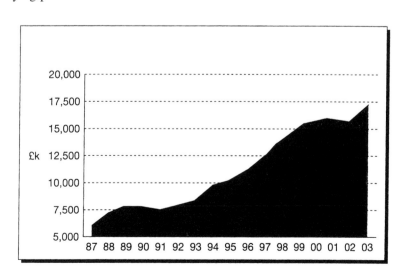

Source: Industry sources/Zenith Media

Figure 22.1 *Growth in total advertising media spend 1987–2003*

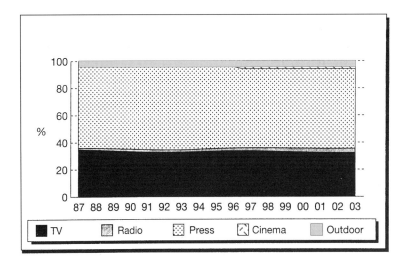

Source: Industry sources/Zenith Media

Figure 22.2 *% share of adspend by medium 1987–2003*

Television

The UK is unique within Europe in that almost half (currently 43 per cent) of all TV viewing is of channels which are funded by a licence fee and carry no advertising – BBC 1 and 2. This has implications for advertisers, as the lack of access to a large proportion of the viewing audience serves to raise the price of reaching people through the available channels. The average UK home has at least two television sets, with 20 per cent having three or more. More than three-quarters of homes have a video, and a quarter receive satellite or cable, a figure which is expected to rise to 45 per cent by the year 2000.

The advent of successive new channels – Channel Four in 1982 and over forty satellite stations since 1985 – has not served to increase the commercial viewing audience significantly. Rather, it has merely tended to fragment it. Against this, it is hoped that the advent of the new near-national Channel Five service since 1997 will help to draw viewers from the BBC's channels into an environment where they can be reached by advertisers.

Nor has the awarding of ITV licences to the highest bidder, which took place in the last franchise renewal round of 1990, served to improve ITV companies' output as measured by the audiences they achieve. The 1996 Annual Report from the Independent Television Commission (which is responsible for regulating UK commercial television) shows that while programme investment is static in real terms, the ITV companies' profits and shareholder dividends have risen steeply. Inflation in the cost of reaching their target customers is running well ahead of RPI, and is thus a major concern among advertisers. This is seen in particularly

stark relief by those who also operate in other European markets, where they are seeing the cost of advertising remain static or even falling as new channels come to air.

The near future will see the start of digital broadcasting, which offers the opportunity to fit many more channels into the existing terrestrial and satellite wavebands. Rupert Murdoch's British Sky Broadcasting has already stated its intention to broadcast up to 500 new channels, many of these being used to run movies starting at 15-minute intervals to maximise audience. (This is known as 'near video on demand.') Further off, we will see the much-vaunted convergence of broadcasting, computers and telecommunications becoming a household reality. As the television screen becomes a multi-purpose item in the home of the future, capable of accessing many channels, some offering interactive services, some downloadable programmes (true video on demand) and some very narrowly-targeted, so the range of communication channels available to advertisers will burgeon, but so will the fragmentation of audiences.

National press

Whereas many other countries are characterised by stronger regional press media, the UK has a very strong national press, though circulations are in long-term decline as newspapers gradually give ground to new, usually electronic media. The market is also characterised by fierce competition between a few powerful media owners. Price promotion, first exploited when News Group cut the cover price of *The Times* to 10 p in 1994, has proved to be a powerful and sometimes enduring method of building circulation and readership share, albeit at considerable cost. Only players with deep pockets can afford to play at this table!

The 1980s saw the arrival of several new titles, notably in the Sunday market – the *Independent*, *Independent on Sunday*, *Sunday Correspondent* and *News on Sunday*. The first two still survive, though both experienced difficulties which resulted in their being acquired by Mirror Group Newspapers two years ago, evidencing the consolidation and even closure that characterised the national press in the 1990s. This trend was given further weight in 1996 when News Group finally pulled the plug on *Today*, the ailing mid-market tabloid it had bought from its founder, Eddy Shah, back in 1987.

Yet amidst this turmoil, 1996 saw the launches of several new titles – maverick Tom Rubython's *Sunday Business*, which is understood to be circulating less than 100,000 copies each week at the time of writing, and the *Planet On Sunday*, which holds the record for the dragonfly of the media world, only lasting for a single launch issue before its backers withdrew support! Sections continue to proliferate, often launching and then closing at will; the UK's 19 daily and Sunday newspapers currently have no less than 100 sections.

Magazines

Despite increasing competition from other media, principally broadcast, the magazine industry is buoyant. The number of consumer magazines has risen 20 per cent to about 2,200 in the past ten years, while cover price increases continue to outstrip inflation.

Over the last five years, an entirely new sector has grown from nowhere to cater for the young men's market, and EMAP plc, previously a publisher of regional newspapers and specialist magazines, has become one of the country's largest consumer magazine publishers.

Publishing technology and low entry costs maintain healthy competition in the market as new players constantly enter at the bottom end to challenge existing titles. This fierce competition forces publishers to keep close to their readers. Those that do, succeed, while those who lose touch atrophy and are absorbed into others or scrapped.

Radio

Commercial radio stations have been broadcasting in the UK for just over 20 years, and the medium has recently shown signs of maturing. Its revenues have climbed sharply, and the share of total advertising spend it achieves has breached 4 per cent for the first time. Much of this success is attributed to the Radio Advertising Bureau, an industry-wide generic marketing body which aims to facilitate the use of radio by removing all the barriers to its purchase.

There are presently 174 stations of very different size and editorial complexion across the UK; from the national stations like Classic FM to small local stations such as Bay FM in Blackpool, from general entertainment stations such as Capital in London, to dance specialists like Galaxy FM, based in Bristol. The dominant player in the field is Capital Radio plc, which is both one of the largest owners of radio stations and, through its MSM subsidiary, also controls nearly two-thirds of the market for national airtime sales.

The last London-wide FM licence before digital broadcasting arrives on the scene is about to be awarded, the favourite contenders being music-based stations which promise to cater for a younger, independent music-oriented audience. At last, some would say.

Cinema

Cinema has enjoyed a renaissance over the last decade, with almost every year reporting admissions higher than the last. In 1996 they were thought to be about 126 million.

This is attributed to two things: the movies themselves, particularly ever more spectacular (and expensive) Hollywood blockbusters and surprise successes, like the British hits 'Four Weddings And A Funeral' and 'The Full Monty'; and the refurbishment of cinemas, usually in the form of multiplexes, multi-screen centres with parking and restaurant facilities.

Carlton, holders of the London weekday and Midland ITV franchises, have recently diversified into cinema by buying Cinema Media, the sales house responsible for some 80 per cent of all cinema airtime. This is seen as a 'good fit', as cinema's strengths with the young may enable them to strengthen their overall sales proposition, given that ITV is relatively weak in the Southeast and does not get younger audiences.

Outdoor

Although it is still the medium of 'men up ladders with bills and pots of glue', the major outdoor site contractors have risen to the competitive challenge presented by other media by upgrading the quality of their plant and the way in which it is presented.

Much of this, it must be said, is due to a French invasion. Both J C Decaux, who operate precinct sites, and Havas Avenir, owners of roadside contractor Mills and Allen, have brought a new professionalism to the market which the other players have been quick to emulate. Two sizes now dominate the field: 48-sheet (20-foot by 10-foot) roadside panels and 6-sheet 'adshels' (illuminated bus shelter sites). More 'ultra-visions' – sites comprising rotating prisms which show three different subjects on the same (usually premium) site – are also appearing, indicating that the revenues they can generate far outweigh their higher initial capital cost.

New media

If media were ranked not by revenue but by the column inches of coverage they receive, the Internet would currently be the biggest medium of all! Yet beneath the vast hype, the medium is, nevertheless, growing almost exponentially and is truly both international and cosmopolitan. There are now over 200,000 UK-based web sites alone.

It also provides challenges to advertisers wishing to exploit it successfully, as it offers its audience the opportunity to edit not only its contents but its very appearance. Advertisement content and placement alike thus have to be reconsidered from the ground up, making new demands of advertisers and their marketing-services suppliers.

Computer games have become significant advertising media for those targeting youth, while screensavers are now widely used to target domestic and office environments, and are particularly popular in a business-to-business context.

New-media consultancies are burgeoning to capitalise on the opportunities presented by these 'new' media, and the first media sales house which facilitates advertiser access to genuinely relevant sites has recently been launched.

CONCLUSION

The UK and indeed the global media scene is experiencing more change than it has ever seen before, and this rate of change is further set to increase. Yet as has been described in the US, the major established media 'brands' continue to enjoy the bulk of audience patronage – for example, the networks still take about 70 per cent of all TV viewing, while ever more channels compete for the rest. This model is likely to show the way forward in the UK for the next few years at least.

Sources for all data: Industry sources/Zenith Media

23

Public Relations – Managing a Common Language

by Peter L Walker FIPR, President, The Institute of Public Relations;
Executive Chairman, PIELLE Consulting Group

In a global economy and the world of international trade and investment, money still talks. But while the bankers, politicians and management provide briefings, unions, consumers, communities and pressure groups have also discovered their voices. No surprises then that public relations, the management discipline dedicated to managing communication effectively, has become the strategic bridge for international investment and marketing success.

THINK GLOBAL – ACT LOCAL

'Think global – act local' is a mantra trotted out as the underpinning philosophy by most modern international manager advisers. Like so much of today's management speak, however, it was coined before it took a millisecond for a message or news to travel from California to Cannes in France or Little Rock to Liverpool in the UK's north west. It may still be a great maxim for personal behaviour but as a credo for effective communication in a modern world, it is an invitation to court disaster.

It is no coincidence that public relations in the UK and the US started to organise itself as a coherent management function 50 years ago. No coincidence either that the lessons of effective communication have been learned together and across continents, as international trade and investment have become the growth engine of the modern world. The challenge for the modern multi-national manager is knowing, or at least learning, how to tap into this deep well of expertise and use the specialist management resource effectively.

When Nestlé's frozen food management team decided to bring Stouffers' Lean Cuisine brand into the European market, they spent eighteen months working with their public relations professionals planning a communication strategy. It was a strategy that looked beyond launch publicity and marketing communication, to employee and community relations where the new products were going to be manufactured, to issue management in a world obsessed with health. Mergers and acquisitions today can flounder on the rocks of misinformation, disinformation, effective and well-organised single-issue pressure groups. Consumer protest can disrupt any inward-investment plan or market-development strategy driven by financial or commercial logic alone.

A GOOD PRESS

'A good press' – media relations are still the key role and raison d'être for investing in public relations by most organisations. Hardly surprising when journalists and a free press are still most feared, probably because they can be least controlled. In today's UK the public relations professional has devised and developed computer-based techniques and programmes for evaluating media comment, plotting and tracking issue development and the impact of messages targeted at individual, sectoral markets and audiences.

For any organisation opening the door to Europe, investing in public relations in the UK is not a soft option or fuel for a 'feel good factor'. This is now a hard, essential commercial decision, where outcomes can be measured against clear strategies. The starting point has to be clear: agreed and shared management and operational objectives. We all know that good communication is two-thirds about effective listening. Taking advice on how those strategies need to be communicated in key markets with core stakeholders across Europe means using your public relations professional as part of the strategic input, not just as energetic and skilled output.

The UK's financial public relations community has led the world in the mass marketing of equities, the key driver in the successful privatisation of state assets. It has produced a partnership with the financial communities in London and Europe that enables the professional city and financial public relations players in the UK to play a unique role in inward investment, mergers and acquisitions across Europe. In today's Europe, inward-investment plans and cross-border acquisition strategies are conducted against a regulatory and legislative framework structured to protect consumer, employee and community interests. Stakeholders as well as shareholders have rights to information, demand appropriate communication and, frequently, consultation. A threat to good management? Not if you use the best UK public relations professionals. These are opportunities to build the relationships, secure commitment and support that any best management practice strategy needs.

Working with experts who operate to a recognised set of operational, ethical and technical standards is an essential. Shared values and common understanding can bridge any cultural differences. In the UK today, the Institute of Public Relations sets the standards for public relations practice. A quick look at its membership structure is the best indicator of the breadth and depth of specialist management skills and expertise to be found in the UK today. City and financial public relations – investor relations; internal communication; marketing communication or, as the EU now calls it, commercial communication; government relations and lobbying, crisis communication management; these are some of the specialist skills any international manager can look for in the public relations professionals he or she works with in the UK.

As part of the process of working with organisations as they become accountable to stakeholders worldwide, the public relations profession in the UK has itself become accountable. Standards, even professional and for skills sets, have been carefully defined and developed. In the UK today 12 universities offer first and second degrees in public relations as well as post-graduate diplomas, each of them accredited by the Institute as the lead professional body. Continual professional development programmes and technical skills training seminars and events create an ever increasing pool of professional talent and expertise.

The UK's position on the dateline and its status as a media hub have enabled the UK public relations professional to become a bridge to a new Europe beyond the boundaries of the common market. Common standards, a common language for communication and a shared appreciation of regional and national variations and ambitions make the best in UK public relations an essential partner for any US management team.

Even when businesses are well established in UK and European markets, management, operational and organisational changes can succeed or fail if the communication of the core messages is left to chance. Bombardier, one of the world's best managed businesses, is a major European player in ground transport. When a European acquisition triggered the creation of a single worldwide corporate brand, a pan-European public relations programme drove the key messages out to governments and markets and down to employees and customers. Working to common standards, using a common language, even though each national audience was talked and listened to in their own language, five in all, was not just an exercise in logistics. Long-term strategies, development programmes and market developments were all factored into the underpinning messages. According to the Chairman of one of the UK's biggest financial institutions 'Every organisation's reputation is at risk if its performance gets out of line with expectation'.

Expectations can be set at the right levels by effective communication and that means using professionals in public relations. Public relations professionals in the UK today reflect the investment that 50 years of professional development have given to a management discipline that is, according to Sir Colin Marshall, Chairman of British Airways, 'the essence of good management'.

24

UK's PRCA: Your Window on Europe's Best PR Services

by Adrian Wheeler, Chairman, Public Relations Consultants Association

Well-managed and effective public relations is an essential component of successfully entering and building market strength in Europe. Good PR in Europe's diverse national economies is vital but presents North American corporations with challenges that often surprise. For all its growing legislative and commercial harmony, the EU comprises widely and subtly different cultural traditions. Penetrating the European market successfully means recognising the innumerable variations in attitude, taste, ethics and expectations, and adjusting product messages to take account of national, regional and even local susceptibilities.

Public relations consultancies specialise in knowing how to present a company's case in the most effective manner to a wide diversity of audiences: governments; regulators; trade customers; consumers; consumer groups; employees; local communities; and of course the media, who act as one of the most powerful channels of communication with these and other important audiences. Much of a public relations consultancy's work involves creating good relationships between its clients and the media who influence public opinion, and this is one area where local knowledge and well-established connections are of the highest value.

For a North American corporation addressing the European market, public relations is usually high on the list of priorities. When City of London Telecommunications (COLT – owned by Fidelity of Boston) first arrived in the UK, for example, it hired a public relations firm before the first metre of fibre-optic cable was put in the ground. COLT knew that building understanding and support among the key London media would take time and effort. As a result, the company's business launch, months later, was covered accurately and enthusiastically by the press. COLT is now expanding its operations into other major European cities.

For Cotton Council International (CCI), the export promotion arm of the US cotton industry, a multi-country European PR programme was vital. CCI needed to get its quality messages across to a wide range of trade and consumer audiences in four different European markets: UK, Germany, Italy and France. The answer was to establish core messages and communications properties which could be 'localized' by PR consultancies steeped in the local traditions of the national markets and the very different media which serve them. Attitudes to the US vary widely in European countries and from sector to sector. 'One size fits all' is a recipe for disaster, so experienced marketers like CCI aim to capitalise on local knowledge to adapt and adjust core messages according to national circumstances.

How does a US corporation go about developing a European PR programme to support its marketing objectives? With very few exceptions, US companies base their operations in the UK, and manage the rollout of their European PR from the UK. Apart from the obvious language factor, there are numerous advantages in co-ordinating a European campaign in the UK. Top of the list is the sheer size and sophistication of the British public relations industry. Starting post-war hand-in-hand with US pioneers like Carl Byoir, the UK PR industry has grown to the point where it is today equal in size to that of the rest of Europe put together.

Virtually all the major US PR groups maintain London offices and networks of offices or affiliations across Europe, while a sizeable majority of the UK's top 100 PR consultancies have well-established European operations with long experience of managing multi-country programmes for US and the UK clients. Many of these companies maintain offices or partnerships in Brussels, and many have experience of running public relations and public affairs programmes in Central and Eastern Europe, Russia and further east. How can you tell which consultancy has experience relevant to your industry and also offers the geographical scope to support your expansion into your chosen markets?

A good starting point is the UK's Public Relations Consultants Association (PRCA), which was established in 1969 and has 160 member consultancies representing 80 per cent of the UK's PR industry by value. Nearly all the large, international groups belong to the PRCA, as well as many specialist firms, for example, in healthcare, information technology and investor relations, who represent clients across all or part of the EU. The PRCA introduced the world's first Consultancy Management Standard, a guarantee of quality, on 1 January 1998, and maintains close contact with other international PR associations as the secretariat of ICO, the International Consultants Organisation. Most significantly, the PRCA offers a state-of-the-art referral service, PReview, to help clients find the best consultancy for their needs.

Using PReview gives clients an automatic guarantee that the consultancies recommended are bound by the PRCA's stringent financial and performance standards. The service is also confidential, so clients can use it to carry out reviews of alternative consultancies as well as to find their first consultancy in the European market. PReview serves major corporations and small firms alike, with three different options costing from just £50 to £650 for a fully-guided database search and personal assistance with the selection process. PReview's database will match your requirements against the PRCA's entire 160-strong membership according to the size, locations, sector experience, disciplines and expertise you specify. PReview's trained staff are familiar with the problems clients face and can pass on the benefit of their experience of assisting others to make the right choice first time.

Clients' relationships with PR consultancies tend to be long-term. Microsoft, for instance, entered the European market with the British PR consultancy Text 100 and is still with them today. The European marketplace is complex and full of pitfalls for the unwary; what works in Milwaukee or Manitoba may not work at all in Milan, Madrid or Malmo. UK PR firms have been finding ways to manage market and media diversity in Europe for over thirty years. The PRCA's PReview service enables you to home in on those consultancies which have exactly the right European credentials and to get them working, quickly and efficiently, on your European development programme.

25

London as the Gateway to Communicating to Europe

by Michael Murphy, Chief Executive, Shandwick Europe

General Eisenhower was one of many Americans who have regarded the UK as a possible springboard for invading Europe. For him, of course, it was a matter of consolidating forces safely in allied territory before the 'big push'. For modern business leaders, the metaphor of advancing across enemy territory is not very helpful, yet often, when it comes to choosing a city from where America's big corporates can speak to mainland Europe, they choose London.

London's status as one of the world's top financial centres, both at the heart of the EU – holding the presidency in the first half of 1998 – and yet also facing across the Atlantic, makes it an obvious candidate. Even when these corporations establish their European headquarters in Brussels or Frankfurt, they often choose London as the place from where their European public relations will be coordinated.

Why? Every case is different, but there are some common reasons:

- because the UK may already be their biggest market in Europe, and it often makes sense to start from there;

- because public relations in the UK has had a 10-year head start over mainland Europe to mature as a profession. Germany and France may have exciting and new PR markets, but London has been developing innovative PR techniques longer than any other city outside the major US capitals, as you would expect of a city which continues to play such a pivotal role in the development of the culture of the English language. Many of the newest techniques have been pioneered in the UK: coordinating across Europe and building on best practice means that the best thinking can be exported and then adapted to other markets;

- because of the English language. For a big American corporation peering across the Atlantic, London uses a common, if not identical, language. It also has a related Anglo-Saxon culture with a ring of familiarity for US executives: they understand that the diversity of cultures and traditions of mainland Europe will be a challenge for any international communicator;

- there are a number of pan-European media outlets which are based in London, from Sky and CNN to *The European* and the *International Herald Tribune*.

For these and other related reasons, London has become a thriving centre of communications for international firms like Shandwick, Hill & Knowlton and Burson-Marsteller jostling for business. Shandwick, with its coverage of 23 markets in this region, is ideally placed to advise US-based clients on getting to grips with pan-European communication campaigns. Let me use three of our clients as examples – Owens Corning, Adaptec and Medtronic.

Owens Corning

The US building materials manufacturer Owens Corning realised in the early 1990s that it would have to build a global strategy if it was going to keep its dominance in the American market. The company's market share in the UK was less than five per cent, but by buying the insulation division of the British company Pilkington, it suddenly found itself the market leader in the UK, and opted to use this established base as a springboard into Europe.

Building materials present a classic example of local-market differences facing US multinationals wanting to expand into Europe; housing materials vary from market to market as the diverse styles of homes in Amsterdam, Athens and the Alps show.

There is a marked variation in the world between the well-insulated flats of thriving Bremen in Germany and new homes designed to let in light and keep out the heat in Naples. Not only are the materials different, but the construction industry itself depends on different skills, traditions and organisation of labour.

These variations are felt even more sharply when it comes to communication. You can send out English-language press releases from the US headquarters, but the chances are that they will not be understood – still less acted on – in the varied regions of Europe unless they are adapted not only to the local language, but also to local style and culture. That is where international PR networks can help.

Owens Corning had been a Shandwick client in the US for a number of years and the office in London handled the initial announcement about their UK insulation business. The team went on to develop a system of communications that ensured local adaptation of the company's key messages through Shandwick's offices in Madrid, Rome or Paris. As a result, when Owens Corning's reinforced plastics products were used to reinforce the cable trays inside the Channel tunnel or for building a bridge in Denmark, this message could be fed through the international trade press, as well as the various local media, and adapted for best effect. The messages are disseminated around the world, but only an expert on the ground can advise on what will be of interest to, say, the editor of an architectural magazine in Catalonia.

Adaptec

What is true of building materials is also true in the IT sector. The successful adapter card manufacturer Adaptec is based in Silicon Valley and has a European headquarters in Brussels, but it chose to organise its European PR through Shandwick's IT specialists in London. From there, a staff of five, speaking a range of European languages, coordinates the European PR work carried out by local agencies in France, Germany and Italy. The London office receives regular press releases from Adaptec's Californian headquarters and must decide if they have any relevance to Europe. Product launches, press tours and the overall European PR strategy are coordinated from London, as they have been for four years now. The London team and the three agencies in the other countries are all specialists in IT public relations.

The London team plays a vital role for Adaptec, assisting the client's Brussels-based senior staff member to oversee all marketing communication activities. They are in regular contact with Adaptec's headquarters, keeping executives there informed about ongoing progress and issues arising in different corners of Europe. This process fulfils dual functions. Initially, its aim is to increase awareness of Adaptec in Europe, and in return it provides the client with a dependable source for market intelligence.

The arena of medical devices is even further removed from those of building materials and technology. The medical press is more international than the building-material and architectural press, yet health care systems across Europe are diverse.

The European medical system is completely different to that in the US, and within Europe you will find many variations. Whereas patients in the UK gain access to hospital treatment via their general practitioners, in Germany they would think nothing of going straight to the hospital to seek treatment. So, for similar reasons, major health conglomerates often choose London as their European beachhead. The US company Medtronic, for example, has been running a campaign to promote a new treatment for Parkinson's Disease in five European countries, France, Germany, Italy, Sweden and the UK.

Medtronic

Medtronic is the largest manufacturer of medical implantable devices in the world, including pacemakers and heart valves. Their head office in Minneapolis wants to keep its finger on the pulse of its communications effort worldwide, making sure the stories peddled about them around the world remain consistent. When it comes to the nuts and bolts of communicating in the European market, this requires an agency on the spot, with local-market knowledge. Shandwick has established a global healthcare task force that coordinates the efforts of its healthcare specialists around the world and it understands these subtle cultural differences very well. That is one of the reasons why Medtronic chose Shandwick at the beginning of 1998. PR staff dedicated to the Medtronic account now keep in touch with each other by phone, e-mail and fax across Europe day by day and Shandwick feeds back progress reports on the launch campaign progress in each European market to Minneapolis every 24 hours.

For all three of these examples, pan-European coordination is about getting the local focus right. It is about giving local PR offices enough authority to translate the corporation's core messages and communicate these to a diverse range of audiences.

Of course there is a paradox here. The trend towards decentralising the delivery of PR has been emerging just as corporations increasingly want to control the messages which they are putting out about their brands across the world. It is up to PR specialists to organise systems which allow them to combine both ambitions, to shape the message and adapt it locally so that it can be understood. The trick is to get enough of the right procedures in place without disempowering the local input.

It's not just the PR industry which has been struggling with this paradox. It is the same issue for global executives trying to shape their organisations without losing the initiative at the coal face. In the same vein, the EU faces the challenge of making a difference to the continent as a whole without diluting local cultures. The million-dollar question remains, how to use that valuable local knowledge while keeping strategic control over the process. The exact balance between central control and local innovation has to be tailored to each organisation, but in the 1990s big corporations such as TNT Express Worldwide, Compaq and Digital have been tackling the communication issues by appointing a single PR agency around the world.

TNT Express Worldwide, for example, does little or no brand advertising, which means that the majority of its marketing messages are disseminated to 48 countries worldwide by public relations techniques and direct mail. Initially, this was delivered through a string of disparate agencies, but it soon became apparent that running the coordination through a single network from a London hub provided a more streamlined approach.

Another, almost directly opposite, approach is the one used by international retailer Marks & Spencer. Its PR programmes are managed separately in different markets. This is possible thanks to the company's own strongly centralised culture providing the context and thereby empowering individual country managers to translate the company's values into local terms. Shandwick facilitates best-practice sharing between markets and provides centralised crisis management counselling.

No matter how the strategy is delivered, the industry, particularly in the UK, has been looking at improving and automating many of the coordination and evaluation functions critical to the management of effective public-relations programmes. In order to gain meaningful feedback there is a need to establish a common framework of measurement criteria which is relevant to the client yet does not lose sight of the specific market conditions. Again, each communication programme requires a varied range of solutions, which

is why Shandwick has developed its own proprietary programmes.

The STEP Programme

The first, The STEP Programme (Shandwick Toolkit for Evaluation and Planning), enables PR executives to identify the best evaluation products available to support each stage of a PR programme from planning to implementing, monitoring and then evaluating its effect. It is delivered to employees via a Web-site which knits together systems providing information on print and broadcast media, as well as the Internet, cross-referencing coverage with audience data, and weighing it according to its influence around the world or in different sectors of the domestic market.

Shandwick Collaborator

The second tool is the Shandwick Collaborator, a Web-based information management application, which allows an agency in London to coordinate the work of other offices across Europe by creating a kind of 'virtual' account team. It means that some of the difficult coordination and information sharing can be handled electronically while the account handlers can spend more time on what they do best: developing strategies and applying creative thought.

Collaborator has two main components: a centralised database, allowing team members to draw on a shared list of contacts, including details of media, government officials, financial analysts and other target groups, updated every month, and a collaborative work environment, where team members brainstorm and exchange ideas wherever they are located around the world.

The application is tailored for each account, and includes common document postings, event calendars, activity reports and instant access to TV, radio, press and Internet clips, so that the team can respond to events as they unfold around the world.

The pressure from the client side to implement effective multi-national campaigns without relinquishing control has provided new challenges for the industry. A direct result is the emergence of a new skills set, new techniques and new systems – like Collaborator and The STEP Programme. Communicating messages to the multi-layered cultures of Europe is an enormous challenge and it may be that the polyglot culture of Brussels or the media expertise of Hamburg may eventually compete with London as the communication centre, but they have not managed to do so yet. For the time being then, London is the gateway.

26

Leading Europe in Communicating with Stakeholders

by Gloria Walker, ABC

Advances in travel and communications technology mean that people everywhere are receiving the same messages, buying the same products and seeing the same brand names from Boston to Bangkok. The new century will see communicators everywhere working with the forces which have affected communicators so greatly in the 1990s: globalisation; technology; reputation; effectiveness and practitioner skills.

Many of us have seen cases where the drive for globalisation has created an opposing force for maintaining regional, local or traditional businesses and values. Due to the advances in communications technology, people everywhere are interconnected. International markets are no longer dominated by corporate behemoths. Anyone with the ability to establish a web-site can now find himself a player in rapidly emerging markets and new businesses around the world. The technology explosion does have a down side, however, as people are faced with a daily barrage of information. We as communicators must cut through this information overload to ensure that our stakeholder audiences are receiving information necessary to building and maintaining positive relationships with us and our organisations.

Working in Europe means approaching some traditional communications practices and issues in a different way. Here are some observations which may be of help as you build your stakeholder communications with European audiences. Within Europe, the UK is a leader in communications practice. Many international consulting firms have London offices serving clients throughout the UK and the rest of Europe. Offices are often available in other European capitals.

UK CONSULTANCIES

Consultancies in the UK tend to specialise in a particular area of communications practice – financial public relations, corporate public relations, internal communications, change management, political and public affairs, sector public relations. The term 'public relations' can be misleading, as this term generally means media relations, particularly press, not the broader definition usually meant in US public relations, although this is slowly changing. Someone working in the UK or elsewhere in Europe can find himself employing a number of consultancies to support communications with specific stakeholder groups.

Alongside the international practices are a rapidly growing number of national and regional consultancies which offer a variety of services. The staffs are smaller and the clients more local, so a wider brief can be accepted and fulfilled, generally with very good results.

US multinationals have found that they need to translate their corporate culture to employee groups in countries with different cultures and languages. While English may be the language of business and widely used in pan-European programmes, it is appropriate to work in the local language, particularly for effective employee communications and community relations. The local management team may speak English, but many employees don't or won't.

European business has been slow to recognise the value of communications in achieving corporate goals and increasing competitiveness. Examples of effective communications programmes from US-based multinationals have demonstrated the effectiveness of communications and increased awareness of the need for a different approach to building relationships with stakeholder groups.

TOMORROW'S COMPANY

In January 1993 the Royal Society for the Encouragement of Arts, Manufactures and Commerce (RSA) brought together senior executives from 25 of the UK's top businesses to develop a shared vision of Tomorrow's Company. The Inquiry's main objective was to stimulate greater competitive performance by encouraging business leaders and those who influence their decision-making to re-examine the sources of sustainable business success. The Inquiry found that an inclusive approach was needed toward business leadership, people, investment needs and to society in general. Writing in the final report, Sir Anthony Cleaver, Chairman of the Inquiry, stated that he believes becoming a Tomorrow's Company 'is fundamentally a leadership issue . . . Leadership that has the courage to put across a consistent message which is relevant to all stakeholders – giving the same vision of the company to shareholder and employee, to investor and supplier, to customer and to the community at large.'

The Tomorrow's Company study is seen as a blueprint for company action. Its findings were supported when in 1994 the results of another study were published. The then UK Department of Trade and Industry and the Confederation of British Industry issued the findings of their study of over 100 best British companies. The study, *Competitiveness – How the best UK companies are winning*, found that nine out of ten of the most successful companies meet four key criteria: they are led by visionary champions of change; they unlock the potential of their people; they know and exceed the expectations of their customers; and they constantly introduce new and differentiated products and services.

These criteria are probably familiar to US companies, but the fact that the UK government recognised them as central to maintaining competitiveness meant that the issues of change, training and development, customer satisfaction and product development were now central to corporate strategy in the UK and, increasingly, across Europe. The growth of the Single Market in Europe also means that companies have to take every opportunity to improve their competitiveness and they are looking for examples of best practice to adapt to their own situations.

To refer again to Tomorrow's Company:

As the world business climate changes, so the rules of competitiveness are being rewritten. The effect is to make people and relationships more than ever the key to sustainable success. Only through effective relationships with and between employees, customers, suppliers, investors and the community will companies anticipate, innovate and adapt fast enough while maintaining public confidence. The company whose communication with all these groups is not rooted in consistent values will expose itself to lack of credibility, loss of confidence and damage to its reputation. This increasing interdependence is amplified by the global power of the media.

This emphasis on competitiveness has created a climate for communications. Companies are providing more resource for the provision of effective communications with stakeholder groups. Today there are more professional communicators than ever working in Europe and that number will increase as the role of communications is fully recognised and appreciated.

The Industrial Society in the UK undertook a study last year to develop a profile of Leadership in the 21st century. Some of the factors have clear implications for communicators: 'capable of providing and sharing a clear vision and direction; constantly encouraging, stimulating and supporting others; ready to communicate, communicate, communicate!'

This readiness to communicate bodes well for us as communicators as we enter the 21st century. Many communicators within the UK are practising at the highest levels using communications tools to great effect. Case studies abound on such topics as communicating financial information; underpinning a major change programme; gaining credibility through measurement; communication strategy for acquisition and integration; supporting first-line managers in a change environment; crisis management; building an in-house public-affairs function, and numerous others.

Reading case studies and other publications from European companies can be a useful way of developing an understanding of communications practice. Some resources which could be of use are *Strategic Communication Management* from Melcrum Publishing and the *Journal of Communications Management* from Henry Stewart Publications.

Professional associations offer another way of becoming familiar with communications practice. In the UK, the Institute of Public Relations (IPR) is the largest organisation for individuals. Through its London-based headquarters, the IPR and its vocational, regional and special interest groups provide services to more than 5000 public relations practitioners throughout the UK. Similar national organisations exist in a number of European countries.

Internationally, the International Association of Business Communicators (IABC) is a global network that inspires, establishes and supports the highest professional standards of quality and innovation in organisational communication. IABC has more than 13,000 members working throughout the world, with Europe its fastest growing region. The European region provides a vast resource of experience and advice for other communicators starting to work outside of the US. Services are available through IABC's European office in Brussels or through chapters in Slovenia, Belgium, the Netherlands and the UK.

In many ways, working in Europe is similar to working in the US, especially since communications is recognised more and more as a critical factor for corporate success. Companies have visions, but these visions must be communicated to those in the organisation who will help turn visions into realities. Management makes decisions, but they must communicate with others to get information, select the best decision alternative and implement the decision. Managers plan, decide, handle conflict and motivate; all these actions, and many others, require participation in the process of communication. Indeed, communication plays a critical role in the process of moving people toward shared organisational goals.

Being an effective communicator in Europe requires all of the skills familiar to US practitioners, as well as some additional ones. Effective communicators are proactive in approach and networked with contacts in a number of important audience groups. They plan and focus their work to achieve organisational objectives. They are results-oriented and measure progress. They take a global approach and are sensitive to local and cultural differences. They work to improve understanding, support, loyalty and retention for their organisations, or for their clients. They are strategists as well as tacticians. They have management's ear as well as the organisation's heart.

Effective communicators can be found working throughout Europe and their value is increasing, particularly in this era of continual change. Smythe Dorward Lambert found in a UK study that communication is never more vital for an organisation than when it is in the throes of change. 'New messages, often very difficult ones, need to be clearly understood by both internal and external audiences to ensure that they feel neither confused nor ostracised,' the study concluded. But how effective are communicators at delivering these messages?

A survey of executives by Watson Wyatt Worldwide isn't encouraging. The surveyed executives said that the most important objective for a communications programme is informing employees about company changes and company goals . . . When asked how well their companies perform these communications tasks, executives gave their companies low marks.

This raises the issue of competencies and standards, an important issue facing the further development of the communications industry in the UK and increasingly throughout Europe. As more programmes operate across borders, communicators will have to demonstrate a range of skills and competencies not just in their traditional areas, but in leadership, management and other areas affecting organisational competitiveness. Attending conferences and workshops will not meet the need for keeping current with developments in communications practice and new media practitioners will have to adopt life-long learning as part of their professional codes of practice and require professional development opportunities in their employment arrangements.

Overall, communications in the UK is a dynamic, growing industry. Many practitioners are highly competent; consultancies offer clients a range of services to meet the information demands of stakeholders. Companies effectively use traditional media, such as newsletters, press releases and videos, and many have been successful in integrating new media – intranets, web-sites, business television – into the communications mix.

In today's changing organisations, everyone recognises the need for effective communication with stakeholders. More and more, communication is recognised as a strategic function as well as a daily deliverer of corporate progress. Just as the US has set the example for the UK, the UK is setting the example for Europe. Best practice is being shared from colleague to colleague, from company to company, from consultancy to consultancy as communications and those who practise it are taking their rightful place at the top of the organisational structure and enabling organisations to maintain competitiveness and build fruitful relationships with stakeholders.

Gloria Walker, ABC, holds BS and MA degrees in journalism and public relations from two American universities. Throughout her career she has gained experience in the US and Europe in corporate and internal communications, public relations and public affairs. She is a member of the Institute of Public Relations and its Government Affairs Group. She is an accredited member of the International Association of Business Communicators and a past president of the UK chapter. She is currently working as a consultant in strategic communications and is pursuing a doctorate in social psychology at the London School of Economics.

27

Visual Communication: Increasing Corporate Effectiveness

by Wayne Drew, Chief Executive of the International Visual Communication Association (IVCA)

The use of visual media for corporate communication dates back to the 1920s. Even then, business leaders saw the importance of communicating with their staff and shareholders. Film was the original medium, but now video is the core of the industry with other sectors such as corporate events, multimedia, the Internet and business television rapidly catching up. With such diversity and rich potential, the award-winning UK visual communications industry offers a range of effective and directional solutions to a variety of business challenges. It is a highly successful sector with a turnover of more than £1.6 billion ($2.64 billion) per year, which is projected to grow to £2.5 billion ($4.1 billion) by 2001. This is considerably greater than UK film production, including lottery moneys, and programme for programme is in excess of the output of the BBC.

Each year, the visual communication industry's finest achievements are acknowledged at festivals throughout the world, including the IVCA Awards, arguably the biggest event of its kind. More recently the New York Festival awarded five gold medals to one UK company alone for its outstanding success. Yet, ironically, in general terms, the industry has neither received the recognition it deserves, nor has its contribution been fully appreciated amongst potential markets.

The International Visual Communication Association (IVCA), the largest trade association of its kind in Europe and with affiliates world-wide, is working to redress this situation. As well as rewarding excellence and creativity within the 'hidden industry', the IVCA also promotes the business benefits of corporate communications. Working closely with the Department of Trade and Industry (DTI), the IVCA is about to embark on a programme targeting the commissioners of corporate products. The Commissioners' Programme

recognises commissioners as the lifeblood of the industry, and is designed to maximise the reach and impact of their work. It has three objectives:

- to increase the profile of commissioners,

- ensure the provision of key business intelligence; and

- to further awareness of the latest developments within visual communication.

It is only once commissioners fully appreciate the business value of corporate communications, that the industry will really maximise its potential. The image of corporate communications has to move on from being just 'a corporate fashion accessory'; it has to constantly and systematically demonstrate just how effective it can be.

THE ROLE OF THE IVCA

An effective trade body provides the latest information for its members and acts as a forum to aid sector development. The 'business case' for visual communication unifies our industry and the IVCA advances this through the provision of corporate intelligence and by offering commissioners and producers strategic networking opportunities at the highest level.

New ideas are essential to every industry and the IVCA is the centre for the latest information, advice and discussion on all aspects of the industry. IVCA publications, which include the unique *Visual Communications Handbook*, are leading guides to the sector for producers and commissioners. The regular *Meet The Challenge* seminars and the IVCA Roadshow deal with such issues as how to measure effective communication, communicating change, and crisis management. The IVCA also provides its members with expert advice and offers over 50 different support services, ranging from governmental lobbying to free legal and PR help-lines so members have access to expert advice.

The IVCA, therefore, performs an important role for the industry and is recognised by both the UK government and the foremost companies as a vital body to the development of the sector. The IVCA recognises that government has a role to play in improving competitiveness, but believes that the prime responsibility must lie with industry itself. The Association has an important role to play in helping industry meet the challenges from increasing competition and to ensure that its voice is understood at all levels of the legislative process. These sentiments were recently reinforced by The Rt Honourable Margaret Beckett MP, President of the Board of Trade. Announcing the widest ranging consultation of business undertaken by any British government, she called for a dynamic new form of partnership between Government and industry to maximise the competitiveness of UK industries.

Partnership action is not a new concept for the IVCA: it is at the very heart of its mission. Through strategic partnerships the IVCA:

- works to represent the visual communication industry's interests at all levels of the legislative and regulatory process;

- works productively to improve the sector's competitiveness and growth;

- supplies considered information and advice to members;

- promotes good public relations and communications;

- promotes exports and other market opportunities;

- promotes training and education;

- promotes standards and product/service quality;

- promotes innovation and technology transfer.

In order to achieve these objectives, the IVCA has produced a number of business programmes dedicated to developing the profile of the sector and guaranteeing its standards are of the highest order. They include raising the sector profile, market development, the provision of business intelligence, suitable training and the stimulation of debate and discussion on all aspects of industry. Also available are management assessment procedures such as ISO 9001 to support their development, a monthly newsletter, regular screenings of new

corporate programmes for commissioners and producers, and a training and recruitment scheme.

Visual communications techniques and services

All forms of visual communication represented by the IVCA have a distinct set of business benefits. It is vital that corporate commissioners have a clear understanding of what each medium can contribute to the success of their businesses. All too often errors are made in communication spend by client companies through a lack of understanding of the best ways to target their campaigns.

Each form of visual communication has specific business benefits which, strategically used, can greatly enhance the reach and impact of the corporate message.

Face-to-face communication (such as events, conferences and exhibitions) has several major advantages over the more mass-marketing tools. It allows for tight targeting with very little wastage, and is active rather than passive communication. It provides opportunities for interaction and dialogue, and enables the three-dimensional, simultaneous use of several media. This multi-layered communication can be explicit and implicit in tone, texture, design and feel, which enables the client to present a substantial story communicated with less constraints on time and space. Such sophistication enables brand personality to be expressed and encourages relationships to be formed and beliefs exchanged.

Video communication

Video communication is most effective when productions are from an environment in which the client considers the production company to be an extension of their own team. In such a context, video can produce highly effective and measurable results. Video contains a powerful sense of sight, sound and motion which can win hearts and minds, change attitudes, motivate, instruct and engage. A well-produced video delivers a clear and consistent message while often giving an audience access to people and places they might not otherwise encounter. Research has indicated that a video mailer is six times more effective than a printed mailer. Its use for public relations is excellent, allowing companies to promote themselves to a wide variety of audiences from shareholders to the media. Similarly, for sales and marketing, video can be designed to support presentations by illustrating the character of the product, or it can stand alone – either by mail or for use within the exhibition environment. It is also an excellent medium for training, as it is portable and repeatable. It can explain complex subjects clearly, visually demonstrating how something is or should be done.

Interactive media

Interactive media remains an alien concept to many people. Indeed a recent IVCA series of focus group surveys indicated that fewer than 10% of corporate commissioners had any significant understanding of its business benefits. Simply, it is the unique combination of video, sound, graphics and software with the added benefits of allowing interaction. Multimedia is not confined to CD-ROM. The age of the Internet/Intranet and the World Wide Web enable interactive multimedia to be distributed as widely and as easily as needed.

Interactive multimedia benefits from the best of both software techniques and conventional media. Used properly, the product feels substantial and extensive, and creates a greater sense of user involvement and control. As a result of this flexibility, one product can provide a range of options for users with different skills, abilities and experiences.

The IVCA's mission is not to teach business the language of multimedia, but to teach multimedia the language of business in order to make relevant this significant and rapidly developing British industry.

The World Wide Web

The World Wide Web has substantial potential for communicating business messages throughout the world. In 1997, there were thought to be 60 million homes and businesses connected to the Internet. By the year 2000, the figure is expected to be 250 million.

Despite the flourishing Web, few companies are maximising the potential of the growing marketplace. Many companies have websites as a passive status symbol, rather than using it as a valuable business accessory. It is no longer enough to have a poorly maintained site; the leading businesses are now using the Web for sales transactions, training programmes and regular staff communications. It is a policy that works.

Business Television

Business television via satellite couples the impact of a 'live' television broadcast with the accurate targeting of satellite technology. Business television is a private network, delivered via satellite from a fixed site to multiple sites throughout the world. Problems of security can be overcome by programme encrypting, and satellite links can be two-way, allowing managers to have immediate access to all of the relevant staff. The speed and precise delivery of message has made business television the fastest growing sector of corporate communication.

Visual communication

The visual communication industry is underpinned by a network of hire and facility companies which provide producers with a rich resource of professional audiovisual services. No two facility companies are identical and each will offer a different combination of technology and experience. Similarly hire companies supply equipment on either a 'dry' or 'wet' hire basis (dry hire is equipment only, wet hire is with technicians to install and operate). Many of the rental companies are also able to offer full-blown technical management services for the staging of events. All should be able to advise on the latest technological developments and the most appropriate equipment to suit the requirements of their clients.

The IVCA is a repository of detailed case studies and examples of best practice gathered from both the producers of visual communication and the associated support industries. Together with its library of members' showreels and award winning products, it can also provide access to over 1500 expert practitioners who have agreed to stand by the Association's code of practice. As such, the Association is a living index of a great British success story.

28

British Design Expertise

by Jeremy Myerson, Consultant, British Design & Art Direction

As North American businesses explore market opportunities in Europe, there are two ways of looking at the prospects. One is to naively treat the entire continent as a single entity – the United States of Europe – which can be approached with a singular business offer undifferentiated from the home market. The other is to adopt a more sophisticated outlook which recognises that the enormous market and lifestyle diversity across Europe requires inside knowledge of the consumer dynamics of different European countries and a more differentiated approach to product and service development.

This is not simply a matter of diligent market research, but extends to the entire proactive process of tailoring your products and services more closely to the needs of European users and communicating benefits effectively through advertising and promotion. The key in all of this is well-targeted design. As Edith Cresson, European Commissioner for Research, Education and Training, recently commented: 'Design is what gives us the edge over our competitors.'

What exactly do we mean by design ? We tend to think of design purely in terms of designed artefacts – products such as cars, laptop computers or posters, for example. But design is a process as well as an outcome, a problem-solving process by which ideas are turned into material things and business strategy is made visible. Design consultants support business primarily in three main areas:

- *product development*, which extends from the generation of new concepts right through to prototyping and production;

- *communication*, which includes all aspects of corporate identity, branding, packaging and multimedia; and

- *environmental design*, which relates to the design of retail and leisure interiors as well as offices and exhibitions.

Whatever business you are in, design consultants can help you reach European consumers through smarter product development, more-focused marketing communications and better service environments. Europe has a long-established design industry, which has emerged from the rich creative and artisan traditions of its different regions, and is characterised by a network of small studios. According to a recent research study by the Netherlands Design Institute, the total European design consulting industry contains nearly 10,000 firms, most of which are highly specialised and employ less than 25 people.

THE UK: EUROPE'S DESIGN LEADER

Within this somewhat fragmented European design scene, one European member state stands out: the UK. The UK is a dominant design player in the region. Today the UK has one of the largest and most sophisticated design industries in the world. Seven out of the world's largest international design consultancies are British and a third of all Europe's design firms are to be found in the UK, an estimated 3,000 firms employing more than 20,000 designers.

Although most of these firms are small, the 100 largest UK design groups in the sector account for nearly three-quarters of the UK design industry's estimated £100 million ($165 million) turnover. These larger groups are most active in working with international clients, including many North American companies, and in developing the reputation of UK design abroad.

The UK design consulting sector is supported by a commercial, educational and governmental infrastructure which is instrumental in encouraging innovation and the development of best practice. For example, the UK has a sophisticated design-management and marketing community within business and industry which increasingly recognises the importance of design as a commercial tool. According to the Netherlands Design Institute, the UK actually spends more on design services annually – $2.4 billion – than any other European country. This figure is even more than the German expenditure on design ($2.2 billion) and nearly one quarter of a total European design spend of just over $10 billion and rising.

Meanwhile the UK's system of design-education and training, which constantly renews the profession's pool of talent, is among the largest and most comprehensive of its type in the world. It ranges from primary and secondary school provision to postgraduate level and continuing professional development. The real competitive edge, however, is to be found at higher-education level, where nearly 200 UK universities and colleges offer around 120 different subjects in art and design.

There are currently more than 62,000 students taking full-time courses in design-related subjects. Every year around one third of Europe's 30,000 design graduates are from the UK design-education system. Design departments in UK colleges and universities are not just producers of professional designers. Many are R&D centres in their own right, developing new skills, techniques and thinking which enrich the UK design industry.

In the context of a symbiotic relationship between design education and the profession, government support is vital. In the UK, the Departments of Trade & Industry, Education & Employment, and Culture, Media & Sport are all playing key roles in supporting the design industry, which has rightly been identified as a vital national resource. Many of the world's most familiar products, brands and environments for such organisations as Nike, Swatch, Philips and Disney have been designed in the UK, although this is not always common knowledge. Did you know, for example, that UK designers were responsible for US systems furniture by Herman Miller, French champagne labels for Moet & Chandon, or the architectural remodelling of the German Reichstag in Berlin? As Prime Minister Tony Blair recently observed: 'the UK was once the workshop of the world. Today we can say with pride that we are the "design workshop of the world" – leading a creative revolution'.

HISTORICAL DEVELOPMENT

Given the current positive commercial, educational and political environment for UK design, how did this position of strength first develop? Although design is largely concerned with envisaging and visualising the future, here it is instructive to look to the past. UK

design has deep historical roots stretching right back to the tradition of craft creativity evident in the stained glass windows, royal regalia, flags, heraldry and tapestries of medieval times.

The true origins of the modern design industry can be traced to the first stirrings of the Industrial Revolution in the mid-eighteenth century, and in particular to the pioneering work of ceramics manufacturer Josiah Wedgwood (1730–95). Wedgwood's family ceramics business was the first in the world to mass-produce goods. It pioneered production techniques and a division of labour that anticipated Henry Ford's model of manufacture by 150 years. Wedgwood used simple, practical design to target a new consumer group, the expanding middle classes. His famous black basalt teapot, for example, was produced to show off the bleached white hands in vogue among women at that time. He also pioneered the use of newspaper advertising.

A century later, following rapid industrialisation and the consolidation of Wedgwood's achievements, the UK could claim the first industrial design consultant of the modern age: Christopher Dresser (1834–1904). From 1862 onwards, Dresser gradually built up a large and thriving freelance practice, designing glass, ceramics, tableware and wallpapers for popular use, and was swiftly able to boast that 'there is not a branch of manufacture I do not design patterns for'.

Dresser can be seen today as an early example of a designer who was commissioned to create new designs specifically to boost sales for a company. Importantly, he laid the practical foundations for the twentieth-century design profession, which became increasingly allied to mass production and mass marketing rather than arts and crafts. When two UK designers, Milner Gray and Misha Black, established the UK's first modern multi-disciplinary design consultancy, Design Research Unit, in 1943, the horizons of the professional designer immediately broadened, a process accelerated by the Pop art and design creativity evident in the UK in the 1960s.

By the 1970s UK design firms had begun to sell their skills overseas, primarily in Europe and North America. In the 1980s and 1990s this trend accelerated with the setting up of global design networks to meet international demand. The creation of the European single market in 1992 was a particular boost to UK designers advising companies from around the world on how to crack the European business scene.

THE ROLE OF D&AD

A key feature of the growth and development of the UK design industry over the past 30 years has been the level of institutional support by professional design bodies in the UK. In particular UK Design & Art Direction (D&AD) has played a highly significant role in supporting British design since it was first set up in London in 1962 by young graphic designers and art directors keen to promote their creative skills.

D&AD today is a professional association and charity working on behalf of the design and advertising communities. Its remit is to set standards of creative excellence, to promote this concept in the business arena and inspire the next creative generation. D&AD has a membership of about 1,300 leading professionals as well as students, colleges and associates. Its most familiar programme is its 'Yellow Pencils' design and advertising award scheme, which attracts more than 14,000 entries worldwide. The best of these are published in the D&AD Annual and CD-Rom, and shown in exhibitions around the world.

High priority is given to D&AD's education programme, with its range of activities focusing on undergraduates, recent graduates and tutors, and popular Student Awards scheme. But there is also a major business-user focus, especially in Europe where, for example, in autumn 1998 D&AD is working with the Department of Trade & Industry to develop an exhibition about creativity in the UK. This exhibition will focus on UK innovation, design and communication in a way which is tailored to the audience's needs. It will itself be an exemplar of culturally sensitive design and will tour key European markets.

DOING BUSINESS IN EUROPE

The expertise of UK design firms – and the activities of D&AD in particular – are significant in the context of the challenges that face North American companies aiming to do business in the Europe of the new millennium. In particular there are three major challenges ahead: technological, economic and environmental.

Rapid advances in technology

The first concerns rapid advances in multimedia technology which have brought moving image, sound and interactivity into the traditional domains of the communication designer. In all areas of business, digital communications, from corporate Web sites to interactive retailing, are changing the way Europeans are working and spending. UK designers are defining many of the new design techniques of the multimedia age. The UK today has 20 Internet hosts per thousand people, twice as many as any other European country. D&AD has introduced a new Interactive Media award in the D&AD Awards, so that business clients can see the most outstanding examples in this important area.

Economic challenges

The second challenge is economic. North American businesses will want any design investment in Europe to deliver a measurable commercial payback. In the past designers have been vague at best about defining in precise financial terms the impact that design decisions make on business performance. However the UK design industry has pioneered many emerging techniques to track and monitor commercial design effectiveness, and D&AD has worked in partnership with such organisations as the Design Business Association and Institute of Practitioners in Advertising, to promote award winners which are not only creatively excellent but also commercially effective. The message is that good design ideas sell, and the success of such well-known brands as Orange, Stella Artois and British Airways reflects this notion.

Ecological challenges

The final challenge for North American firms doing business in Europe is ecological. Europe, especially northern Europe, has much more stringent environmental legislation than other parts of the world. In 1967 there was just one environmental law passed by the EU, and in 1970 just four. By 1994, this had risen to 48. Aware of its own power in specifying and using materials and energy, the UK design industry is at the forefront of the green movement to conserve, reuse and recycle resources. In particular it is working to encourage a more sustainable approach among clients and can offer valuable 'green advice' to companies new to European markets. This is just one of the many benefits US firms can derive from commissioning a UK design consultant.

29

Boxing Clever: UK Offers Packaging Expertise

by Gerry Berragan, Chief Executive, Institute of Packaging

Lateral thinking is at the heart of good packaging technology. The UK packaging industry has put this to good effect and has the enviable reputation of being well advanced in the development of packaging materials, converting techniques, container design, machinery, and transit packaging and logistics.

There is a sizeable and healthy packaging manufacturing base and consequently a strong research and development armoury. UK manufacturers are well aware that packaging should protect and market contents effectively and should never cost more than absolutely necessary to do both jobs well. So economic production, flexibility and sound investment to meet customers' everchanging needs have been paramount in packaging companies' business plans.

To illustrate that in statistical terms, the value of UK packaging materials production is, according to PIRA International, valued at around $13 billion. That represents 1.3 per cent of GDP, a per capita production of $228, and makes packaging the ninth largest industry in the UK – ahead of the pharmaceutical industry, for example. To put it in perspective, it accounts for a healthy share of the total European production of $102 billion and the global figure of $475. The industry employs around 150,000 people.

All sectors are well represented. The figures split into the five main materials as follows:

- paper and board $4.91 billion (37 per cent);

- plastics $3.51 billion (26 per cent);

- metals (ie mainly aluminium and steel cans) $3.24 billion (24 per cent);

- glass $0.73 billion (5.5 per cent); and

- wood $0.73 billion (5.3 per cent).

The industry, following global trends, has become more concentrated in ownership, particularly in those sectors requiring continuing large investment such as paper and board raw materials, plastics, films and metals. This has not only allowed UK-based companies to operate more cost effectively with a far more efficient buying operation, but has also allowed them to provide at least a continental, if not global, approach to multinational customers and give confidence of supply for companies seeking to do business Europe-wide.

In oriented polypropylene film, for example, where barrier developments continue apace to provide solutions for snack foods, confectionery and biscuit packaging, the latest move has seen UCB Films of Wigton acquiring the £50 million Propafilm OPP business from ICI. It has boosted its world tonnage to more than 80,000t. BPI (British Polythene Industries) is another example of an acquisitive company that has grown to become the UK's major force in polythene films supply and David S Smith, a fully integrated paper and board company, has strengthened its base with continental acquisitions.

The UK packaging business is far from being UK-only based or indeed owned, however. In a world of increasing globalisation there is a strong influence from both other European countries and indeed the US. US companies can have confidence that many of the multi-nationals they have dealt with back home are also firmly established in the UK. Crown Cork CMB dominates in the metal-can field. Lawson Mardon, the Swiss-owned food and tobacco packaging supplier, which operates in North America, has a strong UK presence in both flexo and gravure printed films and laminates and cartons.

The other side of the coin is a thriving number of medium-sized companies which come up with innovative solutions to customer needs and design agencies second-to-none in three dimensional and graphics design. Indeed UK packaging designers are recognised as world leaders; many US agencies try to tempt individuals across the Atlantic! Their real strength is an ability to take a brief from the start of a product concept or relaunch and design a package that not only sells its contents on the crowded supermarket shelf, but also takes into account production, filing, ability to run on a line, logistics, ease of use by the consumer and hence create the desire to repurchase.

Take PI Design International, for example. With headquarters in London, it has full service studio offices in Brussels, New York and Cincinnati. A major strength is its facility not only to provide graphic design, but also to create container shapes by translating the computer based design to equipment which produces a solid 3-D model. It combines the skills of brand strategy, graphic and structural packaging design, packaging development and prototyping. Long-term partnerships include Procter & Gamble, Heinz, Kraft Jacobs Suchard, Johnson & Johnson, Shell International, Pepsi Cola and Reckitt & Colman.

Business director Chantal Bordet believes that 'the design business has changed a lot in continental Europe. But it has still a long way to go to catch up with UK standards.' It recently rejuvenated packs for a Scandinavian leading chocolate drink. The O'Boy brand, owned by Kraft, had remained in the same packaging since its introduction some 20 years ago. The brief was to give the product a 1990s feel without losing the brand's distinctive character. In the process, the powdered version was taken out of paper into a composite container of paperboard with a plastic reclosable cap, whilst the concentrated version was launched in a plastic bottle. The brand has an 80 per cent share of the market.

Coleman Planet seeks to be 'global in perspective yet individual in approach'. The Planet design agency is now owned by the US-based Coleman Group. Jacobs' Club brand was staring at relegation from the Premier League of chocolate snacks. Coleman Planet began the design process not simply by looking at the pack design, but started with the bar itself. It redesigned the chocolate coating with the word Club raised in 3D across the bar to give impact and a chunkier impression without increasing the chocolate content. This was followed by a bold graphics statement on the pack. The result was a design that communicated a strong, youthful personality to the brand.

Influences on packaging style have changed dramatically over the last decade. The UK is characterised by the strength of its retailers; that has meant a packaging industry has evolved capable of jumping to it, and fast-tracking total packaging solutions for new brands and FMCG promotions. Demographic change – more single households, the rise in grey purchasing power, and their special needs, the move to healthy eating, and a demand for pack security – has led to expertise in producing innovative designs for easy opening and closing with tamper evidence. Brand protection has meant a call for pack design to foil the copy cats. Package minimalisation in design has reflected concern for the environment coupled with sound economics. To sum up, a pack that stands out, either through graphics, materials and three-dimensional design, or by consumer-friendly design, which uses the minimum of materials, is the goal constantly requested and which UK producers have become accustomed to handling.

Frequently, those most successful packages have been the result of a close development partnership between supplier/designer and end user, something at which the UK company is particularly adept. For example, up to 8,000 hours of nursing time have been saved in the administration of one vaccine, and so been made available for patient care by the use of an innovative labelled syringe developed by pharmaceuticals company Evans Medical and Croydon-based Jarvis Porter Dolphin Ltd. The solution is seemingly simple, yet every detail was thoroughly thought through and called upon extensive research on various materials adhesive combinations. It was recognised as the most innovative pack and awarded a Gold Award in the Institute of Packaging Starpack design awards. A peel-off clear vinyl label not only identifies the vaccine and remains on the syringe for security reasons, but also includes a tear-off portion which is used to transfer the details quickly to the patient's record. Its development has allowed Evans Medical to export its vaccines to 20 countries including in excess of two million to the US. The circumference of the syringe barrel is shorter than the label. This means that the label overlaps. It is designed to adhere to itself so that the perforated transferable portion is in no danger of being torn off accidentally. However, the label surface coating ensures that the adherence from label to label material is less than that of label materials to glass. The nurse doesn't have to prise the portion off with a finger nail or scissors, they simply pull on a raised corner, achieved by a pattern surface release coating.

Strong branding and security of brand were required for Colgate-Palmolive's range of toothpaste and toothbrushes last year. The packaging produced by BPC Taylowe of Maidenhead made extensive use of holographics – a technique at which the UK is a world leader. Real skill was required to protect the hologram on the toothpaste carton so a transparent blue ink was developed. However, the package designed for the toothbrush range not only matched and complemented the carton, it also meant the development of holographic foil blocking to the polyester PETG material used as the pack substrate. A process was developed to allow an increase in pressure on the foil and substrate and thus force the two substances to gel. One problem overcome forced another into the open. PET melts at 70 degrees C and the foil needs a higher temperature to be applied. The solution was seemingly simple but not initially obvious: by using a full sheet covering of foil as an insulator between PET and the heating surface, BPC Taylowe ensured that no PET came in contact with the cylinder.

Although the main consideration of the design brief taken by Rexam Corrugated North East from Flymo for its lightweight lawnmower – the Micro Lite – was protection from damage in transit packaging. Cost savings were also an essential goal, as was the need for the pack to 'sell the product'.

Building on an already strong partnership between the two companies, Rexam and Flymo chose a previously unused pack style for this type of product. Instead of a case with top and bottom flaps that require sealing and a number of separate fittings, a one-piece case was developed with integral fittings. The result was an extremely strong pack with further benefits in logistics and packing. Reduction in component parts meant less materials, and using only one pallet for the delivery of an order has meant a reduction in factory storage space and a tidier production line. Less glue area has meant a cost saving and there are clear environmental benefits.

A five-colour graphic treatment results in good shelf presentation to the case, which also has to stand out against the competition. Cost saving is 23 per cent over the previous pack.

To steal a march on the competition is always the name of the game. By the clever use of thermochromic inks – that is, inks that change colour at different temperatures – Smurfit Labels gave US-owned Sara Lee a winner in its pack for Matey, a children's bubble bath. In what was the first use of these types of inks on sleeves, the label is shrunk around a shaped bottle. Each bottle is in the shape of a character whose face and costume change when the bottle is placed in the bath. One of the inks, thermochromic blue, disappears at temperatures of 25 degrees C.

Sounds simple? Not really. Shrink sleeves have always been printed photogravure using solvent-based inks. Thermochromic inks are water-based and are difficult to dry when printed on heat sensitive shrink film. In addition thermochromic ink can be damaged by solvents used for inks in the other colours of the design. On top of this, the print was difficult to monitor as the heat generated in the print and production made the thermochromic element disappear! Smurfit overcame all these problems and the product has been extremely successful in the market.

30

British Film Production Resources

by The British Film Commission

The British film industry is a powerful and prolific force. The excellence of British production houses and industry professionals has long been recognised, although international recognition of British films is not always consistent. Films such as *Four Weddings and a Funeral* and *The Full Monty* are effective in bringing the British film industry to the forefront of international media and often result in much excitement and speculation about a brave new future. What the British Film Commission (BFC), the industry itself and the Government jointly consider to be the top priority, however, is maintaining our strong international reputation as a production centre and a creative hotspot to ensure that the current successes do not simply result in temporary hype.

Fundamental to this whole mission is the UK Film Commission Network (UKFCN), co-ordinated by the BFC. The BFC was set up to encourage international producers to base their productions in the UK and, with the commissions which comprise the UKFCN, provides support to those filming here by directing them to industry professionals and organisations best suited to their needs. The UKFCN has grown steadily to over 25 offices throughout the UK and concentrates on pro-actively creating business in the UK, providing a comprehensive and specialised service to anyone who is considering making a film in the UK.

Through the Network, producers can gain information, very simply and at no cost, about locations in their particular areas, locally based facility houses, crew, equipment and much more. This offers an unrivalled and impartial service which is indispensable to any foreign producer who is unfamiliar with the UK. An important example is that there is more to the UK than period drama! Although the range of medieval villages, stately homes, castles and waterways is impressive, there is a huge choice of alternative locations on file at all of the regional film commissions, available to foreign producers. For instance, the James

Bond film *Tomorrow Never Dies* used the US Air Force bases at Lakenheath and Mildenhall for its scenes set in Okinawa, Japan, and Stanley Kubrick's *Eyes Wide Shut* for Warner Bros was filmed at the unusual Elvedon Hall, which is built in the sumptuous style of an Indian palace. This is a welcome service for producers, production managers and location scouts, both financially and logistically when planning productions.

There are over a hundred studios throughout the UK ranging from those suitable for small shots to those able to accommodate mammoth sets and post-production. Soho, in London, is also a busy centre for post-production, housing some of the best equipment and facilities in the world. International producers often use their services and experts to create some of the spectacular special effects and/or the soundtrack recordings required for major films, even if the movie was actually filmed abroad. Image-manipulation facilities for commercial and feature production can all be located in less than a square mile as well as at the two largest studios, Pinewood and Shepperton.

The latest example of UK production capabilities in action is the recently released *Lost in Space*, which was shot at Shepperton Studios and post-produced in London. A number of highly specialised special effects and image-manipulation production houses and the animatronics specialist facility, Jim Henson's Creature Shop, collaborated on skills and resources to produce over 500 effects.

The UK has long had a history of producing creative animation work in film, television and commercials, winning international awards annually and Cardiff's animation festival is a 'must-see' fixture for international animation producers. The US-based company DreamWorks – headed by Steven Spielberg, Jeffrey Katzenberg and David Geffen – is currently working with the UK animation Oscar-winning company Aardman Animations on the company's first full length feature, *Chicken Run*. Cambridge Animation Systems based in East Anglia was also chosen by the US company to supply its animation software. The BBC has also just launched the television series *Stressed Eric* in collaboration with the US-based Klasky Csupo.

DreamWorks has not just confined its production interest in the UK purely to the UK's animation sector. Last year it filmed the World War II action feature *Saving Private Ryan,* starring Tom Hanks, here, using production facilities, crew and actors.

The UK production environment is regarded as being highly flexible and competent. The work force is largely freelance, allowing more non-UK producers freedom to employ a wider range of UK professionals and technicians working to the individual production schedule and requirements of a specific project. It is also a proven incentive to foreign producers that the UK has low cost of employment payments, more usually known as fringe costs. Overall, work and pay structures are much simpler, which enables the whole process of transatlantic co-production to be streamlined. At the same time, the studios have long been four-wall facilities, allowing productions to hire in separately crew, technicians and facilities rather than the traditional system where producers used the studios' on-site facilities and work force.

The British Government recognises the importance both economically and culturally that the production industry plays in achieving a positive image for the UK, its industries and its people. This was clearly illustrated by the formation of a joint governmental/cross-industry Film Policy Review Group which identified areas of working practice to be looked at in order to further stimulate investment in all aspects of the film industry, including production, distribution and the marketing of British films to the public both internationally and at home. Most importantly, this initiative showed how the industry and the Government are now more united than ever in providing a clear message about the importance of the UK industry, its assets and talents. The group is taking a longer term view which will see a fundamental strengthening of the whole industry.

The industry is also looking at introducing initiatives in order to formalise and 'reign in' the different strands of film production. This will cover everything from qualifications to distribution. Placed high on the industry's priority list as an initiative to receive additional support is Skillset, the organisation which is funded by the industry to oversee training issues and policies on the introduction of industry standards and qualifications. With a view to the long-term, Skillset seeks to ensure measures of competence for individuals contracted to work on productions and to harmonise qualifications with other European countries.

THE BRITISH FILM COMMISSION

Attracting inward investment, whether in the shape of productions coming to the UK or in building new production facilities, has been the fundamental objective of the BFC. The BFC has always realised the importance of maintaining links with the UK's strongest film production partners and in particular US producers. Initiatives undertaken to achieve this have included a series of inward and outward missions. The BFC's UK awareness visits have provided North American producers with the opportunity to see UK facilities, such as locations and studios, and have resulted in producers returning to the UK with productions such as *101 Dalmations* for Disney, *The Man Who Knew Too Little* starring Bill Murray for New Regency, and *Basil*, starring Christian Slater for Kushner-Locke.

The BFC's key outward mission was the first UK film industry conference to be held in Los Angeles last year, presenting the range of UK film talent and expertise to US professionals. The one day conference bannered 'Framing the Future' brought together UK industry experts and professional advisers and senior US production decision makers to discuss all aspects of film and television production in the UK. The support for this outward mission was provided by the DTI and industry partners.

Synergy between the BFC's strategy and the initiatives proposed by the Film Policy Review Group has most recently occurred with the decision to establish a liaison office in Los Angeles. This will enable the UK film industry to have a first point of contact close to the major studios and production companies.

Whilst US productions are important to the UK industry, they are not the only focus of BFC promotional activity. Maintaining and building relationships with European producers is also important and is undertaken by participating in co-production events, meeting programmes and at international events such as the Cannes Film Festival.

The UK has always held a strategic position in the international film industry as a production partner and a stepping stone between the US and continental Europe. As the world becomes a smaller place in this age of co-production partnerships and industry collaborations, the BFC intends to ensure that the UK plays a central role.

31

Training and Education

by Stefan Stern, The Industrial Society

In recent years, when UK politicians have been pressed to respond to the question, 'What are you going to do to raise the competitiveness of UK companies and their employees?', the handy one-word answer has been: 'Trainingandeducation'.

Motherhood and apple pie have had to move over to make room for Trainingandeducation. The repetition of the word 'training' as the answer to so many of the challenges facing business conceals a somewhat uneven picture of UK business activity. The best UK companies train and develop their employees rigorously, they make a reality of the slogan which declares that 'our people are our biggest asset'. The worst employers do not train enough and poach staff rather than develop their own.

Any US company wanting to know what approach a potential UK partner takes to training should ask for an HR (Human Resources) strategy document, or other statement of intent, plus an indication of annual spend on training. Do employees get 4.5 days of training a year each, which is what the best firms offer, on average (according to Industrial Society figures)? Is at the very least one per cent of the payroll bill being spent on training – again the minimum figure that good employers invest?

Training has long been identified as an area where strategic, co-ordinated action is required if UK employers are to make the most of the talent on offer. But training has also fallen into the politically controversial area where the tradition of voluntarism, that is, proceeding through voluntary action, clashes with some politicians' instinct to legislate to compel employers to act in a certain way. A potted history of the most recent developments in the field of training in the UK reflects this tension between voluntarism and legislation. In 1988 Mrs Thatcher's Conservative government went a long way to overhauling radically the arrangements UK employers had become accustomed to. Industry Training Boards, with levy-raising powers, disappeared, to be replaced by a national network of Training and Enterprise Councils (or TECs – Local Enterprise Companies [LECs] in Scotland). TECs are local, employer-led independent companies contracted to the Secretary of State for Education and Employment. Their purpose is to improve competitiveness by providing training for work and encouraging local enterprise. There are now over 80 TECs in England and Wales, and over 20 LECs in Scotland.

Companies are now *encouraged* to invest in training, but are no longer compelled to do so (as in France, for example). The traditional and widespread apprenticeship model, still prevalent in Germany, has largely disappeared in the UK. In its place stand a series of vocational qualifications, National Vocational Qualifications (NVQs), awarded by colleges of further education, and in theory recognised and accepted by employers as qualifications of value (attainable from level 1 – a fairly modest qualification, to level 5 – regarded by many as equivalent to a university degree). Commitment to on-the-job NVQ training is another sign that UK employers take training and development seriously.

The most widespread and best recognised quality standard for training in the UK is the Investor in People (IiP) award (see Chapter 12). Awarded by the TECs, the IiP award signifies that an employer is offering a high standard of training and development to its employees. After a relatively slow start-up, IiP has now become recognised as an industry-wide standard. Like an ISO quality mark, IiP is regarded by many employers as a minimum sign that a company is worth doing business with. The majority of UK employers now have either IiP or are working towards it – a process which may take up to two years. IiP status has to be renewed at three-yearly intervals, when it is re-assessed by TEC officials.

The UK picture is not, however, an entirely rosy one, in spite of the major efforts and reforms described above. In 1993 the National Advisory Council for Education and Training (NACET) set 'Lifetime Learning' targets for the year 2000, 60 per cent of employees to reach NVQ level 3 and 30 per cent to reach level 4, both of which look unlikely to be met. NACET also stated recently that as many as a third of staff received no training at all, and that NVQs were unheard of in many firms. Now, while the UK, like the US, has experienced several years of growth, the UK economy is running up against severe skills shortages in certain areas, pushing up pay rates and increasing inflationary pressures.

Verdicts are mixed. While employers are happy to have broken free from the days of compulsion, it is not clear that firms are doing enough to train and develop their employees. While NVQs have gone some way to remove the traditional pro-academic bias in the UK and have allowed employers and employees to design mutually beneficial, recognised qualifications, the take-up level has not been high enough.

The changing world of work, with rapidly developing technology, has perhaps outpaced the best-intentioned of employers as to what is necessary in the field of training. Perhaps no compulsory or overly rigid scheme could have risen to the challenge either (see France and Germany). The need to 'upskill' is today very well understood in the UK. The government's Department of Trade and Industry, the sponsor of this book, has published no less than three White Papers (government documents) on competitiveness in recent years, highlighting the need for UK companies to perform. A Darwinian process inevitably takes place, whereby good employers who invest effectively in training are better placed to meet the challenge of competition. Unless a company is planning to compete in a low-wage, low-skill sector, most UK employers accept that the high-skill, high-value-added sectors are where the future lies.

So how should a company train and develop effectively, getting value for money from its investment? The Industrial Society has long argued for better *training needs analysis* and better *evaluation* of training as the answer. Simply put, companies need a very clear picture of what their training need is now and in the immediate future (further down the line is perhaps anybody's guess). Measure how well you are currently doing, benchmark – quality defects, product time to market, customer satisfaction and retention, employee morale and turnover – against competitors. Identify the training needs, invest in them, and measure again after a few months. This proper evaluation of training has delivered value for money for many UK employers, who are controlling their training costs much better than in the past.

The UK training methods, while developing quite fast, still display many traditional characteristics. While CD-Rom and on-line methods are growing in popularity, 'classroom' learning, guided reading and videos are all still popular. Self-managed learning is growing as a concept, whereby individuals are encouraged to design their own learning programmes and are given support for this by their employer. Learning resource centres can be provided to help in this. Training can be better fitted in around the demands of work and also be a complement to it.

The challenge in the UK, as elsewhere, revolves around this issue of developing a *learning culture*. We have all entered the era of lifelong learning, where no employee can feel certain of remaining with the same employer throughout a working lifetime. Employees need to acquire new skills on a continuous basis. Employers have an important role to play in fostering this learning culture, even if, in the UK at least, they are not compelled to. A clever counter-argument would state that employers do indeed face the commercial imperative to train and develop their staff. One special element of the UK employment scene needs to be mentioned in this chapter. After the election of a new Labour government in May 1997, the new administration set about making good its election promise, to get 250,000 unemployed young people back into work – the 'New Deal'. The New Deal has been extended to cover older and long-term unemployed people as well.

The UK, even after several years of healthy growth, still contains many unemployment 'black spots' and indeed probably experiences a much higher level of unemployment than some official figures would indicate. The New Deal is a major undertaking, financed by nearly £4 billion ($6.6 billion) of targeted taxation, to develop new work and training opportunities. Employers have several ways of participating in New Deal, in particular by taking on unemployed people and offering them work and learning opportunities. A £60 ($99) per week subsidy is available to employers for taking somebody on, £75 per week ($124) if the person has been long-term unemployed. While the commitment sought from employers is significant, including the obligation to provide training for new recruits, the early indications are that the New Deal has really tapped in to a large pool of undeveloped and neglected talent. New Deal represents a powerful opportunity for any employer conducting business in the UK.

In the UK the argument for dedicated training has been won. Business people setting up in the UK will find no resistance to the idea that skills levels have to be raised. With the help of networks such as the TECs, colleges of further education, the employment service and its New Dealers, employers should find a welcoming framework of support. Many training providers, not least The Industrial Society, stand ready to provide a service in what is a competitive market.

The new government's reforms, in employment training as well as in social security, place a new emphasis on the value and necessity of work. With low inflation, more or less steady growth and a newly invigorated workforce, the prospects for doing business in the UK have not looked better for many years.

32

Research and Development Plus Skills and Quality

by Invest in Britain Bureau

The UK makes an unbeatable offer to inward investors: high technology, high skills and high quality production. The country is renowned for its research and development, not least in the pharmaceuticals and multimedia industries. Home to the world's leading drug companies, it also leads Europe in biotechnology.

Cambridge, Surrey, Warwick and other universities attract growing numbers of high-tech companies seeking first class expertise. There are now over 50 science parks in the UK with close links to the R&D base in universities, creating clusters of mutually supporting high-tech industries with access to a skilled workforce. Mitsubishi Electric's decision to locate its European R&D centre in digital broadcasting in the UK owed much to Surrey University, where it is based (see below). Science parks are just one of several supportive institutional arrangements for transferring knowledge to private industry.

The world's leading companies choose to conduct R&D in the UK because many of the world's top scientists are from the UK. One such is Dr Simon Campbell, head of the research operations in the UK of US pharmaceutical company Pfizer. In 1997, he became the first non-American to receive the American Chemical Society's prestigious E.B. Hershberg Award for important discoveries in medicinally active substances. Inward investors tend to be among the most technologically sophisticated global companies, both seeking and expecting a skilled workforce in host locations. That is what they can expect in the UK.

In Northern Ireland, Kainos Software Limited, a joint-venture software house between Fujitsu subsidiary ICL and Qubis Limited of Queen's University Belfast, has expanded since 1986 to employ 130 people. Frank Graham, managing director, said: 'Kainos was originally set up to take advantage of the number of skilled computer personnel in Northern Ireland and that is why we have been able to grow so quickly.'

With its high-tech industries, R&D strengths and highly skilled workforce, the UK is a centre for quality production. A study of the world's automotive-supply industry by US management consultancy McKinsey reports that two thirds of the participating UK companies reached the top levels of quality management, 'giving them in total the highest quality level in Europe'. Quality takes many shapes and sizes. For example Coca-Cola Bottlers (Ulster Ltd) has now won Coca-Cola's Quality Excellence Award for ten consecutive years and was also presented with the Northern Ireland Quality Award in 1996/97.

CAMBRIDGE SCIENCE PARK

Cambridge Science Park has been a magnet for inward investment since it opened in 1973. The second company to move into this high-quality 130 acre site was a Swedish firm now owned by Pharmacia. Of the 75 companies on the site, 23 are foreign owned, with parents based in the US, Germany, the Netherlands, France, Sweden, Norway and Japan. Cambridge University is world famous for its scientific research and there are strong links between University scientists and high-tech companies in the park. For example the director of the Toshiba Research Centre, the first strategic research laboratory that Toshiba located outside Japan, is Michael Pepper, professor of physics at the University.

A recent arrival at the site is the US-owned biotech company Innovir Ltd, which synthesises modified oligoneucleotides, targeted at disease-causing genes, or used for genomic or pharmaceutical research. Managing director Nigel Davis said: 'Innovir was drawn to Cambridge because of its proximity to international cutting-edge science and technology.'

Hi-Tech Logistics have extensive experience stretching back over many years of developing and managing total supply chain solutions, starting life as the distribution operation of IBM in the UK. It became an independent business at the end of 1993 as a joint venture between IBM (40%) and Tibbett & Britten PLC (40%) with the employees holding the balance of the shares and quickly made its mark in providing appropriate solutions to solve complex logistics challenges. Its own direct staff, currently some 500 people, deliver the key management, technical and control duties world-wide.

Since its establishment, Hi-Tech Logistics has developed rapidly as a major player in the movement of high technology equipment and won significant new business with a number of blue chip companies. Target market sectors include retail as well as manufacturers and suppliers of telecommunications equipment, electronics, computers, electrical products, hydraulics, optical equipment, medical equipment and light industrial equipment.

We provide a tailored mix from our range of services for each client who experiences a unique service provision specific to each of his/her needs. This service is often provided in a multi-user environment so that our clients enjoy the benefits of dedicated service and multi-user cost effectiveness.

Each of our clients relies on the key element of our Supply Chain Management portfolio which is effective management afforded by the application of high level skills and efficient information and communications technology. Amongst our customers are IBM NCR, ICL, Racal Datacom, Daewoo Electronic Sales, Linn Products, Binatone Telecom, Belkin Components.

In the United Kingdom, we operate from 4 main Operating Centres and use a network of 13 Parts Centres for express deliveries nationwide.

Through our own facilities and those of our partners and sub-contractors, we develop, install and manage operations wherever in the world our clients have a requirement. We have the capacity to operate in every European country and in up to 90 countries world-wide. Our basic country operation usually revolves around a consolidation and cross docking facility, which may or may not be a stocking point for our clients. The key focus is on the application of management and professional logistics skills to deliver excellence in the context of service quality and cost effectiveness for all our customers. We operate in support of both the parts and finished goods supply chain, prior to and after manufacturing and / or sales.

One of Hi-Tech Logistics' key strengths is the expertise of its IT professionals, who can develop contract logistics solutions that balance clients' need for both service and cost efficiency. The whole supply chain management process is controlled by a computerised logistics management system which ensures complete product and order traceability.

We operate a high speed distribution service for urgently needed products. We can despatch goods in as little as 15 minutes from the receipt of order, and have sophisticated systems for an extensive range of pick, pack & despatch activities for product merging and order assembly.

The company is able to consolidate components and assemble products for delivery to the end user. In addition, it offers inspection and testing, condition and quality reporting, re-badging, configuration and customising services.

We can deliver anywhere, to warehouses, offices or individual addresses in bulk, or as a single item to the point of need, and we have trained personnel who can install pre-configured equipment. We take away unwanted packaging for reuse as environmentally sensitive recycling.

Our ability to offer full product refurbishment facilities in-house as well as a comprehensive repair facility allows us to offer unique total supply chain solutions.

Our services are provided in accordance with the requirements of BS EN ISO 9001. The Quality Management System relating to the design, development, installation, and maintenance of Hi-Tech Logistics application software for its distribution activities has received BSI TickIT certification. TickIT is a DTI quality initiative aimed at the software and IT industry.

'Ceiling' the finishing touches on Europe - from Britain

On first glance at the map, the UK might not appear the epicentre of Europe, but closer scrutiny reveals it to be ideal springboard for companies looking to establish themselves in the European market.

One US company, Armstrong Building Products, which manufactures ceilings, and which has European headquarters in the UK, along with two manufacturing plants, is able to treat the distribution of its UK-manufactured products throughout Europe as if they were domestic movements.

It has achieved this through a close working relationship with P&O Trans European, a US$ 1.3bn turnover pan-European logistics specialist earning some 70 per cent of its revenues outside the UK in the wider European market and employing some 7,400 people through the continent.

P&O Trans European is no stranger to the demanding requirements of multi-nationals and ranks companies of the stature of Ford, General Motors, Esso, Reckitt & Colman, Procter & Gamble, Compaq, Dow Chemicals and 3M among its customers.

Armstrong Building Products is part of the US$5.2

bn turnover Armstrong World Industries Inc, has had a presence in the UK since 1925. "I would say that the UK is a natural stepping-stone into Europe for US companies," remarks logistics manager building products Europe, Nick Buckingham.

"One clear factor is the language and possibly there is more similarity in the UK and US in culture than there is between the UK and some of Continental Europe. Society, business methods and politics are aligned," he says.

The UK has also historically offered a fairly low cost base, and there's another benefit: "For distribution outside Europe, the UK is perhaps one of the best places to be and shipping rates from the UK to the Middle East or Asia for instance tend to be more cost-effective than from other places in Europe," says Buckingham. A significant percentage of Armstrong Building Products' production is UK based, with a large proportion of this production being channelled into the wider European market.

The building products division has been manufacturing in Newcastle's Team Valley for the last 50 years and more recently at Stafford in the Midlands, supplying specialist ceiling or interior product distributors with a range of ceiling tiles and ceiling tile support systems.

"Armstrong Building Products actually started in the Team Valley and then built a ceiling plant in Germany and other plants in Europe were acquired. We literally see the UK as part of a European network," explains Buckingham.

"This is now particularly relevant since the borders of Europe came down on 1st January 1993 opening a whole new chapter in distribution," points out Nick Scott-Gray, the Armstrong Building Products account manager at P&O Trans European. He urges prospective clients entering the European market via the UK to think not simply about distribution, or simply about manufacturing, but a combination of both, taking into consideration quality and cost of labour, location of raw materials and key markets and local infrastructure.

Taking all that on board, and with the use of innovative pan-European logistics services, the English Channel/North Sea need not prove such an obstacle, as Armstrong Building Products has discovered.

For five years P&O Trans European has ensured that Armstrong Building Products never feels on the periphery of Europe when it comes to getting its products in place, on time, in good condition and at competitive cost.

Armstrong Building Products has been rationalising its supplier base and transport/logistics is no exception. P&O Trans European has remained a core player. "They have proven themselves the most suitable and more European than a lot of distribution companies," declares Armstrong Building Products' logistics manager.

"P&O Trans European actually started moving our products from our UK plant to the Continent and now moves probably 90 per cent of inter-plant, inter-distribution centre activity," he adds.

A number of factors contributed to the successful involvement. "One was our ability to offer a total integrated and pan-European logistics solution," explains Scott-Gray. "Armstrong Building Products was used to dealing with lots of different hauliers for different routes but we can offer interchangeability on trailers and can line up ten trailers on their site and allow them to load to wherever they want and we'll deliver," he adds.

"Our northernmost port is Teesport, not far away from Team Valley, Armstrong Building Products' main

UK site, and we make it cost-effective on haulage costs." The ability to handle volumes, cope with peaks and troughs and offer the size of fleet and wide range of logistics services were also key.

Armstrong Building Products' sites are in Germany (Munster), the Netherlands (Groningen) and France (Pontarlier and Valenciennes near Lille) and involve the movement of significant full-load, line-haul units each year with P&O Trans European - both to/from the UK and between those mainland centres. The line-haul conduits from the UK are the P&O North Sea Ferries services operating between Teesport and Rotterdam in the Netherlands and Belgium's Zeebrugge.

Products are carried between plants in special curtain-sided trailers holding 40,000 sq ft of ceiling, along with some direct-to-customer shipments, particularly to Ireland where P&O Trans European group companies have a wealth of experience.

Logistically, companies can manufacture in the UK to tight deadlines with no worries about keeping their mainland European distributors effectively replenished. Success is down to synchronisation and co-operation. Suspended ceilings are probably the last part of a construction project to get into a new or refurbished building, and with inventory reductions in vogue, construction companies are understandably reluctant to hold unnecessary stocks. They are equally reluctant to keep workers waiting for the goods. The balance has to be just right and the pressure is always on.

E-mail between the two companies helps keep all parties informed on progress. "We know exactly what the timing requirements are and we work to those and we know when we are going to receive deliveries," explains Buckingham. "These expectations are built into what we promise to our customers down the line." A 48-hour transit from manufacturing plant in the UK to Armstrong Building Products' mainland plants is a normal expectation in the Armstrong Building Products/P&O Tran European relationship, which has intensified over the last two to three years.

Armstrong Building Products' operation is cost-driven and demands the flexibility to move production around European plants as the market dictates. Pan-European logistics, much vaunted but in practice still a fledgling concept for most operators, is essential.

To a company establishing a base in the UK, P&O Trans European has an extensive European coverage, both in terms of hardware and skill. Among service elements are full and part load truck services and group roll-on/roll-off ferry services to Europe from the UK ports of Teesport, Hull, Felixstowe, Dover and Portsmouth.

There are no less than 190 company-owned sites across Europe, comprising transport, warehousing and distribution centres, and, including operations with exclusive partners in southern Europe, the number of locations rises to 260. Some 8 million sq ft of warehousing is operated.

The portfolio includes the ability to hold stock throughout Europe, or centralise stock holding and top-up using its substantial resource of 10,000 road transport units.

P&O Trans European permeates every corner of the continent with traditional strengths in Benelux, Germany and the central industrial belt encompassing Northern France, Northern Switzerland and Northern Italy, and in emerging Eastern and Central European markets such as Poland, the Czech Republic and Hungary where warehousing and distribution facilities have been established. The company offers various sizes of containers and can meet the increasing expectations placed on rail transport through its own fleet of railroaders for road/rail combination, along with the essential block train services from Northern France to Spain and Italy and from North-West Europe to Poland and the Czech Republic and regular services with Austrian train operator OBB, as well as the Rhenania Intermodal barge service using the environmentally-friendly inland waterways.

Its range of container and swap-body equipment should prove ideal for these longer distances where rail is advantageous on cost.

Further afield, the services of a sister-company, P&O Global Logistics, are on hand to facilitate inbound goods from all over the world.

The gamut of P&O Trans European's logistics services can smooth the path of companies setting out on their UK/European quest and valuable advice is at hand to set the cornerstone of effective operation by designing an individual solution based on the locations of customers, the frequency of required deliveries and quantities.

That could mean consolidating consignments centrally in the UK on behalf of customers to route more cost-effectively through to mainland Europe, working alongside customers on their premises in order to move closer to the production on a day-to-day basis, constantly improving transportation

arrangements and overall lead times and costs, or carrying out inventory and supply chain management with full track and trace visibility through high level of systems integration or exchange of EDI messages.

As an example of this partnership approach, Scott-Gray recently spent six months at Armstrong Building Products' locations evaluating all processes involved in the distribution interface. A number of recommendations were made, including the setting-up of a central desk in Germany to handle all Armstrong Building Products enquiries for movement requirements anywhere in Europe.

"That gives us better control and reduces Armstrong Building Products' telephone calls and administration," says Scott-Gray.

Other specific service components for Armstrong Building Products include customisation of trailers for maximum cargo protection and load volumes. Ceiling products are not the easiest of cargoes to handle; one damaged tile could put an entire ceiling project in jeopardy.

As further testament to the close partnership between the two companies five trailers have been liveried in Armstrong Building Products colours and logo and dedicated to this contract.

Yet further co-operation is possible. There has already been an increase in direct-to-customer deliveries and P&O Trans European is keen to offer Armstrong Building Products wider logistic choices in the European market, including storage and secondary distribution - especially as Europe continues to 'grow'.

"We have been doing investigative work over the last two years, specifically looking at Central and Eastern Europe," reveals Buckingham "We haven't made any decisions yet but we have been looking at the different options and once we reach capacity on our network of distribution centres we would look very seriously at the type of relationship."

There are impressive successes on which to build. P&O Trans European has helped Armstrong Building Products to keep its freight rates competitive in an increasingly competitive market, admits Buckingham. There are other factors too. "It is the support the company has given us as we have become more European," he says. "P&O Tran European has been happy to look at us as a European organisation and that has made its overall offer attractive to us."

Is Europe Without Boundaries a Dream?

Probably not when you have every corner of Europe covered. And can offer an integrated logistics network of 190 offices and depots. With a commitment to customer satisfaction in the European market. It's total service - and it has no boundaries.

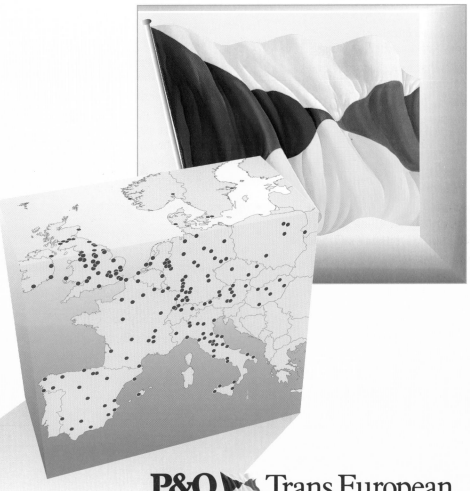

P&O Trans European

Peninsular House, 11/13 Lower Brook Street, Ipswich, Suffolk, IP4 1AQ England
Telephone +44 (0) 1473 581234   Facsimile +44 (0) 1473 581299

ONE NAME, ONE EUROPE

Cambridge Science Park forms the nucleus of a cluster of high-tech industries. There are currently over 1000 advanced-technology firms in the Cambridge area and the proliferation of biotechnology companies is Europe's highest concentration in this dynamic new sector. In 1997, US software giant Microsoft invested £60 million ($100 million) in establishing a basic research lab at Cambridge University. Microsoft's chief technology officer, Nathan Myhrvold said: 'Our goal with this research lab is to create a home for those world-class researchers based in Europe who want to develop innovative new technologies and have an impact on the lives of millions of people around the world'. In addition, Microsoft announced a £10 million ($16 million) investment programme in small Cambridge-based technology companies to help fund growth in the UK IT industry.

Pfizer

In November, 1996, US pharmaceuticals giant Pfizer opened a new £35-million European R&D building at Sandwich in south east England. It forms part of a total capital expenditure of £300 million over the past five years. Pfizer has also more than doubled its R&D spending since 1990, with over £200 million spent in the UK in 1996 alone.

Such investments have been made because of the success of UK scientists at Sandwich, who have discovered three of Pfizer's most successful products. One of them, amlodipine, used to treat angina and hypertension, is the company's largest selling product ever, with sales of £1.2 billion ($2 billion) in 1996. The other two are doxazosin, used to treat cardiovascular diseases, and fluconazole, used for life-threatening fungal diseases. Since Pfizer's UK operations began in 1954, its Sandwich site has grown to employ over 1500 scientists. In 1997 the company won its fourth Queen's Award, its second for Export Achievement.

Several of seventeen new pharmaceuticals in the final stages of development were discovered at Sandwich. They include a treatment for migraine, an anti-fungal for serious infections, a treatment for heart failure and a new class of broad-spectrum agents to treat cardiac arrhythmias.

Mitsubishi

Mitsubishi Electric's decision to make the UK its European R&D centre in digital broadcasting technology marks a further vote of confidence. The new Visual Information Laboratory is located in the Surrey University Research Park, Guildford. The lab intends to forge close links with the university and its strong research teams in image processing and multimedia technologies.

It is developing the technology for products to emerge from digital broadcasting and the resultant convergence of broadcasting and computing. Mitsubishi's prototype products include digital satellite set-top boxes, a 40-inch digital-plasma-display TV panel, a slim-line digital still camera and an Internet TV, incorporating a Web browser within a widescreen TV.

At the opening in January 1997, Dr Toshio Itoh, global head of Mitsubishi Electric's R&D, highlighted three reasons for the investment:

- volume of existing research

- Surrey University's 'outstanding results in practical applications, including image processing, with an open door policy towards companies'

- the cluster of firms engaged nearby in information, communications and broadcasting technologies.

33

Why the UK is the Call Centre Capital of Europe

by the Invest in Britain Bureau (IBB)

IBM was among several inward investors announcing plans for new or expanded pan-European call centres in the UK in 1997. Its help centre at Greenock supports some 2000 customers a day in 16 European countries and focuses on complex technical support for dealers and large corporate customers. The centre is building up to 750 agents. Polaroid Europe also announced plans for an international business centre in Glasgow to consolidate all international customer-service activities in Europe, Africa and the Middle East on one site. It will build to a workforce of 150 over three years.

Florida-based Alamo Rent-a-Car chose Brighton for its restructured pan-European reservations centre and now employs more than 100 multilingual agents. Kingston Technology, the Japanese-owned California memory chip maker, launched its European customer-service centre at Sunbury on Thames. Its 150 staff will manage European logistics, provide free multilingual technical support, and coordinate European sales and marketing activities from a new 40,000-square-foot site.

Following a major new contract with American Express, telemarketing giant Matrixx Marketing of Cincinnati expanded its Newcastle call centre, specialising in out-sourced telephone marketing, to increase sales, lower costs and improve customer service for major companies. The US's SITEL Corporation acquired the UK's leading telebusiness bureaux, the Decisions Group and the Mitre Group, with a total of 1330 agents.

Development of the UK call centre market has been driven by growth in financial services, software companies, airlines, hotel groups, car rental firms and others. There are over 4000 call centres in the UK, a growing number of them pan-European. Early liberalisation of UK telecommunications and consumer acceptance of the teleculture environment were the important drivers, as were flexible working practices and the availability of multilingual speakers.

A 1997 report by the consultancy Datamonitor Technology Practice predicted that the UK would easily lead among European countries in the rapid growth in call centres through the year 2001. It had 123,200 agents or 45.6 per cent of the European total and was expected to have more than 250,000 by the year 2001, retaining a clear lead for the forecastable future. The UK has over 150 local, regional and national public telecommunications operators, around half of them cable companies, and costs have been among the world's cheapest. In 1996, the equivalency rules which had limited international simple resale services to certain routes were lifted. Lease-line capacity can now be provided on any route.

1997 saw the launch in the UK of the first diploma in call centre management outside North America, on behalf of the Call Centre Management Association (CMA), Europe's first professional body of its kind, which was set up in 1995. The diploma – equivalent to a post-graduate qualification – requires students to attain three certificates in call centre management, business strategies and resource management.

Spokesman Roy Bailey explained: 'A main function of our professional body is education and there is a need to address formal qualifications as the call centre industry continues to grow. A management diploma in telecommunications has existed for some years but this does not take into account the marketing and people-management aspects required to operate call centres. The new diploma will fill this gap.'

IBB sponsored one of the first London-based 'Implementing and Managing Pan-European Call Centres' conferences in summer 1996 and has been participating in a full programme of major international call centre conferences in Europe and North America.

Lucent Opens the Gateway to Europe's Communications Revolution

As the barriers to telecommunications competition are rolled back across the European Union, customers are demanding more and suppliers are challenged to provide increasingly elegant solutions. Lucent Technologies has already built a highly successful business presence in this environment by delivering communications to organisations enabling them to deliver quality service to their customers.

Lucent Technologies - a $27 billion company created in 1996 - is dedicated to providing organisations with the most innovative communications solutions. With Farnborough as its head office in the UK and Ireland, Lucent Technologies Business Communications Systems (BCS) develops, manufactures, markets and services advanced voice and multimedia communications solutions, including call centres, private branch exchanges, keysystems, and voice processing systems for businesses worldwide.

The company's portfolio of solutions has been designed with a clear vision of future communications development and with an understanding of the convergence of telecoms, computing and information technology. Lucent's leadership in the call centre market demonstrates this approach. The company's extensive research identified that customers wanted built-in flexibility to match the evolving requirements of their businesses. Lucent responded with the DEFINITY® Call Centre, an expandable system that can be configured as required. This approach has succeeded - an independent study last year by Dataquest showed that Lucent is the number one supplier in the high-end call centre market and has now established itself as market leader across Western Europe.

Lucent is also at the forefront of new developments in telebusiness and, with a predicted 35% of all call centre access coming from the internet by 2000, has an established internet call centre product in the market. This allows agents to manage email enquiries, talk to customers via an internet connection and share product and service information on web pages simultaneously - all with the management support and measurability of a standard call centre environment.

Messaging has also been an area of significant growth for Lucent, reflecting the dominant business trends of mobility, collaborative working and customer care. In the UK alone, just 12 years ago there were less than 1,000 voice mail systems, today there are over 15,000 - and more than 50% of these have been installed in the last three years. Lucent has a 35% share of this market worldwide and offers a wide range of products including platforms that are able to deliver messages across different communications media - for example voice mails that are deliverable as internet messages and faxes that can be converted into voice mails.

The increasingly business-critical nature of communications services for corporations has led to many requests for Lucent to supply its expertise as well as its products. Through its Services division Lucent now provides dedicated technical support, system health and security audits, project management for system integration and disaster recovery services.

Additionally, Lucent offers a Managed telephony Services option for those organisations who wish to focus their investments and resources on their own core competencies.

Lucent's product portfolio does not only address the needs of larger corporations. For medium-sized businesses, Lucent launched the groundbreaking DEFINITY® ProLogix™ Solutions last year. The DEFINITY ProLogix delivers Lucent's proven and advanced communications technology at an affordable price for medium-sized companies. Mindful of customer demand for scaleability, Lucent designed the DEFINITY ProLogix to serve

from 40 to 400 stations and its flexibility extends to the system's features, which are also upgradable. A set of Application Starter packages has been designed for growing businesses that want to sample a feature, cost-effectively, before choosing to add its full capacity later on. The ProLogix Starter packages include Automatic Call Distribution (ACD), Networking, System Administration and Wireless features.

For smaller enterprises and home offices, Lucent has applied the same "customer first" philosophy by producing the new EuroGeneris keysystem. Designed to allow businesses to expand from two to 128 extensions, the EuroGeneris provides unlimited call distribution options. Calls can be routed to an individual, a whole department, or central switchboard. With an eye on the requirements of the smaller business, installation of the EuroGeneris is simple and its easy-to-follow instructions make it operational with minimal training, while built-in features enable customers to monitor and manage calling costs smoothly.

Lucent understands the importance of offering all sizes of organisations the benefits of the latest advances in communications technology. Whether the requirement is for a call centre, telephone and messaging system, or support services, Lucent consistently demonstrates a world-class ability to harness technology to meet customers' evolving business requirements.

Part 5
Business Locations in the UK

AMERICAN AND CANADIAN COMPANIES SCORE AT ASMEC

The importance of minimising risk and maximising resources cannot be stressed enough, and that's a key market advantage that the Asmec Centre delivers to every client. The Asmec Centre is unique - it's a high tech serviced office complex established in the centre of Bracknell in the Thames Valley specifically to house and assist UK subsidiary companies of American and Canadian businesses moving into Europe.

Set up by David Janes, an executive with experience of working in the IT industry both sides of the Atlantic, the Asmec Centre offers 24,600 sq ft of prestigious, high tech office space. The individual offices can accommodate from 1-25 staff, and clients have use of four luxuriously furnished, and specially equipped conference and board rooms.

EASE THE TRANS-ATLANTIC TRANSITION

The whole team at Asmec, however, prides itself on extending the service element of its business to the extreme. Not satisfied with providing fast, flexible, short term leases on prestigious offices, the Centre goes out of its way to ease the pain of the trans-Atlantic transition. The team will line up meetings with consultants qualified to take companies into Europe - from accountancy, tax, marketing and legal advisors, to head-hunting and executive placement agencies. "We make a point of finding out exactly what each company wants and where it stands in the procedure of setting up a base over here", comments Asmec David Janes. "We make all the introductions and , in short, take away the hassle. We also understand that American and Canadian businesses operate in a completely different timezone, and the UK subsidiary executives by necessity have to work late ... so we work late". This comment comes from the heart. Janes had a enquiry on the evening of one December 23rd from a canadian company wanting to set up a Uk operation between Christmas and the New Year. Their needs were completely satisfied. In fact a company could be up and running within an hour.

Asmec, however, really scores with US and Canadian companies because of its investment in technology. Located as it is in 'Software City' in the centre of Britain's 'silicon Valley', the Centre is well ahead of other centres in the provision of leading edge technology services to its customers.

ISDN

Even at the time of its launch back in 1993, Asmec was the first business centre to introduce voicemail and digital, programmable telephone handsets for its clients. Since then it has consistently beaten other centres by being the first, for example, to introduce ISDN-2 per desk, so that all clients can have access to high speed data transfer facilities. As the majority of its 54 clients are UK subsidiaries of US, Canadian or European companies, the large majority in the IT industry, this facility is critical.

THE INTERNET

Both high speed large bandwidth and low speed internet connection services are now part of Asmec's standard offering. For high speed connection, Asmec has installed an on-site router which connects directly via a dedicated large bandwidth pipe to a main computer maintained by VAS-NET, an internet service provider. This service allows unlimited use for a single monthly payment. The comprehensive internet access package offered by Asmec extends to include the provision of e-mail, web site space, creation and maintenance, and domain name registration.

CONSULTANCY

Not content with providing the hardware and software products necessary to facilitate this level of service, Asmec has now gone one-step further to add even more value for its clients. With the appointment of a dedicated IT/ Telecomms Manager, the company is now able to add to its services with the provision of technical consultancy skills. Network maintenance and technical back-up are now utilised by several businesses within the Centre.

THE FUTURE

But even with all these technical commitments, David Janes is still looking for ways to take Asmec, and its clients into the next Millennium.

Video conferencing is currently being installed, but Janes considers that to be a standard offering. Asmec is also introducing, in the very near future, branded telephone charge cards, which will enable tenants to make calls from anywhere in the world, simply have the cost of the call charged to their monthly bill. Currently, Asmec can provide mobile telephones for its clients, but is keenly awaiting the next development of DECT telephones which can be used in and around the office as normal internal phones, but which can also be taken off-site and used as mobile phones.

Another innovation is the availability of short or long term rentals on equipment needed by growing companies such as multimedia Pentium PC's and laptops, modern and network cards, colour printers and LCD projectors. Companies can even hire mobile exhibition stands. All these facilities reduce the need for capital investment by both small and inward investment companies.

In conclusion Janes adds; "Business centre are not about just renting out furnished office space, but providing a full high-tech service that enables the clients to focus on the key issues of their business, such as sales, growth and profitability".

ΛSMEC
CENTRE

34

Business Locations in the UK

ENGLAND

Competition for inward investment within Britain is heating up as regions attempt to market the various advantages of their respective regions. This section looks at some regions at the forefront of attracting inward investment.

The Cherwell District Council based in the towns of Banbury and Bicester is a strategic location with easy access to London, the West Midlands and the UK motorway network. Since 1992 1000 new jobs have been created per year and 75 acres of land have been developed for employment purposes (there is more than 200 acres of development land still available). There are already a number of overseas firms set up in the area including DeBoer Structures of the Netherlands and Schenck Automation Systems Ltd, Mannesmann Dematic and Hella Manufacturing, all from Germany. Clustering within a 50 mile radius are component manufacturers, Formula One race teams, World Rally Champions, IndyCar manufacturers, UK Touring Car teams and Formula 3000 and 500cc motorcycle competitors. The food industry is also well represented.

The major benefit of Essex is its huge pool of labour with the second greatest concentration of employed residents in the UK. Set strategically between the two fastest growing regions in the UK – the South East and East Anglia – it has an excellent communications structure and a broad-based economy. This diversity is a source of great strength as less dependence means the region has more resilience during lean periods. In a recent survey of 700 Essex companies, 45 per cent of respondents anticipated the need to recruit new staff in the near future.

Bolton has bounced back from the demise of its traditional cotton industry, helped by having an adaptable workforce with a strong work ethic, a range of leisure options and an excellent transport infrastructure providing a 'total work environment'. In addition the Bolton City Challenge is a private/public partnership which aims to create opportunities for investment.

Derby is the centre of an easily accessible transport infrastructure. It has a diverse economy centred upon its engineering excellence. It also has a highly skilled workforce, a competitive cost of living and Derby Marketing, a centralised source of information for businesses seeking to locate in the area.

Brighton and Hove has a large pool of skilled labour culled from the two universities. 8000 students graduate every year. It has a vibrant business culture with the accent on creative and technology sectors – the area has a full ISDN network. It also has some of the lowest property and operating expenses in the South East.

Guernsey is not just a finance centre – manufacturing and non-financial services make up 10 per cent of the island's export earnings. It has a unique position with a stable government free of party politics which ensures companies can plan for the future with confidence.

So UK regions are competing hard for investment and each offer their own significant advantages for businesses seeking to relocate.

SCOTLAND

World-class companies are investing in a world-class location as investors take the high road to Scotland.

Results from 1996/97 show the Scottish Enterprise Network attracted 86 inward investment projects involving planned investment of more than £3.1bn. Scotland recently won the UK's largest inward investment by Hyundai, who are now on site with an investment totalling £2.4bn. The completed semi-conductor plant will ultimately generate 2000 jobs. This is just one of a number of American and Pacific Rim companies investing in the north. Motorola last year completed a £250m expansion of its Scottish semi-conductor plant and now employs 2500 people.

The Scottish Enterprise Network has a powerful package of financial assistance to support business growth and enhance investment returns. A comprehensive database of Scotland's commercial and industrial property is being developed to provide market information on available floor space for companies, investors and developers.

Clarkmannanshire Council has a central location less than an hour's drive away from Glasgow and Edinburgh, plenty of space set in an area packed with beauty, history and top-class business accommodation.

CHERWELL – NORTH OXFORDSHIRE

There's a well-founded confidence about the business community in Cherwell, North Oxfordshire. It's an air of success that dates back to the early 1990s and the opening of the M40 motorway.

The area, based on the towns of Banbury and Bicester, became a strategic location for businesses wanting easy access to London, the West Midlands and the UK motorway network . . . and it seized its opportunity readily.

Since 1992, a number of national and international companies have been attracted to North Oxfordshire, generating 1000 new jobs a year. Some 75 acres of land have been developed for employment use, and a new spirit of vibrancy has brought similar growth and prosperity to long-established businesses in the area.

Small wonder that North Oxfordshire's economy is improving faster than almost anywhere else in the South East. With well over 200 acres of development land still available, the area offers virtually unrivalled opportunities to acquire prime, high visibility sites close to key motorway junctions.

Away from the M40, there's plenty to reinforce the upbeat feel of an area poised to be at the heart of 21st century prosperity.

In the thriving town centre of Banbury, historic 18th century properties provide an elegant streetscape and are a top choice for professional firms seeking accommodation of character. At the opposite end of the town, the Castle Quay centre is set to become a shoppers' paradise with 18,580sq m of retail space with such names as Debenhams, BhS, Woolworths and the Burton Group. In all, the £80 million centre, bordering the Oxford canal, will provide 30 new shopping units and 1400 parking spaces.

Bicester, a 'shopping village' which opened in 1995, is currently attracting more than three million visitors a year. With tourist destinations such as Oxford, Blenheim Palace, Woodstock, Warwick and Stratford on its doorstep, the village regularly attracts around 40 coaches a week, 70 per cent of which are international. The rest of its customers are drawn from an affluent catchment area stretching to a 70-mile radius.

On the A34 to the south of Bicester, there are plans for a £20m leisure complex which would include a multiplex cinema, ten-pin bowling alley, hotel, restaurants and pubs.

Linking, surrounding and almost 'gift-wrapping' these bustling commercial centres is the rolling Oxfordshire countryside, with its picturesque villages, quiet country lanes and meandering waterways, all of which contribute to a much-envied environment where quality of life assumes a natural importance.

The North Oxfordshire success story didn't just happen – it had to be worked at. The Economic Development Unit at Cherwell District Council liaises closely with its partners, the Cherwell-M40 Investment Partnership, to advise and assist companies considering locating to the area.

Help available includes:

- information on commercial sites and premises;
- assistance with planning and development issues;
- tailored relocation 'packages';
- specific information on the local economy and the North Oxfordshire area in general.

The Partnership is also keenly aware of the need to maintain a training network to meet future needs and has a close working relationship with the Heart of England Training and Enterprise Council, local universities and colleges, and the Chambers of Commerce.

Perhaps the most telling testimony to North Oxfordshire's pre-eminence is provided by those industries and individual companies which have already decided to make the area their 'home'.

Increasingly these reflect a growing international status. De Boer Structures of Holland chose Banbury for their UK headquarters and have enjoyed phenomenal growth ever since. Germany is represented by Schenck Automation Systems Ltd, Mannesmann Dematic, and Hella Manufacturing.

Elsewhere Alcatel Network Systems and Bertrand Faure Limited wave the flag for France, while Switzerland, Korea and the US also feature in the 'who's who' of the North Oxfordshire business community.

The motor industry is particularly well represented. Close links already exist with major car manufacturers like Rover, Jaguar and Renault, while Aston Martin's runaway success, the DB7, is manufactured in Bloxham, just two miles from Banbury.

The food industry is also well represented and Kraft Jacob Suchard, one of the area's biggest employers, has announced a £1.5million update to its 1960s-built coffee processing plant.

A very important contact!

Bicester Park Distribution Centre, which has planning permission for a rail link to the Oxford-Bletchley freight line, has already attracted Tibbet and Britten, which distributes Mars confectionary products, and Bibby Distribution. A further 28.2 acres is available offering serviced plots ranging from 1 to 12.6 acres.

Elsewhere there is growing interest from high-growth, knowledge-based new technology firms and parallel proposals for a new Innovation Centre to encourage research and development facilities in the area.

Cherwell, North Oxfordshire, is geared up for the businesses of tomorrow . . . but you could be part of it today.

ESSEX, THE BUSINESS COUNTY

Essex is known as the business county and it's a reputation that it richly deserves. The county offers a number of very real advantages to businesses operating within its borders and promises a great deal of potential for healthy growth. In terms of both population and land area, Essex is one of the largest counties in the UK. In fact, with over 711,000 of its residents in employment, Essex can boast the second greatest concentration of employed residents in the UK. In keeping with the varied nature of the county's business base, this workforce possesses a very diverse range of skills and has shown both adaptability and the enthusiasm to learn new ones.

Its location could hardly be better. Sharing its western border with the capital, Essex is set strategically between the two fastest growing regions in the UK – the South East and East Anglia. This, together with its excellent communications infrastructure, promises business in Essex easy access to very lucrative markets in the UK plus those of continental Europe and the rest of the world.

The circumstances have combined to ensure that Essex has a very broad-based economy. The county's most significant business sectors are currently electronics, rubber and plastics, paper, print and publishing, construction, financial and business services, wholesale distribution, retailing, services and entertainment. Beyond these there's a host of other types of industry and commerce thriving within the county's business community. This diversity is a source of great strength. Since the county doesn't depend on just a handful of major industries for its livelihood and its jobs, Essex is very much more robust in its ability to survive within a lean business and economic climate and is in an ideal position to make the most of a bullish economy.

It has a number of other advantages too, as a glance at our 'Top Ten' will confirm.

The Essex top ten:

1. **Market location**
   On London's doorstep and only a short distance from Europe, it couldn't be better.

2. **Accessibility**
   Stansted (London's third airport), Southend Airport, Harwich Port, Tilbury Freeport and an extensive road and rail network.

3. **Infrastructure**
   A well developed and supported business community with great transport, services and distribution already in place.

4. **Able workforce**
   A large and adaptable workforce with a whole range of skills and abilities.

5. **Development potential**
   Ideally located land and buildings ready for development and/or immediate occupation. Regional Selective Assistance grants are available in certain areas.

6. **Housing**
   Variety and quality – take your pick from rural cottages, 'old English' villages, ancient and modern towns and some of England's newest and most exciting high quality developments.

7. **Quality of life**
   With picturesque countryside, bustling seaside towns, historic towns and much more, Essex has plenty of things to see and do.

8. **Education**
   Consistently excellent education offered by a wide range of schools plus extensive university research and business support.

9. **Continuing growth**
   Essex growth is dynamic and very evident, as you would expect in the business county.

10. **Services to business**
    The Essex Investment Office can provide all the information you need on the opportunities and support available to business working in Essex and those planning to relocate to the county.

This stability together with its strategic significance has ensured that the county remains a net attractor of businesses and that its existing companies continue to

thrive. In a recent survey of 700 Essex companies, 45 per cent of respondents anticipated the need to recruit new staff in the near future.

However, this is only a small part of the total picture. The Essex Investment Office is ready to become the eyes and ears for anyone interested in investigating Essex as a potential location for their business and they'll happily do all the early leg work on your behalf. They'll find you sites and premises, provide relevant research and statistics, ensure that your questions are answered swiftly and accurately and organise any introductions you may need.

The Essex Investment Office provides more than just a central contact point. It maintains an extensive county database and information resources and acts as a focus for the future strategic development of inward investment activity in the county. If there is anything you want to know about the potential offered by Essex, your next best move is a call to Essex Investment Office, whether you're looking for a few facts and figures or an organisation that's ready to carry out all of the early research on your behalf.

BOLTON – A PLACE TO LIVE, WORK AND INVEST

Bolton Council and its economic development partners are determined that the town should be recognised as a focus for business success and growth. Like other towns in the UK, there have been periods of structural economic change and contraction, although in recent years local economic performance has improved and the level of unemployment is now consistently below that for Great Britain and the North West, an achievement due in no small measure to the efforts of the town's business support network.

In Bolton the challenge of economic regeneration and change is being met successfully through a strategic economic partnership involving key players in local economic development – Bolton Council, Bolton/Bury Training and Enterprise Council, Bolton/Bury Chamber of Commerce, Bolton Institute, Bolton College, Bolton Business Ventures, Engineering Employers Federation and of course local companies themselves. This partnership is now complemented by Bolton/Bury Business Link, a 'one stop shop' for business advice.

Addressing the problems and opportunities of economic change was not made any easier in Bolton when, as far back as the 1950s, the town had to contend with the special and more serious problems associated with structural economic decline in the once dominant cotton industry. The task of economic renewal through the diversification and redevelopment of Bolton's economy

American Community Schools, England

Relocation often makes it difficult to provide appropriate education for one's children. The American Community Schools, England, has three outstanding campuses and programs to solve these difficulties. Designed originally to meet the educational needs of American families based in London, The American Community Schools Ltd (ACS) has evolved to serve both American and international families. So successful has the approach been that since the School's inception in 1967 it has grown from 35 to over 2,300 students from 60 countries, the largest American international school in Europe.

Three locations close to London, Heathrow, and Gatwick Airports via the M-25 Motorway, provide well-equipped facilities for Pre-K through grade 13. In stately country settings in Cobham, Hillingdon and Egham, students may choose either a program leading to the traditional American diploma for acceptance into American colleges and universities or the International Baccalaureate (IB) diploma for worldwide university access. ACS is accredited on both sides of the Atlantic and the flexible curriculum is designed to facilitate the transition back to schools in America and other countries.

Globally mobile families are reassured knowing that the IB, comprising the final two years of secondary eduction, is a universal qualification and is now offered in schools located in 70 countries.

In addition to the IB, ACS offers more than 17 Advanced Placement (AP) courses. These AP courses include subjects in science, art, language, history, literature and social science. These courses allow able and highly motivated students to secure advanced standing in American colleges and universities.

The IB and AP programs have allowed recent ACS university placements to such institutions as Yale, Oxford, Cambridge, Stanford, Stockholm School of Economics and University of Tokyo. Both AP and IB courses are offered on the Cobham and Hillingdon campuses.

The ACS Cobham campus is located just outside the village of Cobham in rural Surrey, 30 minutes from the centre of London via British Rail. Set in 128 landscaped acres, the school blends stylish, contemporary architecture with the classic elegance of 'Heywood', the Palladio-Georgian mansion that was once the home of King Leopold of Belgium.

Located 15 miles from central London, ACS Hillingdon enjoys a stately setting in 'Hillingdon Court', a Grade II listed building once the home of the Barons Hillingdon. A six million pound addition to the mansion was completed in 1997 and adds labs, libraries, classrooms, offices, cafeteria, auditorium and gymnasium.

The new ACS Egham campus for 3-15 year-olds is set in 20 acres of beautifully landscaped grounds on the edge of Royal Windsor Great Park. The centrepiece of the school is 'Woodlee', the original Victorian mansion house, featuring grand reception rooms with ornate ceilings and Baroque style fireplaces.

Throughout the grade of all ACS schools, a disciplined but caring environment has produced outstanding test results and the enthusiastic support of the parents, over 92 percent of whom highly recommend ACS to their friends and business acquaintances.

Primarily a day school with an active housing office to assist parents in finding homes within the school's busing areas, ACS also offers five-and seven-day boarding programs on the Cobham campus. These highly-tailored services assist international families whether relocating to greater London or living elsewhere.

Once students enroll they begin to experience an exceptional education that includes a wide variety of extra curricular activities and field trips which are part of the standard tuition payment. Studying marine biology on the Devon coast, seeing Shakespearean plays in the reconstructed Globe theatre in London, or playing volleyball in Athens are just some of the enriching experiences that an ACS student might have in his or her years at The American Community Schools, England.

Setting up Shop

The organisation looking to locate in a new territory faces a daunting task. Even if foreign languages are not a problem there are still issues of real estate and construction law - how you know whom to believe and/or trust is the key issue at the heart of a successful venture. So where to begin? There are firms who specialise in helping organisations to relocate and some of then even offer a 'turnkey' type of operation which, in theory at least, allows you simply to move your people, papers and equipment into finished workspaces on the programmed date. While this may appeal to some, most people prefer more of a 'hands-on' approach, albeit that they still need a project manager to guide them through the local issues and to deal with the plethora of consultants and contractors essential to the implementation of the move.

Whoever takes on the project management ought to have first-hand knowledge of all the important processes and procedures - from the initial appraisal of options, thru brief-writing, site finding, development management, project control and setting-up a facilities management policy and regime. And this is where a UK-based firm called Bernard Williams Associates (BWA) comes into its own.

BWA are unique in that all their senior personnel have been trained and practice in the discipline of facilities economics. This means that they have a thorough working knowledge of all the financial and management aspects of providing and using buildings. To BWA **Facilities** is not just about cleaning and photocopying - it covers everything from development appraisal to creation of a facilities management structure in the new centre of operations; along the way you need the skills of negotiation, construction cost control and benchmarking, all of which are part and parcel of BWA's daily offering of practical advice and management.

BWA's interpretation of 'facilities management' and their 'value management' role in its implementation are portrayed in Fig. A.

Note that assets (or property/real estate) are shown as a sub-set of premises. This is because BWA believe that facilities management is primarily concerned with the usefulness of premises (ie a place of work) although the importance of making a sound investment in the real estate is always at the forefront of their thinking when advising on available options.

Fig. A.

BWA AND VALUE MANAGEMENT

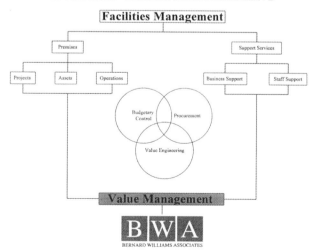

There are three executives divisions within BWA each specialising in particular aspects of facilities economics - Projects Services, Construction Cost Consultancy and Facilities Consultancy.

Each division is headed by partners and associates who understand - indeed have had first-hand involvement - in all 3 of these key areas. **Project Services** is concerned with the front-end appraisal/feasibility and the management of the project from inception to completion: for instance the **Financial Services Authority (FSA)** used BWA to set up and manage the process of finding and procuring the new Canary Wharf home for its 2000 staff - 350,000SF in London's Docklands identified, procured, fitted out and operational in 21-months from a standing start.

Other regular clients in financial services include the **Bank of England**, **Goldman Sachs** and **Salomon Smith Barney**.

The latter two often use BWA to help them with their new overseas offices and this international experience has been augmented by work outside of the UK for multi-nationals like **Shell UK**, **British Airways** and **BP**.

An important part of BWA's professional armoury is their extensive world-wide database of the costs of land, building and facilities services - in fact a leading journal once described the practice as 'the doyen of benchmarking'.

BWA's knowledge of, and track record in, every aspect of facilities operations is unparalleled giving them an unassailable niche position in the field. With the development of the *Frisqué* (**Facilities Risk and Quality Evaluation**) and BQA (**Building Quality Assessment**) programs they now have benchmarking tools of a level of sophistication which renders even their own formerly state-of-the-art technology virtually redundant.

Access first-hand to this data means that BWA can always guarantee their clients are getting the best deal, wherever in the world they want to set up shop. BWA are currently using this database to help **BAT Industries** to set up a value-for-money facilities regime in their new London Headquarters and often use it to help clients such as the **Department of Trade & Industry** make decisions on whether or not to outsource their facilities management activities. BWA have also recently worked successfully with **MAFF**, the **Royal Parks** and **Kodak** in helping them to outsource the management of their facilities and taken an in-depth look at the way **WH Smith**, **DfEE** and **Bass Taverns** maintain the fabric and mechanical services in their premises.

To cap it all, BWA's 540-page book on 'Facilities Economics' is a best seller and is now a standard reference work at Universities and Colleges around the world.

The issue raised at the outset of this article was where you would begin to find someone to trust to help to set up in a new location. Well, BWA have read the story and know the ending…… and that really helps.

BWA *Facilities* Consultancy
Tel: +44 181 460 1111
Fax: +44 181 464 1167
e-mail: bw_assoc@compuserve.com

COST CONSULTANCY & QUANTITY SURVEYING

BUDGETARY CONTROL
VALUE ENGINEERING
PROCUREMENT
QUANTITY SURVEYING

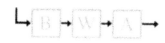

PROJECT SERVICES

PROJECT CO-ORDINATION
DEVELOPMENT CONSULTANCY
CLIENT REPRESENTATIVE
PROJECT IMPLEMENTATION
RISK ANALYSIS
CDM / PLANNING SUPERVISOR

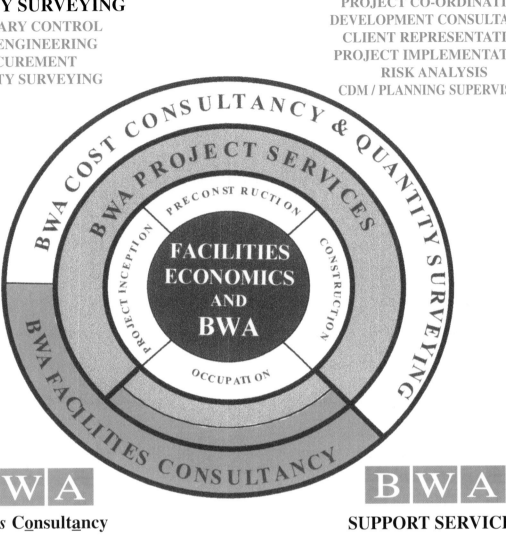

Facilities Consultancy

POLICY & STRATEGY
BENCHMARKING
ASSET MANAGEMENT
FINANCIAL CONTROL
SYSTEM / CONSULTANCY
OUTSOURCING & PROCUREMENT

SUPPORT SERVICES

CAPITAL ALLOWANCES
VALUE ADDED TAX
DEVELOPMENT GRANTS
RESEARCH & DEVELOPMENT
BUILDING QUALITY ASSESSMENT

PROFESSIONAL ADVICE AT EVERY STAGE IN THE BUILDING LIFE CYCLE

Kings House, 32-40 Widmore Road, Bromley, Kent BR1 1RY
Tel: +44 181 460 1111   Fax: +44 181 464 1167   e-mail: bw_assoc@compuserve.com

was met then in a positive and innovative way by the Council through the appointment of an industrial development officer in 1960, the first in the UK. This initiative helped create the diverse economic base and modern industrial estates seen in Bolton in the mid-1990s. However, the Economic Partnership recognises that there is no place for complacency in local economic matters and they are well aware of the size of their task if Bolton's economy is to remain competitive, develop and meet the economic challenges of the next century.

The demise of an industry as powerful and as dominant as cotton undoubtedly created an economic chasm; but the wealth and power associated with that industry (including its many magnates) also provided a legacy, the vision and the means to assemble a physical and business infrastructure capable of sustaining a new generation of industrial and commercial development around which the town would prosper and grow for the future.

Today Bolton's appeal as an investment location is based as much on its natural economic and environmental assets as it is on the availability of financial assistance. The town's natural assets include an adaptable workforce with a strong work ethic, a sound industrial pedigree, a semi-rural location offering quick access to the countryside, 14 golf courses, top quality leisure and recreation facilities, an extensive range of quality homes, superior schools and colleges, excellent motorway connections including an urban motorway, and easy access to Manchester International Airport.

Add to this list a forward-thinking Council, a local TEC dedicated to ensuring that the local workforce is equipped with the skills needed by both today's and tomorrow's industries, sophisticated research and development facilities at Bolton Institute, an award-winning town centre, and you have a self-sufficient town offering companies all the benefits of a 'total work environment'.

The arrival of City Challenge funding proved of enormous benefit to Bolton in that it provided vital funds to create opportunities for investment by upgrading and accessing vacant development land, work which would not have been possible due to the inadequacy of normal mainstream funding through Council budgets. Not only has this helped to achieve the economic objectives of the City Challenge initiative, it has also, simultaneously, contributed to the achievement of both the environmental and social objectives of the initiative by improving the appearance of unsightly land and removing the many unfortunate social consequences of unemployment.

Bolton City Challenge is a private/public partnership in the Halliwell area of the town which has so far generated more than £20m of investment, reclaimed more than 13 acres of land and created 1250 new jobs in the area. One of the flagship schemes is the Tonge Valley, a largely derelict river valley less than a mile from the town centre. While redevelopment of the valley will feature primarily industrial and office uses, there will also be a leisure complex with a multiplex cinema.

Maintaining the competitiveness of SMEs in Bolton through the introduction of new technology and creating an awareness of environmental legislation and the need for innovation is central to the role of the Council's economic development unit. EU funding has been secured for what is known as the BITE project, which is intended to provide funding for awareness-raising amongst Bolton companies in the areas of information technology, innovation, environment and technology. This will then be followed by business audits in individual companies to establish current attitudes and levels of provision and to agree an action plan for implementation by the company. It is hoped that while benefiting the individual companies, the BITE project will also help to create a stronger and healthier local economy in the long term.

Bolton's pride in its industrial heritage and its successful regeneration efforts are matched only by its belief that it is a viable and proven investment location for discerning and forward-looking companies who are able to recognize and evaluate the longer-term advantages of locating in a mature yet vibrant and dynamic town which can set itself apart from other towns and be well placed to remain an economic 'tour de force' in the next millennium.

Middlebrook – much more than just a football stadium

Following the successful completion of the last phase of town centre redevelopment and a practical commitment to the redevelopment of the Tonge Valley, many onlookers must have wondered where Bolton would turn to next to maintain its outstanding and much envied record of achievement in urban regeneration and investment. How could it possibly become involved in any development which would succeed in raising the town's profile to even greater heights? After all, The Market Place, a new hotel (The Moat House), the Water Place, the Excel Centre, refurbished open and indoor markets, The Valley development, The Gates development, two new upmarket night clubs, the prospect of university status and a whole range of town centre improvements aimed at making life more convenient for shoppers and tourists alike have all made outstanding contributions to making Bolton such a talked about town, not just in the North West, but nationally and internationally.

The pundits wondered just what the Council and its private sector partners would come up with next to maintain the town's reputation as an ambitious and enterprising town always prepared to push the frontiers of urban development even further forward. Not to disappoint, it wasn't long before the next development project was announced, one that would, almost literally, rise like a phoenix from the ashes of the former refuse tip at Red Moss Horwich. The project is, of course, the Middlebrook Sports Village Development at Horwich. The centre-piece of this development is the spectacular new all-seater stadium for Bolton Wanderers Football Club. Incorporating architectural and technical features which can only be described as avant garde, the stadium dominates the semi-rural landscape alongside the A6027 at Horwich and is clearly visible from the M61 motorway.

The need to apply commercial criteria to the economics of the Middlebrook Development meant that the football stadium had to be supported by a range of other developments including a cinema, a hotel, retail, offices, housing, leisure and industrial to create a viable overall development which, in effect, has created a mini village within the township of Horwich. The Middlebrook development is now nationally recognised and its contribution to the economic health and vitality of Horwich and to Bolton generally must not be underestimated. Just as importantly, the contribution to the further enhancement of Bolton's image is perhaps incalculable.

From a practical viewpoint, the Middlebrook development will provide a valuable addition to Bolton's 'total work environment', a concept which Bolton considers vital in the constant quest to attract inward investment to the town at a time when competition is fierce. As inward investment opportunities are scarce, Bolton has taken the view that its chances of securing investment would be that much greater if it were able to demonstrate some 'added value' in its package of incentives to businesses. As Bolton considers itself to be a town for the more discerning businessperson who can place a value on the longer-term benefits of locating in the town, this 'added value' was not seen as being of a monetary nature.

One outstanding example of environmental benefit is the extensive and unrivalled selection of golf courses in Bolton, 14 in all, made possible by the town's location within the West Pennines Moorland which not only lends itself to the creation of golf courses but also makes possible a quick transition from an urban to a rural environment. The 'total work environment' also encompasses business support in the form of training through the local Training and Enterprise Council with delivery by various organisations including Bolton

Institute and Bolton College. The newly formed Business Link is establishing a meaningful relationship with Bolton businesses, and the local Chamber of Commerce and Industry, Bolton Business Ventures and the Engineering Employers Federation are key members of the business support network.

The Middlebrook development is yet another strong and positive expression of the town's ambition and a confirmation of the confidence which the private sector has in Bolton as a buoyant and successful commercial centre in North West England. Bolton Council and its economic development partners fervently believe that it has the capability to continue to meet the economic challenges of the next millennium and to maintain a strong, prosperous and resilient economy throughout the period.

DERBY: THE BUSINESS CENTRE OF THE UK

Derby is situated at the heart of the UK and provides easy access to many national and international locations. The major motorway network is just a 15-minute drive away from the city centre and there are rail links to all major cities in the UK. East Midlands International Airport is located ten miles from Derby and operates services to many European capital cities.

To match its excellent location, Derby can offer a diverse economy centred upon its engineering excellence developed by organisations such as Rolls-Royce, Rolls-Royce and Associates, British Rail Research and Adtranz (formerly British Rail Engineering). Derby's highly skilled workforce has facilitated the growth of the city's research and development and hi-tech sectors over recent years.

Derby is able to offer relocating staff competitively priced housing, an extensive and diverse range of shopping facilities, quality health care and excellent primary, secondary and university education. The Peak District and Derbyshire Dales are within easy reach and provide many opportunities for scenic walks and outdoor pastimes. Within the city there is a wide range of sporting opportunities and there are over 20 golf courses within a 15-mile radius. Derby is also home to many historic houses and five museum/art galleries.

Derby Marketing

The partnership philosophy in Derby is highlighted by the success of Derby Marketing in attracting inward investment since its formation in 1993. This recognises the need for a coordinated response to today's invest-

A SUITE SOLUTION

Philip Parris, Chief Executive, Harvard Managed Offices, and President of Executive Suite Association

For more than a quarter of a century, the business centre or serviced office industry has been quietly growing on a world-wide basis, providing purpose-made solutions to meet the needs of changing corporate structures and the increase in global trade and commerce.

Business centres (known in the United States as executive suites) essentially provide a fully equipped business environment, including all the vital infrastructure - human, physical and technological - necessary to allow business operations to establish quickly and efficiently, whilst maintaining close control of costs.

Business centres originated in the US and it is there that the industry is at its most mature, driven by the need of many large corporations to have representative offices in many States. In the UK, and in most other countries, the use of business centres by large corporates has taken longer and it is only with the globalisation of international trade that many have begun to use such facilities to establish overseas representation. This growth in the market for business centres is being enhanced as a result of the revolution in communications. Using the new technologies, large companies now find it more profitable to disperse their operations into smaller business units closer to the market place and business centres provide the ideal resource for this purpose. The fact that serviced facilities are now to be found in all the developed economies of the world, and in many less developed countries, underlines this growing movement.

Companies moving into the UK from overseas often find the process of establishing an office using traditional real estate difficult and daunting. It can take several months to find and secure appropriate premises and, even then, the companies may find themselves locked into long-term lease structures that can become costly liabilities. Business centres, on the other hand, offer instant access and flexibility to expand or contract or vacate at short notice. Likewise, trying to find the appropriate staff in a preferred location can be more difficult than is generally supposed. On the other hand, business centres provide vital business resources and support, and many offer the use of new technology that allows occupiers to learn to operate and evaluate the equipment thoroughly before committing their own vital capital.

An additional advantage of some centres over traditional real estate is in their ability to offer access to business facilities in other parts of the world. My own company, for example, was a founder member of Global Office Network, which currently has some 50 member centres in 13 countries in Europe, Asia and the Far East. Global Office Network partners the US-based Alliance Business Center Network and, together, as Global Alliance Network, they now comprise more then 235 independent centres located in 22 countries, the largest confederation of independent business centre operators in the world. At these locations, clients may take advantage of the best facilities and services as well as access a range of real value added services. If further proof was needed of the industry's growing internationalisation, it came at the end of last year, when I had the privilege to become the first non-American to be elected President of the Executive Suite Association of the US - the world's leading industry association for business centres.

The industry is almost purpose-designed to meet the needs of these new corporate structures, particularly those organisations establishing a bridgehead. Harvard, for example, have been assisting overseas companies, including many American, to set up in the UK for almost 15 years. The speed of setting up a new operation, and the flexibility which the industry provides, will ensure that many more corporations, large and small, national and international, will use such facilities in the future.

ment and development challenges and seeks to provide the investor to Derby with a unique package of information, guidance, support and advice coordinated to maximise the efficient delivery of services to relocating companies.

Derby Marketing is an initiative of the Derby City Partnership – a blend of public and private sector bodies that have joined forces to ensure an unequalled service to all potential investors. Derby Marketing offers the following dedicated services:

- a guaranteed 72-hour comprehensive response to enquiries;

- a full site search facility;

- the creation of a dedicated project team;

- key staff familiarisation visits;

- continued liaison with Derby's business support network.

Derby Marketing partners include: British Gas Transco, British Telecom, Business Link Southern Derbyshire, Derby City Council, Derby Pride Ltd, Derbyshire Building Society, East Midlands Development Company Ltd, East Midlands Electricity, Employment Service, Severn Trent Water, Southern Derbyshire Chamber of Commerce, Training and Enterprise, and the University of Derby.

BRIGHTON AND HOVE

Brighton and Hove is entering a new era of growth. With a new all-purpose council, this new 'city by the sea' boasts an economic strategy in tune with modern business.

The city is linked to global communications by state-of-the-art technology, full ISDN network, digital exchanges and fibre-optic links. Innovative partnerships between business and the academic community are producing a growing knowledge-based sector.

With 8000 graduates a year from two universities, the local workforce is creative and highly motivated.

There are some of the South-East's lowest property costs and millions of pounds of government and private funds available for industrial regeneration.

Thirty minutes from Gatwick and less than an hour from London, the city recently attracted the European HQ of Alamo Rent-a-Car, ROCC Computers and the occupational pensions watchdog, OPRA. Regency architecture and unspoilt downland offer an unrivalled quality of life.

GUERNSEY – THE ENTREPRENEURIAL ISLE

The Channel Island of Guernsey has a long history of business success. From farming and boat building, through to quarrying and horticulture, the islanders have always made a success of their chosen ventures.

One key to the island's success is its location on an historic trade route between Northern Europe and Great Britain. Evidence of the island's importance as a trading centre is found in the numerous fortifications and spacious cellars that span many different eras. Outwardly little has changed. Certainly Guernsey's importance as an international trade and business centre will continue beyond the millennium.

As most people are aware, the island has a reputation as one of the world's most mature and natural international financial centres. Development has been steady over the last 30 years through the sensible policy of encouraging only high quality banking, insurance and investment fund institutions to become Guernsey-based. Currently international finance activities generate 57 per cent of the island's export earning.

This strong financial base has many advantages. The international nature of the island's business activity has secured regular transport links with many of Europe's major business centres, all year round. A strong tourism sector combined with a high degree of business travel has resulted in the quality of service reaching its highest ever level. BAE 146 Whisper jets are regularly used by both major operators and sea travel has been revolutionised in the last few years with the use of fast car-carrying wave piercer catamarans.

All this means that Guernsey, as an English-speaking, readily accessible offshore location, can provide the ideal base for many types of operation. The Guernsey Board of Industry is responsible for the development of the manufacturing and non-financial service companies on the island that account for approximately 10 per cent of the island's export earnings.

Many well-known names are based or have large operations on Guernsey, including Specsavers, NRG (Hashuatec), Ribbon Revival, the International Energy Group, Jones and Bradburn, Simco and Intersurgical. Guernsey exporters manufacture a range of products including pleasure boats, electronics, pharmaceuticals, plastics, office furniture, toys, crafts, textiles and software. Guernsey is also proving to be an excellent base for the headquarters of sales and distributions networks, management partnerships and franchise operations.

Creating environments for your organisation to flourish.

It's a well known fact that if a working environment is comfortable and balanced it's more productive. As one of the leading European distributors of DAIKIN air conditioning equipment, SPACE have unrivalled knowledge and experience of their extensive and pioneering product range comprising over 650 models all with a 3 year warranty. Many of these models are now optimised for use with environmentally friendly refrigerants.

By giving detailed projections on capital costs, running costs and maintenance costs and incredible energy savings means we can be absolutely confident of meeting the exact requirements of each and every project. This confidence extends throughout a national network of over 200 approved installation and maintenance companies with the total support of the SPACE team from design right through to after sales engineering support.

If you need any advice on air conditioning ask the experts at SPACE. Alternatively, take advantage of the fully equipped showroom and seminar facilities at the 30,000 sq. ft. head office. They were built with you in mind. It's another sign of our dedication and commitment to our customers today, tomorrow and far into the future.

Give your office the space to flourish and call us at any of the offices below. You'll soon discover why we're the best in our field.

SPACE AIR
Space Airconditioning plc

Guildford Tel: 01483 504883 ● **Bristol Tel: 01275 341030** ● **Leeds Tel: 01132 822171** ● **Birmingham Tel: 0121 7223223**

Guernsey's unique position and its stable government, free of party politics, ensures companies can plan for the future with confidence. The beauty and tranquillity of the island, combined with an environment ideal for bringing up children, provide an environment ideal for the entrepreneur who accepts there is more to life than work. Whether you like to sail, play golf, swim or just enjoy a good walk, the island has much to offer and all within a few minutes of home or work.

For further information, contact:

Tony Brassell or Kevin Roberts
Guernsey Board of Industry
Tel: 01481 35741
Fax: 01481 35015

Better still, pay us a visit and we will show you the benefits of living on Guernsey – the entrepreneurial isle.

INVEST IN SCOTLAND

Scotland and its economy

Scotland is wealthy in its:

- property investment opportunities;
- skills base;
- high-tech industries;
- business infrastructure;
- academic and research excellence;
- quality of life.

World class companies are investing in a world-class location. Investors, developers and occupiers are finding a fast route into Scotland.

Scotland has plenty to offer industry, including first-class air links, a Euro rail terminal and an excellent quality of life. Scotland has wonderful scenery, golf courses, and excellent products – such as whisky, seafoods and textiles. This is balanced by Scotland's economy – a high-tech base which is attracting a wave of investors from within Europe, the US and the Pacific Rim. They are attracted to Scotland because of its ready access to European and world markets – and its way of life.

Results from 1996/97 show that the Scottish Enterprise Network attracted 86 inward investment projects involving planned investment of more than £3.1 billion. Further, Scotland recently won the UK's largest inward investment by Korean giant, Hyundai, who are now on site, commencing with an investment totalling £2.4 billion. The completed semi-conductor plant will ultimately generate 2000 jobs.

Companies like Chunghwa Picture Tubes and Lite-On, both massive Taiwanese companies, have recently brought huge inward investments into Scotland. They are joining a number of Japanese companies such as Mitsubishi, Canon and NEC who have located their European manufacturing bases in Central Scotland. US companies also play a significant role in the Scottish economy. Leading-edge companies such as IBM, Motorola, Lexmark and Exabyte Corporation are serving their European markets from Scotland. Motorola last year completed a £250 million expansion of its Scottish semi-conductor plant and now employs 2500 people.

The Scottish Enterprise Network

The Scottish Enterprise Network supports economic activity via its network of 13 Local Enterprise Companies (LECs), each of which is responsible for property, business development and skills training in its area.

The network has a powerful package of financial assistance to support business growth and enhance investment returns. Crawford Beveridge, Chief Executive of Scottish Enterprise, says, 'We have made excellent progress in our mission of creating jobs and prosperity for the people of Scotland, and our message to investors, developers and occupiers is that we aim to continue to meet your business needs.'

While it has been another record year for inward investment, the Scottish Enterprise Network is as unequivocally committed to Scotland's own businesses. Massive investment from overseas companies has direct spin-offs for local service providers, which in turn generates significant demand for quality accommodation from those local players. The Scottish Enterprise Network has a role to play in encouraging developers and investors to capture this sector of the market, and look to the very real investment possibilities and opportunities that exist.

RAPID speeds up the investment process

RAPID is an initiative led by Scottish Enterprise which is designed to develop the property market. It stands for Resources and Action for Private Industrial Development. The range of assistance available includes:

- advice and information;

- rental guarantees;

- bank mortgages guarantee scheme;

- rental concessions;

- commercial loans;

- joint ventures;

- grants.

RAPID has the role of encouraging private investment in developments which might not offer sufficient return without assistance. The programme is not restricted geographically, as it is available throughout the Scottish Enterprise operational area and any company or person proposing to develop or refurbish property can apply, although the level of assistance available will vary from area to area, depending upon market conditions. Scottish Enterprise can act as catalyst, partner, hierarchical funder or facilitator. The programme further focuses on providing property for companies locating in Scotland for the first time, as well as indigenous companies, and can also assist companies with expansion space or start-up accommodation.

Until recently, the vast bulk of Scottish industrial property was developed and owned by the public sector. RAPID is now being used to adjust this balance and stimulate development and investment opportunities. In the year 1996/97, £104 million was levered from the private sector for the construction of industrial and commercial premises.

Scottish Property Network

A comprehensive database of Scotland's commercial and industrial property is being developed to provide market information on available floorspace for companies, investors and developers.

Scottish Property Network (SPN) is a joint venture between Scottish Enterprise and the University of Paisley; it compiles information from property agents, property owners, Local Enterprise Companies, local authorities and enterprise trusts. It contains extensive details of stock, availability and prices and has been set up to encourage market activity.

For further information on the Scottish Enterprise Network, the local Enterprise Companies, or details of development opportunities, contact:

Euan Hall
Head of Property
Scottish Enterprise
120 Bothwell Street
Glasgow G2 7JP
Tel: 0141 248 2700
Fax: 0141 228 2395

Space is a little closer to home in Clackmannanshire

If it's space you're after, look no further than Clackmannanshire.

Clackmannanshire lies at the heart of Central Scotland. Nestling against the Ochil Hills and bordered to the south by the River Forth, the area is packed with beauty, history and top quality business accommodation. Its central location means that the major cities of Glasgow and Edinburgh are less than an hour's drive away.

Dumyat Business Park is Clackmannanshire's flagship new centre of business. The first phase of work on the new business park extends to 25 acres with potential for more expansion into the 21st century. The park provides a fully serviced and landscaped environment, offering flexible plot sizes to accommodate any company's needs.

Companies can also get help with the capital costs of their investment thanks to Clackmannanshire's status as an Intermediate Grant Assisted Area for the purposes of Regional Selective Assistance.

As well as Dumyat, the new business development at Alloa West can offer businesses up to 100,000 sq. ft. of flexible open-plan accommodation, all linked with the latest in state-of-the-art SMART technology. Fibre optic links will connect the new business park to purpose built housing, offering new potential for businesses specialising in teleworking.

As well as accommodation, the Council can tailor a relocation package to help with:

- working capital;

- support for training and recruitment;

- advice and funding for business diversification, relocation and growth;

- grant support for management development, training and new technology training.

Part 6
Useful Addresses

Useful Addresses

BUSINESS/PROFESSIONAL ORGANISATIONS

Advertising Standards Authority
2 Torrington Place
London WC1E 7HW
United Kingdom
Tel: +44 171 580 5555
Fax: +44 171 631 3051
Web-site: http://www.asa.org.uk

BCL Immigration Services
3rd Floor, 11–14 Grafton Street
London W1X 4NP
Tel: +44 171 495 3999
Fax: +44 171 495 3991
e-mail: bcl@workpermit.com
Web-site: http://www.visa-free.com/index.htm

British-American Chamber of Commerce
8 Staple Inn
High Holborn
London WC1V 7QH
United Kingdom
Tel: +44 171 404 6400
Fax: +44 171 404 6828
Web-site: http://www.bacc.org/index.html

British Bankers' Association
Pinners Hall
105–108 Old Broad Street
London EC2N 1EX
United Kingdom
Tel: +44 171 216 8800
Fax: +44 171 216 8905
E-mail: rogermiles@bba.org.uk

British Chambers of Commerce
Manning House
22 Carlisle Place
London SW1P 1JA
United Kingdom
Tel: +44 171 565 2000
Fax: +44 171 565 2049

British Design & Art Direction (D&AD)
9 Graphite Square
Vauxhall Walk
London SE11 5EE
United Kingdom
Tel: +44 171 840 1111
Fax: +44 171 840 0840
Web-site: http://www.dandad.org

British Direct Marketing Association
Haymarket House
1 Ovendon Street
London SW1Y 4EE
United Kingdom
Tel: +44 171 321 2525
Fax: +44 171 321 0191
E-mail: dma@easynet.co.uk
Web-site: http://www.dma.org.uk

British Film Commission
70 Baker Street
London W1M 1DJ
United Kingdom
Tel: +44 171 224 5000
Fax: +44 171 224 1013
E-mail: info@britfilmcom.co.uk
Web-site: http://www.britfilmcom.co.uk

British Standards Institution
British Standards House
389 Chiswick High Road
London W4 4AL
United Kingdom
Tel: +44 181 996 9000
Fax: +44 181 996 7400
E-mail: info@bsi.org.uk
Web-site: http://www.bsi.org.uk/

British Venture Capital Association
Essex House, 12–13 Essex Street
London WC2R 3AA
United Kingdom
Tel: +44 171 240 3846
Fax: +44 171 240 3849.
E-mail: bvca@bvca.co.uk
Web-site: www.bvca.co.uk

Business Link Network Company
39 London Road
Newbury
Berkshire RG14 1JL
United Kingdom
Tel: +44 1635 572600
Fax: +44 1635 572601
Web-site: http://www.businesslink.co.uk

Canada-UK Chamber of Commerce
38 Grosvenor Street
London W1X 0DP
United Kingdom
Tel: +44 171 258 6576
Fax: +44 171 258 6594
Web-site: http://www.canada-uk.org

Chartered Institute of Marketing
Moor Hall
Cookham
Maidenhead, Berks SL6 9QH
United Kingdom
Tel: +44 1628 427001
Fax: +44 1628 427009
E-mail: marketing@cim.co.uk
Web-site: http://www.cim.co.uk

Chartered Institute of Patent Agents
Staple Inn Buildings
High Holborn
London WC1V 7PZ
United Kingdom
Tel: +44 171 405 9450
Fax: +44 171 430 0471
Web-site: http://www.cipa.org.uk/cipa/

Confederation of British Industry
Centre Point
103 New Oxford Street
London WC1A 1DU
United Kingdom
Tel: +44 171 379 7400
Fax: +44 171 240 8289
Web-site: http://www.cbi.org.uk

Electronic Commerce Association
Ramillies House
1–9 Hills Place
London W1R 1AJ
United Kingdom
Tel: +44 171 432 2500
Fax: +44 171 432 2501
E-mail: roger.till@eca.org.uk
Web-site: http://www.eca.org.uk

The Factors and Discounters Association
2nd Floor
Boston House
The Little Green
Richmond
Surrey TW9 1QE
Tel: +44 (181) 331 9955
Fax: +44 (181) 332 2585

Forrester Ketley & Co
Forrester House
52 Bounds Green Road
London N11 2EY
Tel: +44 (181) 889 6622
Fax: +44 (181) 881 1088
E-mail: forresters-lon@compuserve.com

Grant Thornton
Grant Thornton House
Melton Street
Euston Square
London NW1 2EP
Tel: +44 (171) 383 5100
Fax: +44 (171) 383 4715

Incorporated Society of British Advertisers
44 Hertford Street
London W1Y 8AE
United Kingdom
Tel: +44 171 499 7502
Fax: +44 171 629 5355
Web-site: http://www.isba.org.uk

The Industrial Society
3 Carlton House Terrace
London SW1
United Kingdom
Tel: +44 171 839 4300
Fax: +44 171 723 7375
E-mail: infoserve@indusoc.demon.co.uk
Web-site: http://www.indsoc.co.uk

Institute of Chartered Accountants in England & Wales
Moorgate Place
London EC2P 2BJ
United Kingdom
Tel: +44 171 920 8527
Fax: +44 171 638 6009
E-mail: tdwright@icaew.co.uk

Institute of Directors
116 Pall Mall
London SW1Y 5ED
United Kingdom
Tel: +44 171 839 1233
Fax: +44 171 930 8040

Institute of Practitioners in Advertising
44 Belgrave Square
London SW1X 8QS
United Kingdom
Tel: +44 171 235 7020
Fax: +44 171 245 9904
E-mail: nick@iipa.co.uk
Web-site: http://www.ipa.co.uk

The Institute of Public Relations
The Old Trading House
15 Northburgh Street
London EC1V 0PR
United Kingdom
Tel: +44 171 253 5151
Fax: +44 171 490 0588
E-mail: info@ipr1.demon.co.uk
Web-site http:/www.ipr.press.net

International Marketing Partners Consultants
US tel/fax: 310/665-1155
UK tel: 011+44+171/828-9400
UK fax: 011+44+171/828-9466
E-mail: intl_marketing_partners@compuserve.com

International Organisation for Standardisation (ISO)
1 rue de Varembé
Case postale 56
CH-1211 Genève 20
Switzerland
Tel: +41 22 749 01 11
Fax: +41 22 733 34 30
E-mail: central@iso.ch
Web-site: http://www.iso.ch/

International Visual Communication
Association (IVCA)
5–6 Clipstone Street
London W1P 8LD
United Kingdom
Tel: +44 171 580 0962.
Fax: +44 171 436 2606
E-mail: info@ivca.com
Web-site: www.ivca.com

Investors in People
7–10 Chandos Street
London W1M 9DE
United Kingdom
Tel: +44 171 467 1900
Fax: +44 171 636 2386
Web-site: http://www.iipuk.co.uk

Law Society Of England and Wales
113 Chancery Lane
London WC2A 1PL
United Kingdom
Tel: +44 171 320 6811/5810
Fax: +44 171 242 1309

Management Consultancies Association
11 West Halkin Street
London SW1X 8JL
United Kingdom
Tel: +44 171 235 3897
Fax: +44 171 235 0825
E-mail: mca@mca.org.uk
Web-site: http://www.mca.org.uk

Market Research Society
15 Northburgh Street
London EC1V 0AH
United Kingdom
Tel: +44 171 490 4911
Fax: +44 171 490 0608

Public Relations Consultants Association
Willow House
Willow Place
London SW1P 1JH
United Kingdom
Tel: +44 171 233 6026
Fax: +44 171 828 4797
E-mail: chris@prca.org.uk
Web-site: http://www.martex.co.uk/prca/index.htm

Shandwick International plc
18 Dering Street
London W1R 9AF
Tel: +44 171 629 9700
Fax: +44 171 499 1752
E-mail: gboyd@shandwick.com
Web-site: http://www.shandwick.com

TEC National Council
Westminster Tower
3 Albert Embankment
London SE1 7SX
United Kingdom
Tel: +44 171 735 0010
Fax: +44 171 735 0090
Web-site: http://www.tec.co.uk

GOVERNMENT AGENCIES

Canadian High Commission
Commercial/Economic Division
Macdonald House
1 Grosvenor Square
London W1X 0AB
Tel: +44 171 258 6600
Fax: +44 171 258 6384
E-mail: td.ldn@ldn02.x400.gc.ca
Web-site: http://dfait-maeci.gc.ca

Department of Trade and Industry
1 Victoria Street
London SW1H 0ET
United Kingdom
Tel: +44 171 215 5000
Fax: +44 171 215 5651
Web-site: http://www.dti.gov.uk/support/index.htm

The Employment Service
'New Deal'
Large Organisations Unit
Level 3
Mayfield Court
West Street
Sheffield S1 4EP
New Deal Helpline: 0114 259 5765/5856/7226

Enterprise Zones
Department of the Environment
Regeneration Division 3
4/E8 Bressenden Place
London SW1E 5DU
United Kingdom
Tel: +44 171 890 3757
Fax: +44 171 890 3759

Invest in Britain Bureau
Department of Trade and Industry
1 Victoria Street
London SW1H 0ET
United Kingdom
Tel: +44 171 215 2501
Fax: +44 171 215 5651
E-mail: invest.britain@iibb.dti.gov.uk
Web-site: http://www.dti.gov.uk/ibb/

Invest in Britain Bureau (Canada)
British Consulate-General
Suite 2800M, College Park
777 Bay Street
Toronto M5G 2G2 Canada
Tel: +1 416 593 1290
Fax: +1 416 593 1229
E-mail: mailto:britcon@igs.net

Invest in Britain Bureau (US)
British Consulate-General
845 Third Avenue
New York NY 10022 USA
Tel: +1 212 745 0418
Fax: +1 212 745 0456

REGIONAL DEVELOPMENT BOARDS

Devon & Cornwall Development International Agency
5 Derriford Park
Plymouth
Devon PL6 5QZ
United Kingdom
Tel: +44 1752 793379
Fax: +44 1752 788660

East Midlands Development Company
2–4 Weekday Cross
Nottingham NG1 2GB
United Kingdom
Tel: +44 1159 527870
Fax: +44 1159 520539

East of England Investment Agency Ltd
2 Quay Side
Bridge Street
Cambridge CB5 8AB
United Kingdom
Tel: +44 1223 461939
Fax: +44 1223 461941

Industrial Development Board for Northern Ireland
IDB House
64 Chichester Street
Belfast BT1 4JX
United Kingdom
Tel: +44 1232 233233
Fax: +44 1232 545000

INWARD
Muirfield House
Kelvin Close
Birchwood
Warrington
Cheshire WA3 7PB
United Kingdom
Tel: +44 1925 830022
Fax: +44 1925 830456

London First Centre
Hobhouse Court
Suffolk Street
London SW1Y 4HH
United Kingdom
Tel: +44 171 925 2000
Fax: +44 171 925 2022

Northern Development Company
Great North House
Sandyforth Road
Newcastle upon Tyne NE1 8ND
United Kingdom
Tel: +44 191 261 0026
Fax: +44 191 232 9069

Scottish Enterprise
120 Bothwell Street
Glasgow G2 7JP
United Kingdom
Tel: +44 141 248 2700
Fax: +44 141 221 5129

South East Regional Investment Ltd
Centaur House
Ancells Business Park
Ancelis Road
Fleet
Hampshire GU 13 8UN
United Kingdom
Tel: +44 1252 761002
Fax: +44 1252 761001

Welsh Development International Agency
Principality House
The Friary
Cardiff CFI 4AE
United Kingdom
Tel: +44 1222 828810
Fax: +44 1222 390630

West Midlands Development Agency
1500 Solihull Parkway
Birmingham Business Park
Birmingham B37 7YD
United Kingdom
Tel: +44 121 717 0909
Fax: +44 121 717 0720

West of England Development Agency Ltd
5 Greenways Business Park
Bellinger Close
Chippenham
Wiltshire SN15 1BN
United Kingdom
Tel: +44 1249 461010
Fax: +44 1249 436626

Yorkshire & Humberside Development Agency
Westgate House
100 Wellington Street
Leeds LS1 4LT
United Kingdom
Tel: +44 1132 439222
Fax: +44 1132 431098

Index

Index of Advertisers